The Ashes of Lou Gehrig
and Other Baseball Essays

The Ashes of Lou Gehrig and Other Baseball Essays

by SEAN PETER KIRST

with a foreword by Harold Holzer

McFarland & Company, Inc., Publishers
Jefferson, North Carolina, and London

LIBRARY OF CONGRESS CATALOGUING-IN-PUBLICATION DATA

Kirst, Sean Peter.
    The ashes of Lou Gehrig and other baseball essays /
by Sean Peter Kirst ; with a foreword by Harold Holzer.
      p. cm.

    ISBN 0-7864-1578-9 (softcover : 50# alkaline paper) ∞

    1. Baseball — Anecdotes.   2. Baseball players — Anecdotes.
I. Title.
GV873.K57 2003
796.357'02 — dc21

                                   2003010995

British Library cataloguing data are available

*Cover photograph: Lou Gehrig (National Baseball Hall of Fame Library,
Cooperstown, NY)*

Manufactured in the United States of America

*McFarland & Company, Inc., Publishers
  Box 611, Jefferson, North Carolina 28640
  www.mcfarlandpub.com*

In loving memory of my brother:

James Dennis Kirst
October 10, 1946–August 26, 2002

Acknowledgments

Countless people, over four decades, helped in the making of this book. I'll run the risk of offering special thanks to just a few, starting with the men, women and children whose stories form this collection. From George Pollack, protector of Lou Gehrig's legacy, to a group of children playing ball on an empty suburban lot, I remain in their debt for the faith they placed in me.

I also extend a profound "thank you" to a trinity of upstate New York editors who transformed my career:

Bill Hammond was my first professional editor, the guy who hired a 14-year-old to work as a regular stringer for the sports department of the Dunkirk *Observer*. Hammond simply accepted the word of another young reporter, Jerome Reilly, that I could do the job. He then approved my earliest foray into baseball history, which dealt with the correct birthplace of one Charles "Piano Legs" Hickman.

Mary Anna Towler, my editor at *City Newspaper* in Rochester, elevated my style and taught me much about the sheer tenacity demanded for any piece of decent writing.

Finally, John Lammers— my friend and long-time editor at the *Post-Standard* in Syracuse — allowed me the freedom to write most of the pieces that make up this book. He shared my passion and delight in any untold baseball story. Without him, I never would have enjoyed the time or liberty to pursue the mystery of the ashes of Lou Gehrig. He is an editor with extraordinary gifts.

I thank Stephen A. Rogers, Mike Connor and Tim Bunn of the *Post-Standard*, who gave the green light for reprinting these columns and essays. Rosemary Robinson, my editor, gave the idea an early blessing. Stan Walker and Molly Elliott, also of the *Post-Standard*, were helpful beyond words in lining up the photos.

I appreciate the patience and assistance of the entire staff at the National Baseball Hall of Fame and Museum, especially Bill Guilfoile, now retired, and Jeff Idelson, who once owned a patch jacket. I appreciate everything done for me by the staff at the Onondaga Historical Association, and by Ron Gersbacher, the long-time keeper of Syracuse baseball lore.

I thank my parents, Jim and Jean Kirst, two baseball true believers who didn't live to see this book; my surviving brothers and my sister, Michael, John and Pamela, who wore basepaths in our back yard before I was even born; Sharon, the big sister I wish I had the chance to know; and the late Joe Overfield, the great baseball historian of Buffalo, who understood so perfectly the glory of lost days.

My oldest brother, Dennis, to whom this book is dedicated, was born on October 10, 1946, one day after Ted Williams bunted for a hit during the great Boston–St. Louis World Series. Dennis bought me my first glove and my first bat. Throughout my life, he looked out for me.

It remains beyond belief that he is gone.

Harold Holzer, a tireless Lincoln scholar with a passion for baseball, wrote the foreword and always found time to encourage me.

Credit is also due to my good friends, Darrell Kaminski and Bob McCrone, who kept inquiring about the progress of the manuscript, and to Michael and Barbara Petranto, who've done so much for my family over the last 12 years.

I offer a special thanks to members of the 2002 Midland Valley Cleaners Little League team, from Elmwood Park in Syracuse: Muhammad Hassan, Jon Grimes, Alex DeJohn, Seamus and Liam Kirst, Nick Sheridan, Steve Thompson, Perry Crain, Chris Davis, Josh Rathbun, Ethan Wojcik, Chris James and Mitchell Hoey. They came from every imaginable city background. Some of them had never even owned a glove. Against the odds, these boys made it to the championship game. They were an inspiration, walking affirmation of why baseball really matters.

Most important, I thank my children, Sarah, Seamus and Liam, whose daily presence is a gift in too many ways to count, and my wife, Nora, who's been with me from the start. She is accustomed to the clatter of the keyboard, late at night.

And she understands— more than anyone —just how much this means.

Sean Kirst
Syracuse, N.Y.

Table of Contents

II. Black Cat

III. Vanished from the Game

Foreword

by Harold Holzer

During the mid–1980s, when I was a young (or so I thought at first) press officer in the administration of New York governor Mario M. Cuomo, I met an even younger fellow — a reporter from Niagara Falls (in his case, genuinely young) — who impressed me from the beginning as unusually savvy, hard-working, and gifted.

The story that originally brought us together was one of the most complex challenges I ever tackled in my role as spokesman for the New York state director of economic development. An ambitious private developer had requested state assistance for a plan to bring a major new economic development project to depressed Niagara Falls. The governor, the state's economic development director, and I all flew together to the Falls to negotiate.

And there to greet us, buttonhole us, question us, and relentlessly pursue us was Sean Kirst, boy reporter extraordinaire.

The events that unfolded in the days and weeks to come proved frustrating, vexing, and in the end, hugely disappointing, and it is no great loss to modern readers that they have been lost to history. The proposed development never got off the ground, although the state made a generous offer to attract it. Throughout the drama, Sean Kirst followed the story day by day, long after other journalists abandoned it for easier fare, until finally it died a merciful death.

At the time, I was more eager than he was to see the chapter closed. But Sean would not give up until he had extracted from us every piece of information we had about the deal-that-never-was, including a good deal of data we would have preferred to keep to ourselves. Not another reporter on the beat had the same degree of curiosity and professionalism — not to mention genuine charm — and most appeared to be twice his age.

Recalling those days, when most local reporters were more adversarial than collegial, I am convinced that Sean and I worked well together because early on, we found a bond that brought us together and gave us something to talk about beyond official business. That subject was baseball.

Sean revealed himself early as a student, fan, and historian, an acute observer of the national pastime, especially as it was played — and relived — on the major and minor league fields of New York State. And he seemed to like my own personal baseball stories (my local friends were tired of hearing them), including that of my experience of witnessing Roger Maris' 61st home run at Yankee Stadium on October 1, 1961. Talk about feeling old (even though I was only twelve at the time I saw that historic game).

Sean ultimately moved on to a bigger beat in Syracuse, and I moved from Governor Cuomo's staff to the Metropolitan Museum of Art, where I have headed the communications and marketing office since 1992. Happily, the Met soon proved a part of Sean Kirst's new beat, and we enjoyed the opportunity to renew our friendship.

As Sean discovered, the museum has long owned a little-known but extraordinarily rich baseball card collection that may well be the largest in the world, larger even than that housed at the National Baseball Hall of Fame in Cooperstown. Phil Rizzuto came to the Met to inaugurate its debut on public view, and Yogi Berra has since visited as well. What an extraordinary thing it is to stand and watch those great heroes staring at the tiny mementos of their playing days.

The collection even includes an example of the rarest of all baseball trading cards, the famous Honus Wagner that the unpredictable "Flying Dutchman" ordered withdrawn from sale when he found out that it accompanied the sale of tobacco. Sean went on to write evocatively about this trove, and quite movingly about the unique New Yorker who had amassed it.

Sean Kirst writes in the same clear, irresistible way about almost everything he tackles: his prose combines insight and verve. But it is particularly incisive when he writes about baseball. It reminds me of the work of the early sportswriters who first turned baseball reporting into an art form. Even in the days of ESPN and instant replays, it is good to read thoughtful pieces about baseball again.

And it is particularly good that the best of Sean Kirst has been collected for this book. Daily newspaper columns are too often relegated to the dust bin of memory, when the best of them deserve to be saved and savored. I suspect that readers who love sport and good journalism will savor the contents of this book for a long time.

Harold Holzer
New York

Harold Holzer, vice-president for communications at the Metropolitan Museum of Art, is also a nationally acclaimed author and scholar on the life and works of Abraham Lincoln.

Preface

These are a few of the tales you will find inside this book:

An attempt to steal Lou Gehrig's ashes from his tomb caused his widow, Eleanor, to take the first steps toward having Gehrig's remains moved to Cooperstown — where Hall of Fame officials considered turning the hall into a mausoleum for the game's immortals.

Less than a day after Ty Cobb was stabbed during a street fight in which the greatest hitter of all time later claimed to have bludgeoned a man to death, Cobb was thrown out trying to stretch a single into a double in a meaningless exhibition game.

The father of American baseball card collecting, Jefferson Burdick, was a recluse and an invalid who never attended a professional baseball game, according to the best knowledge of his closest friend.

Moses Fleetwood Walker, the last African American to play in the Major Leagues before Jackie Robinson, was arrested for the murder of a white man following a brawl on Walker's long walk home from a "baseball errand."

Babe Dahlgren, who took over when Lou Gehrig sat down for the Yankees, went to his grave maintaining that he was drummed out of baseball because of orchestrated rumors that Dahlgren loved to smoke dope.

These stories were almost all written over the past 10 years, as part of my duties as a sports columnist — and now as a metropolitan columnist — at the Syracuse *Post-Standard*. For much of that time, I was lucky to work under an editor, John Lammers, who shared my passion for baseball history.

This collection also springs from a simple truth, first shared with me years ago by baseball historian and scholar Tom Heitz: Some of the last great untold stories about the game and its heroes are hidden away in such Minor League towns as Syracuse.

I was first alerted to the fascinating tale of Burdick, the great card collector, by Luke LaPorta, a Little League pioneer whose own story is also told within this book. As for Cobb, the research behind that story was done by Doug Roberts, a Syracuse lawyer and a good friend of mine, who graciously allowed me to turn his work into a lengthy piece for the *Post-Standard*.

The exchange of letters about Gehrig's ashes was buried in an old file at the Baseball Library in Cooperstown. I went there for another pupose, which I quickly forgot when I stumbled into architectural sketches of a proposed mausoleum for housing the remains of the immortals. Concerning Dahlgren, a casual phone call about his time with the Syracuse Chiefs touched off his passionate contention that the lords of the game had wrongly labeled him as a "pothead."

This book is important to me on many levels, not the least of which is putting all of these stories and tales under "one roof." I have been in love with baseball, and its history, since early childhood. My father, who loved Charlie Gehringer, played softball well into his 50s. My mother shared his passion for the game, as well as a working class fascination for the characters who played it.

She grew up in Buffalo. Her uncle, Donald MacLeod, a Gaelic-speaking Scotch immigrant, used to take her to Buffalo Bison games at the old Offermann Stadium, where a career minor leaguer named Ollie Carnegie was a power-hitting star.

Years later, as a young woman, my mother spotted Carnegie riding a city bus to work. My mother was carrying my oldest sister on her lap, while Carnegie, her hero, was carrying a lunch pail. She felt too much reverence to dare to speak to him, but he offered a smile for her baby. In the telling of that story — in the awe my mother felt, in the link between two worlds— I first felt a kind of beauty that goes far beyond the game.

My mother is long gone, as is Jim Robertson, an old man who lived on my street, near a steel plant, when I was a boy in Dunkirk, N.Y. Mr. Robertson would often stand on the sidewalk, just taking in the breeze. He had some kind of surgery on his face that made it difficult for him to talk, and he often waved to us as we rode past on our bicycles. Someone told me, years later, that he had been a fine third baseman. By then I was a young reporter on a small daily paper. I checked out the story, only to learn that Mr. Robertson had played in an exhibition game against Pie Traynor's Pittsburgh Pirates.

It seemed incredible that such greatness could be tucked inside a pair of green work pants. I went to the house of Mr. Robertson, as I still need to call him, and he pulled out the proof, photographs and yellowed clippings that he kept in a box. He had played semipro ball in the 1920s against such men as Hugh Bedient, a pitcher and a Federal League outcast who in his prime bested Christy Mathewson in the World Series.

From his own team, the Dunkirk Blackbirds, Mr. Robertson recalled such teammates as Ty Tyson, another former Major Leaguer. And in that precious exhibition game — played on an autumn afternoon against the Pirates — Mr. Robertson came up with two hits, even though Pittsburgh won.

I wrote that story, one of my earliest attempts to capture the larger magic contained in a box score. I wrote it for two reasons. It did not seem right for the tale to die with Mr. Robertson. And I knew — in the same way that a late-summer breeze can speak of fall, before it comes — that other people would read and treasure the same story.

This book, then, was created for that purpose. If you are reading it, I assume you are a kindred soul, and I think you will take some pleasure in these stories. You will find within these pages many tales of the immortals, set side-by-side with equally important baseball tales of those of us locked down on Earth.

My mother first taught me the value of that balance. She saw both worlds, in one person, in Ollie Carnegie.

Prologue

It starts on a fall morning when you are eight or nine years old, and your mother allows you to stay home from school. You claim, as she irons, that you have a sick stomach. Maybe it is so, maybe not. The important thing is that she rules in your favor. You follow your mother as she goes through her chores, helping her to change the sheets in your brother's bedroom, where you find a stack of books he keeps piled near his bed.

He is a ballplayer, and your mother coaxed him into reading with old children's baseball books about the Golden Age: John P. Carmichael's My Greatest Day in Baseball, *Arthur Daley's* Inside Baseball, *Ray Robinson's* Greatest World Series Thrillers. *You take the books downstairs, and you sprawl on the living room floor, near a window.*

You begin reading about Enos Slaughter and his "Mad Dash," about Dizzy Dean getting hit in the head while going hard for second base, about Grover Cleveland Alexander's long walk to the mound against the Yankees.

You read about Willie Mays and "The Catch" against Cleveland. You read about the old Giants and the Dodgers and the great civic betrayals. You read about the "Miracle of Coogan's Bluff" and the day Hack Wilson lost a high fly ball, and how Wilson's whole life spiraled into tragedy. You read about Jackie Robinson and how much he endured, and how the abuse — in the end — may have sheared years from his life.

You read all morning, lying on the floor of a rented house in a little factory town, maybe 400 miles away from Yankee Stadium and great cities you can't begin to comprehend. But you are there, in those ballparks. You have grown up around small town baseball games, and you take the scents and the sounds and put them on a bigger canvas.

You see the rust and faded outfield walls of the Polo Grounds. You smell cigars and cut grass amid the diesel fumes of Brooklyn. You see the brick walls at Wrigley as Babe Ruth taunts the baying fans, as the crowd screams and lemons roll toward his cleated feet.

And you see, not far away, the quiet man who is on deck.

Lying there near the window, the books strewn about the floor, you stare at flecks of dust swirling in a beam of light.

Years later, you will know:

They are the ashes of Lou Gehrig.

I

AMONG THE IMMORTALS

1 The Ashes of Lou Gehrig

The National Baseball Hall of Fame is awaiting word from Cal Ripken, Jr. He has promised the hall some artifact from his 2,131st consecutive game, which broke the record Lou Gehrig held for 56 years.

In this case, at least, it will be hard to outdo Gehrig. Nearly 50 years ago, shortly after the 1941 death and cremation of the "Iron Horse," Gehrig's survivors offered the hall the greatest artifact of all.

His ashes.

Hall administrators were so taken with the possibility of obtaining Gehrig's remains that they began to draw up plans on a much larger scale. At that time, players like Babe Ruth and Ty Cobb were still alive. The hall saw Gehrig's ashes as the first step toward a great tomb for baseball's immortals. In one plan, Hall of Famers would have been offered the chance to enclose their ashes in the wall beneath their famous plaques.

It was all deadly serious, so serious that the hall asked its architect to draw up some designs. Then hall administrators sought out municipal opinions on whether a museum could care for human remains. Yet a tight lid was kept on the process, even after Gehrig's widow changed her mind years later.

The "repository for the immortals," as the tomb would have been called, has remained a secret for almost 50 years. The chronology is tucked away in a stack of letters and documents in the research library of the hall in Cooperstown.

And Gehrig's ashes were never disturbed — at least not legally.

After Gehrig's death in 1941 at the age of 37, his ashes were enclosed in a vase in a locked cabinet, part of a larger monument at Kensico Cemetery near Valhalla, N.Y. But Lou's parents quickly decided they wanted the ashes in the Hall of Fame. For a while, at least, so did Eleanor Gehrig, Lou's widow. She was tired of "sight-seers, picnicers (sic) and autograph hounds," reported Paul Kerr, then-treasurer of the Hall of Fame, in a 1949 memo.

Even today, with the Ripken drama reigniting old devotion, fans leave balls and bats and handwritten notes at Gehrig's grave. But in the 1940s, when Gehrig's death was still fresh, the pilgrimage was continuous and not always healthy.

The *Post-Standard*, Wednesday, September 27, 1995; original title: "Hall of Immortals"

Lou Gehrig in spring training. (National Baseball Hall of Fame Library, Cooperstown, N.Y.)

Eleanor felt Gehrig's grave was so besieged by the public that she stopped going there. Some fans, to her, seemed a little too obsessed. There was at least one attempt to steal Gehrig's ashes, according to George Pollack, Eleanor's attorney. Until she changed her mind about the transfer, Eleanor envisioned the Hall of Fame as a safe and quiet place, with built-in protection from an overzealous public.

The hall tried hard to make a secret of the plans to move the ashes. Everyone involved saw the need for what one memo called "discretion." For four years, from the first discussion in 1946 of a small and intimate crypt beneath Gehrig's plaque to more outlandish plans for a "repository for the ashes of the immortals," the hall confined the story to its own staff.

Even now the tale retains a whiff of mystery.

Chet Day, present-day general manager of Kensico Cemetery, said veteran employees recall that Lou's mother wanted the ashes moved, but

Eleanor did not. Eleanor, however, held legal control. The disagreement reportedly became heated.

Hall of Fame documents indicate Eleanor was in favor of the move as late as 1949. Her feelings quickly changed. Within a year, an attorney named John Looman was writing the hall on her behalf, claiming she was upset that a few paragraphs about the plan showed up in a Broadway column in a New York newspaper. The release of that information, Looman maintained, put Eleanor in "a rather unenviable position as far as publicity is concerned."

Because of that leak, Looman wrote, Eleanor had decided to indefinitely put the transfer on hold. Eventually that pause became a permanent decision. The ashes stayed where they were at Kensico.

That letter ends the correspondence in the file about moving Gehrig's remains. But it leaves you to wonder: Was one news leak all it took to change Eleanor's mind? Or was she upset, as baseball historian Tom Heitz speculates, at the questionable taste of making Gehrig's ashes the centerpiece of a baseball Valhalla?

The hall in the late 1940s was undergoing its first major expansion. The architect hired to draw up the plans, a man named Zogbaum, was asked to incorporate a design for a Gehrig memorial and a greater mausoleum. Perhaps that tomb would have been a thing of dignity. Or perhaps it would have trivialized the remains of baseball's greats.

Certainly it would have made it difficult to inter the extended family alongside Gehrig, which is what Eleanor did at Kensico.

Still, the biggest question of all is the mysterious break-in at Gehrig's grave — which may have pushed Eleanor toward switching the ashes to Cooperstown.

For the last 25 years of her life, Eleanor's attorney was Pollack, 80, who now lives on Long Island. He was probably Eleanor's best friend. He still takes care of the estate and serves as family representative, since there are no true survivors. It was Pollack who went to Baltimore on Gehrig's behalf when the record fell to Ripken.

Eleanor never mentioned anything to Pollack about moving Lou's ashes. But she did tell him a story about a person Pollack describes as a "nutty fan," who tried to steal Gehrig's vase from Kensico. The story obviously upset Eleanor, and she never told Pollack exactly how it came out. She never told him if the thief succeeded in taking the ashes — or if they were even returned to their place inside the monument.

Opposite: Lou and Eleanor Gehrig, in a photograph donated to the Hall of Fame by Eleanor. (National Baseball Hall of Fame Library, Cooperstown, N.Y.)

Now, Pollack wonders if that incident might have caused Eleanor to consider putting the ashes in the hall.

In their original will, written shortly before Gehrig died, Lou and Eleanor specifically asked for their ashes to be mingled. Yet, in 25 years, Eleanor never brought up that request to Pollack. Pollack finds that curious, since Eleanor neglected few details. So it affected what he did when Eleanor Gehrig died.

That was in 1984. Pollack bought a new vase for her ashes. He put it inside the small chamber at Kensico, next to Lou's vase. Pollack prefers to think Lou's vase has something in it. But remembering Eleanor's story about a grave-robber, Pollack was not absolutely sure. He did not feel any need to open the vase and take a look, since he felt he met the spirit of the request in Gehrig's will.

In the end, for whatever reason, it has all worked out all right. The vases are locked together in a monument in a graveyard near White Plains. Visitors still leave behind scribbled notes of devotion.

As for Cooperstown, any baseball fan knows this simple truth: The Lou Gehrig in the hall is always young, and far from ash.

George Pollack remains the protector of the Gehrig estate and legacy. He maintains that Gehrig earned a lasting place in the American imagination through a dignity that transcends his epic baseball achievements. Pollack does his best to preserve that reverence. He carefully controls the use of Lou's name or image, and he tries to make sure that any profit from commercial use of Gehrig's name goes directly toward medical research into Lou Gehrig's Disease.

Still, in the weeks and months after the column about Lou's ashes and Cooperstown appeared in The Post-Standard, Pollack grew troubled by the idea that he had failed to honor Lou and Eleanor's original intention. If they wanted their ashes mingled, Pollack wondered, who was he to prevent it?

Yet he also saw his job as being vigilant of Gehrig's legacy, and he carried a hidden worry. He remembered how Eleanor once started to tell him that someone had tried to steal Lou's ashes. She never finished the story. Pollack had no idea if the thief succeeded. It left him with a nagging fear that he might look into Lou's vase, locked inside the vault at the Gehrig family plot, only to discover that Lou's ashes were gone.

Pollack knew how that would play, in the tabloids and the television news. If it was true, he would be helpless to protect Lou's dignity.

Chet Day, general manager of Kensico Cemetery, said he is absolutely certain that Lou's ashes remain inside the vault. Pollack remained uneasy. The weight of the original promise bore down on him. In the summer of 1996, Pollack returned to Valhalla. He brought along the key to the vault at Gehrig's tomb.

To make peace with himself, he had come to a decision. He would open the vault. He would see what was there, and then he would make a decision about mixing the ashes.

Pollack walked to the grave. He put the key into the lock. It wouldn't turn. Pollack stooped over — standing above the balls and letters left by pilgrims — to take a better look. Someone had jammed a penny in the lock. Pollack tried again. He couldn't get the penny out.

It seemed to him to be a kind of sign.

Pollack had his answer. He turned and left, and the vault remained closed. He stopped worrying about what happened to the ashes. The important thing was the love story between Eleanor and Lou, one of the great tales of devotion in baseball history.

"They're together," Pollack says, "at least as much as they can be."

2 Ty Cobb's Violent Legacy

You want a moment, one moment, that defined Ty Cobb, and this is where you find it. In Syracuse, of all places. All the pathology, all the courage, all the ugliness. He took it with him to the plate at Star Park on August 12, 1912, where he stepped in and ripped a first-inning single off Syracuse pitcher Phil Sitton.

It was an exhibition, a meaningless game. Cobb turned the corner and tried to stretch the hit into a double, giving the crowd of 7,000 a taste of his fall-away slide. He was thrown out at second by a minor-league arm, but the attempt itself tells the story of the man.

He had a fresh stab wound in the back. Barely 12 hours before he played that game in Syracuse, while driving to the Detroit train station with his wife in the dead of night, he had been stopped and assaulted by three men. Cobb was stabbed, leaving a wound a half-inch in diameter and a quarter-inch deep.

Years later, Cobb would maintain he chased down one of his attackers and killed him. Pinned him to the ground. Clubbed him in the face with a pistol until his features disappeared. Cobb crouched over the man,

The *Post-Standard*, Friday, April 14, 1995

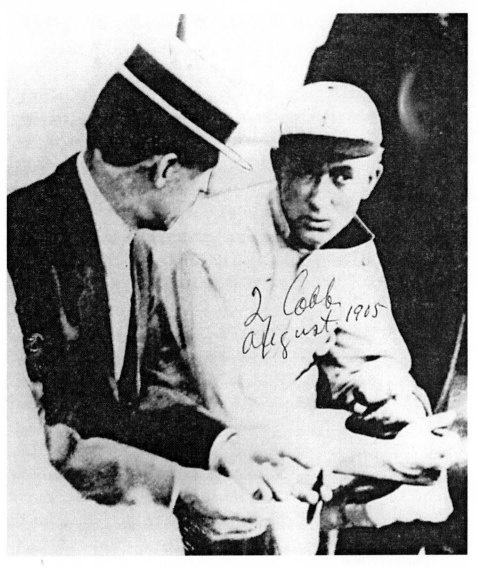

Ty Cobb in his 1905 rookie season in Detroit, with manager Bill Armour. This photograph, from the archives at the National Baseball Hall of Fame Library in Cooperstown, was apparently signed and inscribed by Cobb himself (see page 19).

watched him die, then got on a train and went to Syracuse to play hard in an exhibition.

That is the way, at least, Cobb told the story.

To biographers of an American folk hero, the saga captures the essence of the legend: Ty Cobb, the over-the-top baseball immortal, beating a man to death and then wiping his hands to board the train for Syracuse.

There is only one problem. New evidence indicates Cobb killed no one that night. Indeed, the only evidence that an attack occurred at all was the wound in Cobb's back, a wound that was treated by a Syracuse doctor.

But the real story — a tale of street crime and craps games and a desperate need to win — may say even more about Cobb as a man.

Regardless of whether a man was killed, it was one of the most bizarre and violent episodes in Cobb's career. He had sat out two games in Detroit in the days before the attack. The papers said he had a cold. But Cobb was healthy enough to play an exhibition in Syracuse with a wound between his shoulders. It is reasonable to wonder if Cobb feared for his safety in Detroit.

The Meaningless Exhibition

The day after the stabbing, while rumors he was dead made the rounds in Detroit, Cobb played against the Syracuse Stars of the old New York State League. Fred Burchell, owner of the Stars, had been lining up big-league teams for exhibitions. He wanted to prove to Ed Barrow, president of the International League, that Syracuse could support a higher brand of baseball. The success of the Tigers game hinged on the appearance of a legend who led the American League with a .421 batting average.

In the hours before the game, Burchell huddled with Tigers manager Hughie Jennings to discuss whether the wounded Cobb would play. He not only played, he played to win. He went 2-for-4. He was thrown out three times trying for an extra base and made a running shoestring catch in right field.

The Tigers won the exhibition 3-1, then grabbed a train for New York to take on the Yankees. Cobb had time before leaving to attend a local opera as a guest of honor, where he was presented with a silver shaving kit. He told the crowd, "I am very glad to be in Syracuse."

At the moment, it was certainly much safer than Detroit.

Film Misses Contradiction

There is a recent film about Cobb that stars Tommy Lee Jones. It spends a couple of hours trying to capture his essence, asking whether a man can both be a raging sociopath and yet somehow noble. It includes a re-creation of the assault in Detroit. But it misses the defining moment in Syracuse, when he tried to take extra bases with a stab wound in his back.

Almost all of the historical background on this incident has been provided by Doug Roberts, a Syracuse attorney. Roberts is a lover of baseball research, of the "forensics of the game." He is involved in several "digs" into baseball lore. Throughout it all, he never forgot how as a child he once read of Cobb bragging he killed an attacker on the streets of Detroit.

That account was contained in "Ty Cobb's Wild 10-Month Fight to Live," the same story that provides the framework for the film. Written by Al Stump and published after Cobb's death in 1961, the narrative describes how the 73-year-old Cobb pulled up his shirt to reveal for Stump a scar on his back.

"In 1912, and you can write this down, I killed a man in Detroit," Stump quoted Cobb as saying. "He and two other hoodlums jumped me on the street early one morning with a knife. I was carrying something that came in handy in my early days—a Belgian-made pistol with a heavy raised sight at the barrel end."

Cobb told Stump he drove off the men, then chased one of them into a dead-end alley. "I used that gunsight to rip and slash and tear him for about 10 minutes, until he had no face left," Cobb said. "Left him there, not breathing, in his own rotten flesh."

The graphic nature of the story stayed with Roberts, although he only hit on the local link about four years ago. While scrolling through old copies of The Syracuse *Post-Standard* from 1912 on a separate project, he came upon accounts of Cobb playing here — immediately after surviving an attack in Detroit. This is the way Cobb told the story at that time:

"I was on my way to the station with Mrs. Cobb when three figures leaped out of the dark and stopped me. I stopped the car, climbed out and asked what was the matter. They answered in a foreign tongue and clearly wanted to fight. One of them grabbed me. I hit him back and knocked him down.

"One of the others sailed into me, and while I was fighting him, the man on the ground got up, drew a knife and slashed at me. I dodged and only in time. The knife pierced my clothes and made a slight wound in my shoulder. This frightened the men. They ran off and Mrs. Cobb and I continued to the station. I did not mention it to (manager Hughie) Jennings and did not think anything about it. I suppose when I called a doctor the story leaked out."

The doctor was F.W. Van Lengen of Syracuse.

Search for Answers

The comparison, today, would be Michael Jordan getting stabbed — and later claiming he beat that attacker to death. Cobb towered above baseball at a time when it was the true national pastime. But the story became a blurry mix of history and myth. It reached the point where most biographers accepted Cobb's contention about the killing.

In attorney's fashion, Roberts set out to either prove or disprove that Ty Cobb killed a man — only hours before trying to stretch a single into a double on a little minor league field in Syracuse.

Roberts, who plans to write a detailed account of the incident, contacted Stump. Roberts spent hours in the research rooms of several libraries. He made two trips to Detroit, sifted through records in the coroner's office, met with a 93-year-old fan who remembered Cobb, and scrolled through accounts in old Detroit newspapers. Finding the answer became a quest.

The old man, William McBrearty, knew the streets of the city as they were in Cobb's day. As McBrearty drove Roberts along the same route Cobb would have used to reach the train station, he spoke of how Cobb befriended him when McBrearty was a boy.

McBrearty said the great ballplayer would sometimes pick up the wide-eyed child and his dog and drive them to the ballpark — where McBrearty's dog chased down the Tigers' fungoes.

To McBrearty, Cobb was a kind and patient man. But Roberts was chasing the ghost of another Cobb, a man who bragged of a ruthless killing.

Roberts originally set out to prove Cobb took a life. After all his digging, he left Detroit convinced that Cobb did not kill a man, that the incident did not end in a death.

Stump's most recent book, "Cobb," again contends the killing took place. Stump himself is too ill to conduct an interview. But even Louis Rubin, the man who edited that book, agrees the murder story could have been fiction.

"Cobb got a lot of things screwed up in his memory," Rubin said. "He had a very creative memory for making things look more dramatic than ever."

Shady Characters

Still, what Roberts learned did nothing to elevate his opinion of Cobb. If anything, it convinced Roberts that the assault on the ballplayer was no anonymous attack, that it came out of Cobb's contact with petty criminals in the clubhouse.

Roberts theorizes that Cobb exaggerated when he claimed he killed someone. The Detroit papers — which carried the stabbing as front-page news — mentioned nothing about a body being found near the scene of the assault. Instead of telling the *Detroit Free Press* that he killed one attacker,

Cobb said, "I gave him a whipping and reckon beat him up pretty badly." Cobb boasted that the man, very much alive, then got on his knees and begged Cobb's forgiveness.

And Roberts, who studied every unexplained death reported to the coroner in that period, found nothing of a man bludgeoned to death.

Yet, Roberts learned that the summer of 1912 had been volatile, even by Ty Cobb's standards.

Coming into the season, *Sporting Life* magazine bluntly noted how gamblers were betting big money on the batting title, sure to be won by either Cobb or Joe Jackson. In May, Cobb had been suspended after he went into the stands in New York and started beating a heckler named Claude Luecker, a man who had lost all of one hand and most of his other in a factory accident.

It was reported afterward that "underworld elements" in New York were threatening Cobb's life, but Cobb hardly seemed daunted. While sifting through a thick file of yellowed clippings in the library, Roberts came upon a separate, crumbling paragraph of newsprint. It did not even list what newspaper it came from.

The clipping told of how Cobb in 1912 "attacked ... a newsboy, after a game of craps in the Detroit clubhouse. Soon after that, Cobb was stabbed one night while on his way to the train station. Cobb concluded that the men who attacked him were friends of (the newsboy), and last Sunday night he met the newsboy alone and gave him a beating."

Cobb never publicly told this tale in the days after the assault. He said nothing about his wound to his teammates until he got on the train for Syracuse, where his roommate, Jean Dubuc, noticed Cobb's shirt was soaked with blood.

Unwilling, perhaps, to make known his involvement with street-level gamblers, Cobb didn't even call the police. And he told the Detroit papers the attack was a surprise.

"As far as I know, I have no enemies who would take this method of inflicting injury on me," he said.

That was a joke. Cobb's whole career was a primer in creating enemies.

He once broke his thumb punching a butcher's assistant in a dispute over meat. At the peak of his career, following an exhibition in which he was taunted by a college ballplayer, Cobb allegedly lured the boy to his room for a supposed "apology," then kicked and beat him while two teammates pinned the young man to the floor.

Even the Detroit papers, in 1912, didn't buy that the knifing was coincidence.

"An effort was made to hush up the affair here," the *Detroit Free Press* reported. "But the local police are busy looking for the would-be assailants. Cobb got in wrong with a member of a gang that hangs around the ball-park several days ago when he trounced a young fellow in the clubhouse."

His Legacy

No arrests were ever made in the case. Cobb recovered from the wound, won the 1912 batting title with a .410 average and remained in Detroit. He lived a long life. Even now, as the new movie details, he is remembered as perhaps the greatest and most volcanic competitor of all time.

There is no question he played that day in Syracuse with a stab wound in his back. But was he capable of smashing a pistol into a man's face for 10 minutes? And then capable of walking away from the corpse, going straight to Syracuse and playing as if nothing had happened?

Cobb, to his deathbed, hoped you would believe it. Perhaps he couldn't stand the idea that people might think he got the worst of any fight. But McBrearty, with an 80-year-old image of Cobb still fresh in his mind, neatly summed up what Doug Roberts discovered.

"He might have been a son of a bitch," McBrearty told Roberts, "but he wasn't a killer."

Doug Roberts, the lawyer and researcher whose passion and diligence uncovered this story, is now involved in a daunting project to identify the exact moment portrayed in several panoramic images of old ballparks stored at the National Baseball Museum and Hall of Fame in Cooperstown.

Roberts also continues work on his great baseball quest: He wants "Smokey Joe" Wood elected to the Baseball Hall of Fame.

As for Cobb, the National Baseball Hall of Fame Library has a photograph, apparently donated by Cobb himself, inscribed to a man named "Mac." The photo shows the young Cobb, in 1905, with his first manager in Detroit, Bill Armour. The inscription seems to summarize the whole tale of the stabbing, and the way Cobb later told it.

It reads:

"To 'Mac,' Just a serious 'country boy' being instructed by his first manager, Bill Armour, major league, he was not scared then and never been scared since, in fact he find he doesnt [sic] scare easy. Just before his first game Major League in August 1905. Ty"

◆ ◆ ◆

3 The Memory That Ruth Built

Monday was the 100th anniversary of Babe Ruth's birth. Ted Spencer got to celebrate just a little early. He is curator of the National Baseball Hall of Fame and Museum. In December, he was going about his business on a quiet day when a dignified couple asked for a minute of his time.

They were carrying the one relic of Ruth's life the hall could never find.

"What we always wanted," Spencer said, "was some evidence of the Babe's kindness toward children."

We have all heard the legends about Ruth's good deeds for kids. But the stories are anecdotal. The hall, which is serious about documenting history, had been frustrated in finding physical proof.

Bette Beaumont held it in her hands. She and her husband, Leo, made the pilgrimage to Cooperstown to guarantee their treasure ended up in the right place. Bette, 67, lives in Florida now, but her maiden name is Clark, and she grew up in Winthrop, Mass. More than 60 years ago, that is where her brother, Fred Jr.— an active 7-year-old boy with a full head of curls— became a victim of the polio epidemic.

The doctors made 5-year-old Bette move away, for fear she would contract the same illness. For more than a year, Fred Jr. was confined to the Children's Hospital in Boston. It was a difficult thing for the family to endure. But Fred Sr. was New England regional manager for Oscar Mayer meats. He knew what might lift the spirits of his son, and he had the kind of friends who could make the connection.

They got word to the Babe of what had happened to the child.

In January 1932, the same year in which Ruth's legend would peak because of the "called shot," a letter arrived at Children's Hospital. It was hand-written, beneath a letterhead that simply read, "Babe Ruth, New York." This is what the Babe wrote:

> Hello, Fred
> I have received some very nice reports about you and the nice way you are getting along. Now I want you to keep it up and it will not be long before you will be [sic] and running around. You are

only eight years old, and who knows that someday the umpire will
say, Freddy Clark Jr., now batting for Babe Ruth. Say, Freddy? Will
that be great or not. Now I want you [sic] keep your fight and
think of me.

From your friend, "Babe" Ruth

Fred Clark Jr. never fully recovered. He would die young, at the age
of 42. The letter went into storage at the old family home in Winthrop.
Years later, when her mother decided it was time to leave that house, Bette
Beaumont volunteered to take one last walk around. The place was all
packed up. Her mother, overcome by emotion, stayed in the car.

Bette was about to descend into the basement when she saw a slip of
paper lying on the steps.

It was the letter from Ruth, almost lost in the move. Bette and Leo
put it in a safe deposit box, where it stayed for years. Fascinated, they
taught themselves much of the Babe's history. Bette can tell you, for
instance, that Ruth was meticulous about putting quotation marks around
his nickname because of strict training in the orphanage from Roman
Catholic nuns.

A few months ago, the Beaumonts agreed they should finally do something with the letter. They are at a point in their lives for making those
decisions. You know they could have sold it, for a ton of money. But the
episode during the move whispered to Bette that something bigger was
involved.

Their children, and grandchildren, suggested the Hall of Fame.

That is how Ted Spencer stumbled into this climax to his quest, an
old couple with the relic that will make the Ruth exhibit.

The letter is now at a lab, being chemically preserved. Hall officials
couldn't be happier. What they like is the hand-scrawled spontaneity, reinforced by the missing words and grammatical errors. This was Ruth, at
the pinnacle of celebrity, taking the time to write some kid he had never
even met.

The hall didn't make a big deal this week of Ruth's 100th birthday,
simply because few visitors go to Cooperstown in February. Instead,
Spencer said, the anniversary will be celebrated this summer for the nice-
weather crowds. The letter will serve as a prime exhibit. It will hang next
to a photo of Fred Clark, Jr., as a little boy, wearing a cap and carrying a
bat. Bette Beaumont and her family plan to attend the opening.

They are thrilled about it, although Bette is thinking a lot about her
brother. They were born into a fiery family love for the Red Sox. Fred Jr.
was an athletic child. Without polio, he most certainly would have taken

Babe Ruth, with children, in Vancouver, B.C., 1926. There are many legends about Babe's kindnesses to kids. (National Baseball Hall of Fame Library, Cooperstown, N.Y.)

up baseball. She has this vivid image of young Fred, shortly after he came home from the hospital. He would sit at the ballpark, watching other kids play ball.

"He was such a handsome boy, and he suffered such pain in his life," Bette said. That is why she is feeling so fulfilled this week, amid all this talk of Ruth and his birthday. Her brother has attained his own piece of baseball heaven. With the help of the Babe, he is in the Hall of Fame.

◆ ◆ ◆

4 Babe Was a Smash in Syracuse

An October afternoon, 1928. A car pulls up in the rain at the old House of Providence, an orphanage on West Onondaga Street in Syracuse. It carries a few men in long coats, including a reporter for the *Herald*, who writes this description for the next day's paper:

"Row upon row of shining-faced little kids, scrubbed and brushed to within an inch of their lives, sitting quietly — as only orphans can sit — on rows of straight wooden chairs. Quiet-voiced, kindly sisters bustling about. Every eye glued on the door — every face bright with expectancy. The same expectancy you see on the faces of little kids whose fathers take them to the ballparks every little while. Only these kids haven't any dads to take them into ballparks, or anywhere else.

"And then in walks THE GREATEST MAN IN THE WORLD. No doubt about it. Any one of them would fight to prove it. And, throwing off his hat and coat, he makes himself right at home. Shaking hands with all he can reach; tossing the littlest ones high in the air and laughing uproariously when they squeal; feeling one fellow's pitiful little bicep and kidding him about his 'Gene Tunney muscle'; showing how he swings at a fast one and a slow one. In short, doing just exactly what kids like to have him do."

Babe Ruth.

Ruth was one year past hitting 60 homers in a season. He was five days past batting .625 in a World Series sweep of the St. Louis Cardinals. Ruth was among the most famous people in the world. He was rich, with fine clothes, beautiful women and a lust for living big.

Ruth remains front-page news in 1998. It has been 50 years since the Babe died, an anniversary that has put him on the cover of *Sports Illustrated* and made him the focus of an HBO documentary. His uniform is the centerpiece of a new Hall of Fame exhibit at the New York State Fair. And the interest is magnified by Mark McGwire, who has tied Ruth's best with 60 home runs in a season, a feat that shines a light on the man who did it first.

Seventy years ago, Ruth walked through wet leaves toward the House of Providence.

The *Post-Standard*, Monday, September 7, 1998

The Babe understood. He had been a kid in trouble on the streets of Baltimore, ignored and neglected by an alcoholic father, finally pushed into a Catholic orphanage. He grew up among the forgotten and the castoffs. Yet Ruth, as a boy, soon revealed his potent gifts, and he rose up to change the basic way baseball was played.

He was all about power — big homers, big money, the biggest town, the biggest team. Still, he was an icon for the poor because he never really changed. As local Syracuse baseball historian Ron Gersbacher points out, Ruth first embraced Syracuse orphans in 1922, joining them for a sandlot game at Burnet Park, where 5,000 boys surged around the Yankee hero. Ruth waded in, ignoring dusty hand prints on his stylish new suit.

In 1928 he was again in Syracuse, this time joined by Lou Gehrig for an exhibition game. It was too wet for the Yankee stars to play. Instead, Ruth and Gehrig went for a tour, stopping at a Syracuse University football game. They left for their visit to the orphanage, where Gehrig watched as Ruth gave a short talk.

"Kids," he told the orphans, "I'm no speechmaker. But I want to tell you that if you mind the good sisters and learn your lessons and be on the square, you'll be mighty glad when you get as big as I am. You may not have as much fun as other kids, or as much as you ought to have. But you can all be big men, good men. And you're a mighty fine-looking bunch of kids. As I said, I'm no speechmaker."

"But THEY thought he was," the *Herald* reported, "and that's what counted. And so did Sister Emily, the superintendent.

"'Mr. Ruth, I don't know how to thank you,' she said. 'The children have been talking about you for weeks. ... They've been so excited they couldn't think about anything else. You'll never know what it has meant to them. You can't imagine what such a thing means in a place like this.'

"Several minutes later, after the children had sung their little institution song and given three cheers ... the Babe sat silent in the car. Suddenly, he snorted. 'Can't imagine it, eh?' he said. 'Can't imagine it? The hell I can't. I was in one!'"

That was Ruth, why he still matters. He was better than his myth.

John Timmins, 93, of Syracuse, grew up in the House of Providence. He remembers Ruth's visit with the orphans at a baseball diamond at Burnet Park in Syracuse, in 1922. "We all knew he was an orphan, too," Timmins says. In Timmins' memory, another House of Providence orphan "named Brennan struck out Babe Ruth. I remember (Ruth) was wearing a suit, and he swung so hard at the ball he made a hurricane of dust when he missed — probably on purpose. I remember it like it was yesterday morning."

In 2001, the House of Providence held a reunion of orphans who'd grown up there. Timmins showed up hoping to find someone from his generation, someone else who might remember that era. He was the oldest one at the reunion, by about 10 years, which left him alone with his memories of Ruth.

◆ ◆ ◆

5 A Baseball History Lesson

During my childhood, my old man drove a crane on a coal pile. He rarely showed his face at my school — unless my mother dragged him along to some parent-teacher conference.

Bear with me. This has everything to do with whether George Herman "Babe" Ruth really called his shot when the Yankees played the Cubs in the 1932 World Series.

And that remains important, not because John Goodman made a bad movie about Ruth, but because October marks the 60th anniversary of an event central to baseball mythology.

Did Ruth — while standing in the heart of Wrigley Field, that still-vibrant temple of baseball — predict the exact landing spot for his fifth-inning homer off Cubs hurler Charlie Root?

Getting back to the story, I was half-awake in some forgotten high school class when my old man stuck his head in the door. That was trouble. It could only mean somebody had died, or that I'd better be ready to lie like crazy.

"He's got his road test today," my old man grunted to the teacher, which surprised me — since I wasn't signed up to take it.

It made sense once we got in the car. "Joe McCarthy called," the old man said. "He's calling back in 15 minutes."

That was it. My parents would usually break my neck for playing

---

The *Post-Standard*, Thursday, May 12, 1992

hooky. But my old man was a ballplayer — he had a heart attack after play-ing shortstop, in a softball game, at the age of 54 — and Joe McCarthy was bigger than school.

I had written a stupid, "Geez,-can-I-have-an-interview" letter to the former Yankees manager, then long-retired and ancient in Buffalo.

McCarthy gave a jingle, and the old man came to get me. I went in the house and the phone rang, and a baseball immortal called me by the wrong name.

"Peter," Joe McCarthy said. "Next time send a stamped, self-addressed envelope."

His voice was thin, trembling. He said he didn't do interviews, be-cause he "forgets things." I got the feeling he didn't want any kid to see him in ill health. I was groping for questions when McCarthy made it easy.

"The Babe never called his shot," he said.

He told me Ruth was "gesturing" in anger. The Cubs had been riding the big guy — part of a bitter dispute between the clubs — and Ruth was giving it right back. Then the Babe hit a home run that cleared the wall near the scoreboard by 10 feet.

Awesome, yes. But not mystical, McCarthy implied.

I put down the phone and went back to school.

Now, McCarthy is dead. So are my parents. But the argument about the called shot is heating up again. In the new movie, from what I've read, Goodman is shown pointing to the exact place where the ball touches down.

It seemed the time had come to follow up on the phone call. I burrowed into some microfilm and dug up the Associated Press account of the game, gleaned from the Oct. 2, 1932, edition of The *Post-Stan-dard*.

"Before he connected for (the) blow," the paper reported, "there were two strikes on him and the Cub players, yelling from their dugout, were making uncomplimentary remarks. The Babe WAVED THEM BACK TO THEIR DUGOUT (emphasis mine), raising his two fingers to tell them that there were two strikes on him and to watch out. He connected with the next ball for his second homer, and the Cubs crawled further [sic] back in their dugout."

Son of a gun. I'm glad the old man came and got me.

◆ ◆ ◆

6 Former Chief, 79, Waits for Justice

Don't assume that Ellsworth "Babe" Dahlgren, a former Syracuse Chief, takes pride in his sliver of baseball immortality.

Dahlgren was a reserve first baseman for the New York Yankees on May 2, 1939, when Lou Gehrig finally decided he was too sick to play. Manager Joe McCarthy tabbed Dahlgren to start at first, ending Gehrig's streak of 2,130 consecutive games.

More than a half-century later, Dahlgren rarely speaks of that moment. Instead, he continues to fight for vindication over what he maintains was baseball's first drug scandal.

"I've suffered from it for 50 years," Dahlgren, 79, said by telephone from his home in Bradbury, Calif. "I still carry it around on my back. I was traded eight times because of a story that wasn't true."

He readily distributes copies of his letters to baseball commissioners, seeking some kind of apology. Nothing has happened. So he is working on a book detailing his contention that someone spread a lie about him abusing marijuana.

The rumor poisoned his career, according to Dahlgren, who suspects the story originated with McCarthy.

Al Lopez, a member of the Hall of Fame veterans committee who played with Dahlgren at Pittsburgh in 1944, can remember the whispers.

"I heard something about it, yeah," Lopez said by phone from his home in Tampa, Fla. "It was hard to prove, and I think it was hearsay. But a guy (accused) of something like that, you're not going to want him on the club."

In a sense, Dahlgren's fine play for the Chiefs triggered the events that led to his odyssey. In 1935, his rookie season, Dahlgren started in the infield for the Boston Red Sox. But he was sent to Syracuse the following year, after Boston obtained future Hall of Fame first baseman Jimmie Foxx. During his summer with the Chiefs, Dahlgren lived in a small house near North Salina Street, not far from the stadium.

The *Post-Standard* called him a "classy first-sacker" who batted .318 while driving in 121 runs, still the second-highest total in the history of the team.

The *Post-Standard*, Tuesday, April 21, 1992

The Yankees, impressed by those numbers, brought him up in '37 as a backup for the "Iron Horse." In 1939, after 2,130 consecutive games, Gehrig was diagnosed with a terminal disease that would later be identified as amyotrophic lateral sclerosis.

And Dahlgren was called on to fill Gehrig's spot.

"I'm sick of that, too," Dahlgren said. "I never wanted to be a Yankee. There was no way to replace Gehrig." Still, Dahlgren contributed that year to a great New York team, driving in 89 runs for a club busy winning its fourth consecutive World Series.

Yet Dahlgren said his troubles began when he made the off-season mistake of seeking batting advice from Lefty O'Doul, a retired .349 major-league hitter who lived in San Francisco. O'Doul, Dahlgren said, told a reporter about the visit. A story went out on the wire service poking fun at McCarthy's inability to tutor his own players. "Marse Joe," Dahlgren claims, questioned him about seeing O'Doul and never forgave the first baseman for looking beyond the Yankees for help.

Dahlgren suspects that's when his problems began.

In 1941, the .261 career batter began a five-year tour of baseball that would take him to the Boston Braves, the Cubs, the St. Louis Browns, the Dodgers, the Phillies, the Pirates and finally back to the Browns. He retired in 1946.

It was in Brooklyn that Dahlgren first heard the drug rumors. After the 1942 season — in which he batted .169 — Dahlgren balked at an attempt by team president Branch Rickey to ship him to the minors. During a tense encounter, Dahlgren said, Rickey brought up the allegations about marijuana abuse.

"It was a lie," Dahlgren said.

Dahlgren took his complaint to baseball's commissioner, Kenesaw Mountain Landis, seeking a ruling to clear his name. According to Dahlgren, Landis opened a file after Dahlgren voluntarily submitted to a series of blood tests.

But Landis died in 1944, and Dahlgren maintains the issue died with him.

Nearly fifty years later, Dahlgren said he simply wants a public admission from the commissioner's office acknowledging the blood tests and the meetings with Landis. He has sent that request, without success, to every commissioner except Fay Vincent.

After his playing days, Dahlgren ran a batting cage near his home and spent some time as a hitting instructor for the Kansas City and Oakland Athletics.

It would seem easy enough for Major League Baseball executives to

Babe Dahlgren during his Yankee career. (National Baseball Hall of Fame Library, Cooperstown, N.Y.)

resolve the old man's contention, one way or another, by simply responding on whether a file exists. If it does, Dahlgren said, he wants it thrown open to the public.

Don't look for him to get that chance.

"Basically, our position regarding Babe Dahlgren is that we won't attempt to rewrite history," baseball spokesman Richard Levin said. "We don't see any reason to reopen that case."

Babe Dahlgren died in 1996, at the age of 84. Danny Litwhiler, who played with Dahlgren on the 1943 Philadelphia Phillies, said his old friend was still angry until the day he died, convinced that he'd been ruined by a false rumor spread within Major League Baseball.

◆ ◆ ◆

7 Baseball Makes Immortal a Man, a Romance, an Era

Laraine Day figures it this way. Leo Durocher wanted to be in baseball's Hall of Fame more than anything else in his life. He died embittered three years ago, an 86-year-old man convinced his induction was not going to happen.

Still, Day remains a religious person. She is confident Leo will be in Cooperstown on Sunday, getting a belly laugh out of seeing her accept in his behalf. She was his former wife. Most important, until he died, she was perhaps his greatest friend.

"It would have been the most fitting if he was here to get it himself," she said. "That was all he was living for."

Her role, however, provides perfect symmetry. Forty-seven years ago, Durocher was banned from baseball for a year for "the accumulation of unpleasant incidents in which he was involved," in the words of then-Commissioner A.B. "Happy" Chandler.

The *Post-Standard*, Thursday, July 28, 1994

Leo was accused of hanging out with gamblers. Chandler blasted the manager, known as "The Lip," for saying blunt and nasty things about opponents—notably for calling Yankee president Larry MacPhail "a blowhard."

Within the then-puritanical commandments of the game, Laraine qualified as a major "incident."

She was famous, a beautiful actress. She co-starred with Cary Grant, Spencer Tracy, Robert Mitchum, Gary Cooper. When Durocher first started courting her, she also happened to be married. Forget that it was a marriage in trouble. Forget that no one would blink at the same thing today.

This was 1947. They married in Mexico, on the day after Laraine got her official divorce. An American judge contemplated jailing them for bigamy. "When I married him, we'd never even been out on a date," Day said. "Because my divorce wasn't final, I could only see him with chaperones."

Despite the public heat, Laraine hung in there. She was with Leo in 1951, for Bobby Thomson's pennant-winning homer and the "Miracle at Coogan's Bluff." She was with Leo for the triumph of the '54 World Series, when Willie Mays made the catch that still defines baseball grace.

Year after year, as other managers of his era made the Hall of Fame, Leo waited. He had a barbed reputation. He once said, point-blank, that he would knock down his mother if it would help win a game. And then there were "the incidents."

"I always felt he should have been vindicated for all that many years before," Day said.

As a shortstop, Durocher played on both "The Murderers Row" Yankees of Gehrig and Ruth, and with the gritty St. Louis Cardinals known as the "Gashouse Gang." But it was as a manager that he earned his greatest fame.

His lifetime winning percentage, with the Dodgers, Giants, Cubs and Astros, was .540. He won 2,008 games, three pennants and one World Series. For the last "seven or eight years," according to veterans committee member Al Lopez, Durocher barely missed induction into the hall.

"This year he just got the votes," Lopez said. "I think it helped him to have Bill White come on (the committee), and Yogi (Berra), and Pee Wee (Reese), who was one of his players."

Six weeks ago, Bill Guilfoile called Day to ask if she would take Leo's place at the induction. Leo had been married four times. Guilfoile, the hall's associate director, could have used that as an excuse to duck what

Laraine Day and Leo Durocher, appearing on the *B.F. Goodrich Celebrity Time*, 1950. (National Baseball Hall of Fame Library, Cooperstown, N.Y.)

will be one of the hot stories of this weekend. He could have asked Leo and Laraine's two children, Christopher and Michele. He could have asked Mays, who describes Durocher as a "dear father."

Instead, Guilfoile went with Day.

She is 73 years old, living near Hollywood with her husband, Mike Grilikhes, who was also a close friend of Durocher.

"We were divorced in 1959," she said Wednesday of Leo. "There was no bitterness. We had just become interested in different things and different people. But we always stayed friends."

Day said Leo's public savagery was a self-created thing. The bottom line — prepare the drumroll — is that he was a nice guy, even if Durocher made history by saying nice guys finish last.

"He was a very generous, kind, thoughtful person who put on a great show," Day said.

This is her defining example. The Dodgers went to Cuba for spring training in 1947. Every night, she recalls, Durocher would leave the ballpark for the hotel in the seventh inning. The newspapers claimed he was going back for an extra shift behind closed doors with his new "starlet" wife.

What he was actually doing, Day said, was meeting privately with individual Dodgers, veterans like Reese, convincing them to accept Jackie Robinson as a teammate. Robinson was up against the world in his efforts to integrate baseball. Durocher tried to make it easier.

Day recalls with great nostalgia the fine times in New York, when Durocher's Giants often ruled the National League. After every win, the couple would go to a movie or out on the town. After each loss, they made sure to stay home.

"It wasn't that we were so glum," she said. "Everybody would second-guess. The cab drivers, the waiters. People would stick their heads out of windows and second-guess Leo as he walked down the street. I remember once we had just lost a very bad game, and a cab driver started telling me what Leo should have done. I told him, 'You turn around, shut up and start driving this cab.' I had never spoken to anyone that way in my life."

His favorite players, she said, shared his kind of fire: Reese, Robinson, Mays, Sal Maglie, Alvin Dark, Eddie Stanky. She remembered how Leo would weave yarns about his old teammate and opponent, the great Dizzy Dean — how Dean's wife would break things in the women's restroom whenever her husband lost, how Dean concocted wild new biographies for every new set of reporters.

Day met Durocher in 1941, at New York's Stork Club. She was at a table with Allan Jones. Leo walked in and immediately attracted a crowd. She knew nothing about baseball, much less about Leo. He seemed noisy and arrogant, and she had no wish to see him again.

A few years later, they happened to fly on the same plane from the Los Angeles airport. "I turned to this lady I was with and said, 'Let's hope we don't sit anyplace near him,'" Day said.

When they got on board, Durocher had theatrically saved them two seats. By the time the plane landed, Day had been won over by someone she describes as a funny, charming and warm baseball man. Beyond that, in a fashion she's rarely seen again in her life, she sums him up in one word.

Vitality.

"You could be at a party filled with all the biggest stars," she said. "But when Leo walked in, everyone turned toward him."

It is up to her to pay him tribute Sunday before the baseball world. Even Day, the veteran actress, is feeling a few nerves.

"I'm afraid I won't know anyone," she said. "I'm afraid they'll all have grown old, or changed." But she has great faith in what she calls "baseball people." Durocher always ran with a show biz crowd. When he died, Day said, it was his ballplayers— not Hollywood — who showed up to say good-bye.

"He had been so ill, for so long, that he died without too many friends around," she said.

Day, for her part, never went away. She understood how he always felt branded by the days of "incidents," how he felt his reputation barred him from the Hall of Fame. On Sunday, she will share three brief and telling stories about Durocher, including a vivid memory from the game when Bobby Thomson knocked it out. She believes Leo will be there, enjoying it all. And she has no doubts about where baseball's bad boy wound up.

"I think," she said, "they'll let him have the day off to come down."

Mike Grilikhes reports that he and Laraine Day continue to live quietly in California, "enjoying every day with each other."

◆ ◆ ◆

8 World Series Finally Rings True for Buckner

The ring didn't fit on his left hand. Line drives and hard slides broke all the fingers. The knuckles are huge and the bones are crooked, so he slid it onto his right hand, opened and closed it a couple of times.

Bill Buckner showed the ring to the only guy on the pregame bench, Syracuse Chiefs player Julian Yan, a native of the Dominican Republic. "Magnifico?" Buckner asked. "Yeah," Yan said in a soft voice.

All around them were empty blue seats at MacArthur Stadium, where the crowd was barely 2,000. "That's about it," Buckner said, amused by the irony. He had 2,715 hits in 22 major-league seasons. He won a batting title with the Cubs.

And he came so close to winning the whole thing, to being part of a world championship team.

But Buckner did not get a World Series ring until Wednesday, under moody gray skies in a Triple-A ballpark.

It made him wistful about his three kids, Brittany and Christen and 4-year-old Robert, all far away, back in Boston. And he thought about two shots at a ring as a player.

In 1974, Oakland took out Buckner's Dodgers in five games. That was long before the hard luck of 1986 that became baseball lore, when the wounded Buckner helped carry the Boston Red Sox to the absolute brink of rocking the Mets.

In the sixth game, the Sox had a 5-3 lead with two out in the tenth. The Mets won. The final run scored when Mookie Wilson's grounder skipped under Buckner's glove at first base. A fine ballplayer became a tragic figure, which is a permanent bad rap. The Red Sox blew a two-run lead with no one on and two out. It was a team breakdown.

Buckner is the guy we remember.

He is a batting instructor now in the Blue Jays' farm system. He looks much younger than his 43 years, young enough to still be playing, which he misses tremendously.

"This isn't like being a player," Buckner said of the ring, a heavy chunk of diamonds and gold. "I came very close to a world championship, and it would have been nice. You can't come any closer than the seventh game. But Toronto, it's the kind of organization where they want everybody to feel like they had something to do with it."

He did. Buckner tutored Ed Sprague last summer in Syracuse, and Sprague went up to hit a pinch-homer for Toronto that turned the tide of the World Series.

Still, Buckner is appreciative of his two trips as a player to baseball's pinnacle. "The ultimate goal is to win it all, but just to be there is something," he said. "Ernie Banks, he never even saw a playoff game."

The Blue Jays ordered 235 of the $8,000 rings, and Executive Vice President Pat Gillick crisscrossed the country, handing out most of them. He found Dave Winfield, now with the Twins, in a Chicago hotel lobby. No media, no ovation, just a handshake for the first ring of Winfield's career. "This is what it's all about," Winfield told Gillick.

At Big Mac, the rings sat on a folding table, near home plate. Buckner's name was the first to be called, ahead of Chiefs manager Nick Leyva, coaches Rocket Wheeler and John Poloni, team administrators Tex and John Simone.

Buckner said a couple soft words to Gillick no one could hear, then went to the dugout and slipped on the prize. "Thank you for the great years in Boston!" a Red Sox fan shouted from the first row of the stands.

It was the right thing to say. Buckner reached out to shake the man's hand, and for a moment both of them were touching the ring.

Bill Buckner now lives a quiet life in Idaho. "I've got some real estate stuff going, and I've got a couple of car dealerships," he says. He is happy, he says, for the chance to spend time with his teen-age children. "I don't want to be leaving anymore," he says. "It's just nice to be around, and to be able to do things with them in the summertime."

As for the World Series ring, he keeps it in a case with the rings he received for being on pennant-winners with the Dodgers and the Red Sox, in the same room as the Silver Bat he earned as a National League batting champion. He chooses not to wear the World Series ring from Toronto, although he appreciates how the Blue Jays valued him enough as a batting instructor to make him a part of the celebration.

"It's nice," Buckner says, "but it's not quite the same."

◆ ◆ ◆

9 Baseball History Lofts a Line at a Regular Guy

Sal Durante calls it his "secret life." Every day he gets up in the morning and drives a school bus loaded with kids, where he faces the same trials, the same fatigue, of any bus driver in Brooklyn.

But now and then the phone will ring, and the "secret life" will kick in. Maybe it will be a filmmaker wanting Sal to take a drive to Cooperstown. Maybe it will be the Yankees saying Mr. Steinbrenner wants him as a guest at a game.

Thirty-three years ago, Durante was a teen-ager in the bleachers at Yankee Stadium when Roger Maris ripped a line drive that sailed over the fence. Durante had played some outfield as a boy, and he stayed with the ball from the moment it left the bat. He stood up on his seat and barehanded the shot, and with that he and Maris were linked in history.

At least until someone goes one home run better.

"That was a thrill, and the money was nice, but the whole time I just wanted to give the ball to Maris," Durante said.

It was Roger's 61st home run of the 1961 season, the homer that eclipsed Babe Ruth for the single-season record. Durante fell to the ground clutching the ball. Despite the velocity, the catch did not bruise his hand.

There was a $5,000 reward for whoever caught the ball, and he got popped in the face while he held on for dear life. But the security guards came and pulled everyone off, giving a 19-year-old who delivered auto parts a burst of baseball fame.

Durante initialed the ball before he allowed it out of his hand. It was his means of insurance, to make sure no one tried any switch. It left his mark on a record no one else has challenged.

Until now.

Ken Griffey, Jr. already has 32 home runs. He has gotten to that plateau faster than anyone in history. The All-Star break is more than two weeks away. It is a year of a reputed rabbit ball, just as it was when Maris set the record. Since Griffey has the air of a guy who can do it, a tremor of excitement is going through baseball.

Durante respects Griffey, but he won't yet concede the threat.

The *Post-Standard*, Tuesday, June 28, 1994

"Sure, I hear it, here and there, that he's ahead of the record," Durante said. "But it's happened before. How about Kingman? What he'd have, 31 at the break? They all wear down. This is not an easy record to break."

Looking back, Durante sees his role as destiny. That is why he will resist any hackneyed efforts to get him out into the stands, even if Griffey closes in on the record, even if promoters want his picture waiting for another shot.

It would be too shallow, an insult to Maris. Durante wasn't a regular at Yankee Stadium. He double-dated at the game with his fiancée, Rosemarie, along with one of his cousins and a girlfriend. They made the decision to go that morning. They got off the subway and went to the stadium ticket booth. Just for the hell of it, they asked if there were any seats left in right field.

"The guy looks through the pile and says, 'Sure. Here ya go.'"

Unbelievable. The biggest record of them all on the line, and they walked up and got to sit near the bull's eye. Still, they weren't really thinking about the 61st homer. Durante would have been happy to grab a batting practice ball. But some inner voice warned him to switch his seat with Rosemarie, the same voice that causes an outfielder to shift position by a step.

When Maris launched history from one end, Sal was on the other.

That was the last he saw of the game. The guards brought him down into the stadium to meet Maris, down into the crush of cameras and writers. Durante had instant sympathy for Roger. "I wondered how he'd put up with it, day after day, for all those weeks," Durante said.

He had always been a Mickey Mantle fan, but he immediately switched allegiance. Maris was appreciative, gracious, a regular guy, not the crank that Durante was always reading about.

Maris gave Durante a cigarette lighter that carried the Yankee logo. A month later, when Sal and Rosemarie got married, Maris mailed them a silver gravy dish. And in 1965, Rosemarie wrote to Maris and asked if he'd make time to meet their 3-year-old son. Maris said sure, and they all went out to the stadium, where Roger made a fuss about the kid.

All of this created what Sal calls his secret life. "One day a working stiff," Durante said. "One day a celebrity." One day he deals with screaming kids on the bus. One day, in Cooperstown, grown men call him "sir."

When it first happened, he took the $5,000 in reward money and paid off his parents' debts, and used the rest to buy some furniture. That was big money then, but Durante still had to go out and get a job. He had been a gopher for an auto parts outfit, and eventually he settled in as a bus driver.

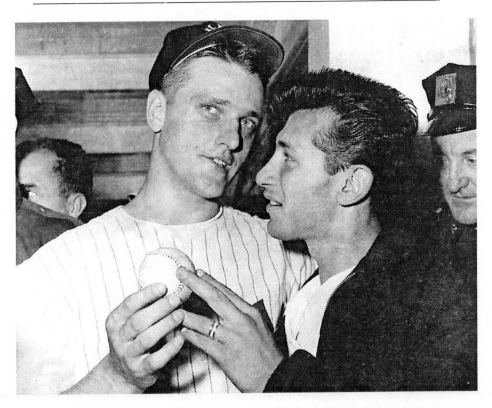

Roger Maris and Sal Durante, after Maris' 61st home run, 1961. (National Baseball Hall of Fame Library, Cooperstown, N.Y.)

He got some strange mail. A woman who grabbed his feet right after he caught the ball asked if he would mail her his shoes. No, Durante said. But he also heard from a lot of regular people, who somehow felt touched by his role in the record.

The years went by. Even as many of his friends moved away, Durante stayed in New York City, held there by his roots. The city seemed to get tougher and colder. He raised three children, became a grandfather. Baseball, to Durante, gradually changed. Maybe it was Sal growing into middle-age, but the love, the passion, drained from the sport. His trips to the stadium declined. In 1985, he looked in the paper to learn that Maris was dead of cancer.

A year later, on the 25th anniversary of No. 61, he made what remains his last trip to the ballpark. Steinbrenner invited him, and he saw Maris' widow, Pat, and her kids. It was an emotional reunion. "A beautiful person," Durante recalled.

A couple of summers ago, Sal was invited to Cooperstown to be part of a documentary. They got out the ball, and one of his initials was still there, faded but distinct.

"It didn't really change my life," Durante said. "But it put me down in history."

He wonders about that, as Griffey keeps up this torrid home-run chase. Maybe it will be just another false hunt. Maybe the record, in the same way as batting .400 or winning 30 games, has become a kind of statistical relic. Yet, Durante has the sound of a man who thinks it soon may fall.

"I didn't get rich off this," he said. "Really, (after the reward) I never made a penny off it. But I would like to stay a part of baseball. What's it like to be part of something, then to lose it?"

It is a question he asks for himself, and for Maris.

Three men, Mark McGwire, Sammy Sosa, and Barry Bonds, have now exceeded Roger Maris' single-season home run record. Yet Durante still lives out his "secret life," a more innocent alternative to the cold-blooded financial issues swirling around some of the home run balls hit by Bonds and McGwire. The Hartford Courant, *for instance, noted how Sal and Rosemarie were among the honored guests at the 2001 screening reception for Billy Crystal's "61*," a film about the home run chase between Maris and Mantle.*

"He's one of the biggest celebrities in the room," Bob Costas told the Courant.

◆ ◆ ◆

10 Bouton's Book Told Sad Tale of Mantle

Bowie Kuhn was more than happy to hurl the first harpoon. Jim Bouton's new book had just hit the stands, and the commissioner of baseball was sputtering mad.

The *Post-Standard*, Monday, April 18, 1994

Jim Bouton, during his career with the Yankees. (National Baseball Hall of Fame
Library, Cooperstown, N.Y.)

It was preposterous, Kuhn said. How could anyone claim that some of baseball's greatest stars were actually drunk on the field?

Kuhn could have been even more specific. The book was "Ball Four," and the star in question was the brightest one of all. And while Bouton wrote 25 years ago with a light-handed brilliance about lechery and drug abuse and pettiness among ballplayers, what really teed people off is what he said about Mickey Mantle.

The essence of which, it is now clear, was absolutely true.

"I was glad to see (Mantle) go in (the Betty Ford Clinic)," Bouton said a week or two ago from New Jersey, where the former Syracuse Chief is now in private business. "I was pleased for him. But I don't take any responsibility for it."

He doesn't see himself as playing a role in making Mantle face the truth. Still, Bouton was about the first person in baseball to refuse to serve as an "enabler." Within the business of alcohol reform and rehab, that is the word they use to describe people who delude themselves about a bad drunk's behavior, who prefer to let it happen and who fear rocking the boat.

"Boat rocker" was among the nicer things the baseball world called Bouton.

That was during Vietnam, the string of assassinations, the free-fall of safety and sanity in U.S. cities. Heroes were failing everywhere. Americans clung to a childhood vision of baseball players. Mantle was perceived as a prince of tragic nobility, a guy of tremendous talent carried down by his bad knees.

Bouton, who had been Mantle's teammate during the decline of the Yankees, popped the bubble. He described Mantle with fondness and admiration. He loved Mantle's irreverence, his sense of humor. He was in awe of his baseball talents. But he also spoke of how Mantle was prone to volcanic mood swings, how he sometimes could be a jerk even to little kids.

And Bouton said, bluntly, that the guy's personality was shaped and defined by alcohol. He talked about Mantle slamming pinch-hit homers when he was so hung over he had trouble standing up. He lamented the early demise of Mantle's career, an end hastened by far too many evenings at the bar.

"Mantle," Bouton recalls, "would miss games because he was so hung over."

That is a crystal sign of alcoholism, when drinking outweighs the basic anchors in your life. Bouton was ostracized, reviled, for saying it. Despite his celebrity, he has still never been invited to any team's old-timers game.

A quarter-century later, with Mantle's liver damaged and his life in danger, Mickey is the one reaffirming everything Bouton said.

You may have seen *Sports Illustrated* last week, the ravaged face on the cover, Mantle's stark account of disintegration inside. It was courageous, and heartrending, but it also makes you mad. What a waste. And what if someone close to Mantle, years ago, had tried to make him face the truth? What if he had somehow found his way to the same kind of counseling available to ballplayers today?

Maybe his career would have survived a little longer, and he would have achieved the .300 career batting average he missed by a sliver. Maybe he wouldn't have those nightmares of being locked outside Yankee Stadium. Maybe this guy who meant the world to countless little kids could have spared his own family a lifetime of pain.

Mantle was not the greatest player Bouton ever saw. He reserves that honor for Roberto Clemente. "A complete person, on and off the field," Bouton said. But Bouton says Mantle had the most perfect baseball body imaginable, and that his talents were on a plane of their own. "He was better hung over," Bouton said, "than anybody else in perfect health."

It's been 25 years since Bouton was labeled a baseball traitor for publishing his book. Yet, he takes no pleasure in the belated proof that he was right. Bouton knew it. So did everyone else in baseball. That was the problem.

Jim Bouton's writing career began when he kept a diary of his time with the Syracuse Chiefs during the 1967 season, "when the Yankees sent me down and I was trying to get back."

He is 63 now, still writing from his Massachusetts home. His newest book, "Waconah Park," a diary-style tale of the battle to save an old ballpark, is expected to get released this year. Asked if he considers himself a ballplayer or a writer, Bouton laughs and says, "I've been a writer ever since my fastball was gone."

Then he reconsiders.

"I never considered myself a writer," Bouton says. "I considered myself a pretty good observer." As for his reflections on Mantle, and the idea that "Ball Four" introduced a whole new kind of sports genre, Bouton adamantly deflects any praise.

"I get credit for all sorts of things that I never intended to do," he says. "I just called attention to the fragility of the lives of ballplayers."

◆ ◆ ◆

11 Now, More Than Ever, a Hero

This is the way Sam McDowell sees it: Mickey Mantle is a hero, now more than ever, even as Mantle fights to survive a liver transplant caused in part by four decades of hard drinking.

"He had the courage to turn it around," McDowell said. "He didn't have to do that. Most people who are alcoholics will die (practicing) alcoholics. Mickey chose the route to recovery."

If you have a drinker in the house, you know what McDowell means. The disease is about mood swings and hangovers, letdowns and abuse, and finally about a brutal death. What Mantle did by drying out, McDowell said, was give himself back to his family.

McDowell, 52, who spent last week in Syracuse working with the Chiefs, came up with the Cleveland Indians in 1961 as a pitcher with one of the best fastballs in baseball. He led the American League in strikeouts five times, but he never broke through to the elite level. There was a simple reason for that.

He is an alcoholic, although he has been in recovery since 1979. His baseball career was one long stretch of binges and trouble. He was out of the game in 1975, at age 32. Finally, pressure from his family persuaded him to get help.

McDowell went back to school to become a certified counselor, and he started working with other alcoholics in baseball. He now runs the Employee Assistance Program for several clubs, including Toronto and its farm system, where he helps players with problems, from alcohol to loneliness. He does the same job for the Major League Baseball Players Alumni Association, which includes such former stars as Mantle.

Still, McDowell won't say if he played a role in Mantle's decision to stop drinking. "That's personal," McDowell said. But he said Mantle's biggest obstacle was always the hard-drinking entourage around him.

"By and large, he was surrounded by these people," McDowell said. "I know of cases where there were interventions all set up to confront Mickey (about his drinking). These people didn't want it to happen." They were apologists, McDowell said, and they helped Mantle nearly drink himself to death.

The *Post-Standard*, Monday, June 12, 1995

The young Mickey Mantle. (National Baseball Hall of Fame Library, Coopers-town, N.Y.)

Despite these "friends," Mantle in 1994 checked into the Betty Ford Clinic in California—which caused McDowell to rejoice.

"The thing about Mickey Mantle, and I'm talking as an individual who had to face him as an enemy, he was one of the most genuine, loving and fun-loving human beings in baseball," McDowell said.

Mantle's decision to quit, at an advanced stage of addiction, was an extraordinary thing. For every guy like Mantle, McDowell said he can name other Hall of Famers—"big, big names"—who never were able to shake off the bottle.

In the 1950s, Mantle could drink all night and no one would say a thing. Now, McDowell said, any player drinking to excess within the Blue Jay system is quickly confronted by a counselor. Those individuals are not publicly embarrassed, but the organization expects them to get some kind of help. Hard drinking is rejected as a baseball way of life.

To McDowell, Mantle's career was an exercise in courage. He remembers seeing Mantle in the Yankee whirlpool, wrapped in tape from his waist to his ankles. The guy often played in tremendous pain, McDowell said, although few fans realized just how much he hurt.

McDowell is confident Mantle's resiliency will bring him back again. Sooner or later, McDowell expects to see Mantle face-to-face, and the old pitcher already knows just what to say.

"I'll tell him I'm glad he's all right," McDowell said, "and that I admire him."

Sam McDowell is involved in building a retirement community for professional athletes in Florida. Yet he remains upset about the people around Mantle who acted as "enablers," who wouldn't allow alcoholism professionals to get too close. "A lot of roadblocks were thrown in our way," McDowell says.

◆ ◆ ◆

12 Fanfare for an Uncommon Man

From the time he was a child, Bob Costas loved Mickey Mantle. Even after Costas became America's premier sportscaster, he carried a Mantle baseball card in his wallet. When Mantle died, Costas said the eulogy.

The two men first met when Costas was a young sportscaster. That handshake was not arranged by Joe Garagiola or Phil Rizzuto or some other baseball icon. It was set up by Don Ross, a restaurant guy from Syracuse with some amazing friends.

"I walked in today and saw the message that Don had passed away and I was saddened," Costas said last week, after learning that Ross, 71, had died Dec. 7. " He's one of the names connected to my earliest memories as a broadcaster."

Ross was a co-founder of Twin Trees restaurant on Avery Avenue. It has expanded into three distinct businesses operated by Ross' sons. The Ross brothers— Donald II, Louis and Ron — said their father was a tireless worker and a big-time advocate of bowling.

"There was a lot more to him than the Yankees," said Ron Ross, referring to his dad's devotion to Mantle's longtime team. Moose Ilacqua, a close friend for 50 years, said Ross would sponsor as many as 30 bowling teams in one season. "He had a great heart," Ilacqua said.

Costas first knew Ross as the president of the Syracuse Blazers, a blood-and-guts franchise in the old Eastern Hockey League. In 1973, WSYR-AM hired Costas, then 21, to handle the Blazers play-by-play.

"He knew I was a kid and that I was overwhelmed," Costas said. That job started Costas on his climb to national celebrity. Yet he remembers Ross for a more personal reason.

Ross' birth name was Donald Rescignano. He grew up as a loyal Yankee fan. When the Syracuse Chiefs became the International League affiliate of the Yanks, Twin Trees turned into a second home for many players.

The Ross brothers said their father flew on the team plane to Thurman Munson's funeral. They recall how Bobby Murcer was short enough to dance on the Twin Trees bar without hitting the ceiling. They said Ross often dined with Yankee legend Billy Martin.

One of the great thrills of Costas' career was covering Mantle's 1974 induction into the Hall of Fame in Cooperstown. The national media swarmed over the village. Costas, a kid reporter from Syracuse, figured he had no chance to interview his hero.

Ross made it happen. "It was in the library at the Hall of Fame," Costas said. A thick crowd pushed and pulled as Mantle walked past. "Hey, Mickey!" Ross called out. Mantle looked over. They made eye contact. Mantle stopped. On a good word from Ross, Mantle spoke with Costas.

Years later, Mantle would help restore his image by giving Costas some dramatic revelations about alcohol abuse. Costas responded with his stirring eulogy. To Costas, in a subtle way, it is all linked to Ross.

As a young man, Ross drove to Yankee Stadium at least 15 times a season. That ended as his health failed. His sons said the 1993 death of their mother, June, sapped much of the joy from his life. Ross lost her a few months before their 50th anniversary.

He lived long enough to become a great-grandfather, and to see his sons expand the Twin Trees tradition he helped create. When Ross died, not quite two months after the Yankees won the World Series, pitching great Whitey Ford sent flowers to the wake.

The Ross brothers say those celebrity friends never changed the essence of their dad, a contention echoed by a guy who knew Ross from both sides. "One measure of people is how they treat other people who aren't seemingly impressive or important," Bob Costas said.

That was Costas, 20 years ago. Don Ross cut him a break.

◆ ◆ ◆

13 The Next Pitch Will Have to Wait

A quiet Sunday morning. My wife and daughter went off to church, the baby was sleeping, my 4-year-old son and I were playing around with a bat and ball.

His back was to the house. He stood above a wooden board thrown down to be home plate, a too-big hat hanging over his eyes. He was struggling with his swing and his stance, but after a while the kid began to hit the ball. He kept asking for another pitch, and pretty soon the two of us were wrapped up in it, the sun burning down, insects buzzing in the weeds.

One house away, a screen door bounced open, our neighbor stuck his head out the door. "Hey," he shouted. "It just came on that Mickey Mantle *died*."

My boy stared at me, the bat on his shoulder, wondering when I would let go of the pitch.

How could I explain? Mickey Mantle died. I looked at my kid, the symmetry almost too much to believe. And I knew that all over the country, as the news spread, similar moments were being frozen for countless Mantle fans.

His story was our answer to the myth of the log cabin. Mantle's dad was named Mutt, a powerful American symbol in itself. He named his son after a great catcher. Mutt would roll a ball to the baby in the cradle. Despite the child's threats to walk away, the father made him hit from both sides of the plate.

Baseball rescued the kid from a life in the mines. He shot up to the majors after two seasons. He hurt his knee in the World Series, then came back to become an American legend. He hit "moon shots." He made a running catch to save Don Larsen's perfect game. He had the epic home run race with Roger Maris.

How do you describe Mantle? You think back on him, from childhood, and it is like a burst of light. You knew of Mantle before you knew how to play the game. In those days, a television presence was a fleeting, black-and-white image on a small screen. No saturation coverage, no ESPN. We all created our own Mantles, which means we all felt distinct sorrow at the news.

The *Post-Standard*, Monday, August 14, 1995

The awe, and the grief, weren't reserved just for the fans.

"He wasn't just a ballplayer," said Gene Woodling, a .284 career hitter and longtime Yankee outfielder, who took my call on a phone Sunday out in his back yard. "Nobody, but nobody, was like Mickey Mantle.

"They talk about Babe Ruth. How many long home runs, really long, did Babe Ruth hit? Two? Three? Four? Mantle hit 30. At least. I know. I was his teammate. I saw 'em. You go to these towns, and they'll say, 'Ted Williams hit one here,' or 'Willie Mays hit one here.' Nobody hit as many long ones as Mantle.

"Not even Joe DiMaggio was Mickey Mantle. I'm not knocking DiMaggio. I'm not knocking Willie Mays. They were great. But nobody bunted like Mickey Mantle. Nobody else could bunt one-hop to the pitcher and then beat it out. That was Mantle."

Woodling and Mantle were teammates on the great Yankee teams of the early 1950s. Woodling saw the way children reacted to Mantle, watched him become much larger than life. All in all, Woodling said, Mantle handled it with grace.

"Naturally, I feel bad about what happened at the end," Woodling said. "But was he the only American to be an alcoholic? How about Ruth? I won't let anyone knock Mantle to my face. He wouldn't hurt a fly. I don't know of any ballplayer who didn't like Mantle. I tell you, he could light up the skies."

Woodling said goodbye, went back to his yard. I called Johnny Sain, now retired in Illinois. Sain was the fine Boston Braves pitcher who went on to be one of the great pitching coaches in baseball history. He spent the last four years of his pitching career as Mantle's teammate.

"I was coaching first base the day he hit the facade in Yankee Stadium," Sain said. "The ball hit the top in upper-left field. If he'd hit it over a little more, more toward centerfield, it would have gone right out of the stadium."

It is hard for Sain to believe that Mantle has joined a more depressing tradition, the line of Yankee legends who have died before their time. Lou Gehrig. Ruth. Thurman Munson. Roger Maris. To Sain, it is particularly hard to separate Maris and Mantle, both for their power and for the way they shared the stage at the same time.

Sain saw Maris shortly before he died, at a reunion in New York. Maris sat down at the same table, and he suddenly leaned over and said with much passion to Sain, "Johnny, sometimes I look back on my career and I still can't believe it. It doesn't seem real. It seems like a dream."

From the harsh glare of adulthood, that is the same way Mantle now appears to many of us. The screen door slammed shut in the next yard.

My son and I were left alone with the news of Mickey's death. The boy is 4 years old. He was waiting for me, the bat on his shoulder.

The best thing for us both was for me to throw the ball.

Gene Woodling, Mantle's teammate and friend on the great Yankee teams of the 1950s, died in June 2001.

◆ ◆ ◆

14 A Mantle Memory: Against All Odds

Bob Hayes couldn't get out of it. He had promised his son he would take him to Yankee Stadium, where Mickey Mantle was running a public baseball clinic. The kid wasn't about to let his dad off the hook, not even if that brain tumor was getting in the way.

"It's August or early September," Bob Hayes recalls. "He's been out of surgery a month. He's lost all this weight and he can't walk 15 feet. We get him home and we tell him we'll do the clinic the next year. He says, 'We're going.' He's being a miserable little (profanity) about it. I ask the doctor and he says, 'If he can handle it, go ahead.'"

They went to the clinic, all of them packed into the family car: John, his three brothers, Bob and his wife, Janet. The year was 1972. The whole family has spent 23 years thinking back on that trip. Everything went wrong to make one thing go right. That's why the phone at their house rang all day Sunday, after friends heard the news that Mantle had died.

John Hayes was 10 years old in '72, the son of a policeman from Tipperary Hill in Syracuse. His dad loved the Yankees, and particularly loved Mantle. "I remember when he broke in, in 1951," Bob Hayes said. "He had

---

The *Post-Standard*, Tuesday, August 15, 1995

Opposite: **Mickey Mantle lays down a bunt against the Cincinnati Reds, 1954 Hall of Fame game, Doubleday Field, Cooperstown. (National Baseball Hall of Fame Library, Cooperstown, N.Y.)**

that attitude and speed and youth. We couldn't wait to get the paper every day to see how he had done."

That passion flowed down to all the Hayes children. John was a fine Little League player, and his jersey always carried Mantle's No. 7. No one worried at first, then, when the kid did some vomiting a few mornings in a row. They assumed it was another pesky childhood bug.

But something about the case bothered the family doctor. He sent John to a specialist, who made the diagnosis. Brain tumor. "When the doctor told me that," said Bob Hayes, "I wanted to take him out right there."

Bob held back. Down deep, he understood the truth. His son's only chance was risky surgery. The operation took 13 hours. For a week after that, the boy was unconscious. The doctors said they couldn't get rid of all the cancer. John immediately went into radiation therapy. His weight dropped to 60 pounds. His dad often had to carry him around the house.

Despite all that, John wanted to see Mickey Mantle.

One month after he got off the table, the kid climbed into a station wagon at 4 a.m. for a ride with his family to Yankee Stadium.

Mantle did the clinic every year. Bob Hayes remembers how the Yankees would hold it between games of a doubleheader. Phil Rizzuto ran the thing. He would routinely pick a few good questions from the crowd to ask the Mick. During the drive, to kill time, the Hayes family scribbled 20 questions on the side of a paper bag.

Hayes remembers that there were 30,000 or 35,000 people at Yankee Stadium. The Yankees, at that time, were no powerhouse. Most of the crowd was there to see Mantle. Rizzuto stood up and made an announcement. He was going to pick 10 questions submitted by the crowd. The winners would all get their pictures taken with Mantle.

The first question he read was, "At what age should you start to switch hit?" John Hayes lit up. It was his question! But Bob looked down at his son and felt sick. They had not written their name or address on the bag.

"What the hell," Hayes told his kid. "We'll still give this a shot."

They went to the room where the winners had gathered. Hayes, carrying his son, hoped he could work out his problem with some official. But it was chaos, at least 100 people packed into a small space. Amid the mayhem, a Yankee administrator started reading off the winners. The fourth or fifth choice was some guy from Connecticut. Nobody answered when they announced the name.

Bob Hayes stuck up his hand. "That's us!" he shouted out.

They handed Bob a slip of paper and sent the family through a closed door, down into a tunnel. The paper held the name of the Connecticut guy. Bob grabbed his pen from his pocket, tried to cross out the other

John Hayes, a 10-year-old weakened by surgery to remove a brain tumor, wanted only to meet Mickey Mantle. A series of misadventures almost kept it from happening. Yet here are the two of them in 1972. (*Post-Standard*)

name and write down his own. It was a nightmare. The pen wouldn't work. He got down on all fours, pushing the pen across the paper like a chisel. Too late. A door opened and out walked Mantle, in full uniform.

What the family remembers is the size of Mantle's forearms, the enormity of the hand he held out to enclose John's. Mantle wrapped one bearish arm around the frail child, pulled him in front of a camera. They took the picture and the family got hustled out the door. Bob Hayes is no schmoozer. He didn't know how to explain what had happened, and he worried the Yankees would get mad at the deception.

They drove home with the Yanks thinking John was a different kid.

This is where Janet Hayes comes into the story. Bob wasn't going to call the ball club. He was ready to give up on the photo. Janet wasn't putting up with that. "I had to try and do something," she said. A club official, at first, doubted her story. "No one," he said, "gets through our security."

An hour later, he called back. He had found the photo and was putting it in the mail.

Bob Hayes now runs the security force at the State Fairgrounds in Syracuse. John, for his part, is doing just fine. He is 32 years old. He lost some hearing and eyesight on his right side, but on the whole he recovered from the surgery quite well. He works for the MONY group as an insurance analyst, and he is an assistant high school basketball coach at Bishop Ludden High School in suburban Syracuse.

"My dad is the main man in my life," John said. "But after that, you know who I'd pick as No. 2."

As for Bob, what he remembers most of all is his son's raw will. The whole story doesn't happen if not for one thing. A month after they removed a tumor from his brain, the kid insisted he was going to see Mickey Mantle.

Seven years after the death of his hero, John Hayes has many photographs of No. 7 hanging in his house. "I don't know what it is about these guys playing today, but it's not the same," Hayes says. "I still idolize Mickey Mantle."

◆ ◆ ◆

15   Sal Maglie Lies Isolated from the World, But Not Alone

Funny the way things stick in your mind. It is Thanksgiving, and throughout the week I have been thinking of a veteran sportswriter by the name of Bill Wolcott, and why he makes sure that he still sees Sal Maglie.

The *Post-Standard*, Thursday, November 26, 1992

"I'm a reporter and I go to the locker room after big games and there are 15 reporters around some star, trying to get to them and talk to them," Wolcott says. "Forty years ago, Sal Maglie had 20 of the best reporters in New York City trying to get to him all the time. It seems like there should still be some kind of reporter there."

There is, but only one.

Wolcott has put in 25 years as a sportswriter at the Niagara *Gazette*. He writes in a simple and elegant way and he is truly old-school, a craggy face with his glasses sliding down on his nose, often armed with his black cigar.

Wolcott learned to read as a child by going over box scores. One of his heroes was Maglie, the sinister "Barber" of major-league lore, who was born and raised in Niagara Falls and won 119 games in the major leagues.

During the 1956 World Series, when the aging Maglie started the fifth game for Brooklyn against some obscure New York Yankees right-hander, Wolcott watched on a black-and-white television at a Sears Roebuck and Co. and he rooted out loud for Maglie to win. History forbid it. Don Larsen pitched a perfect game.

Now Maglie lies motionless in a Niagara Falls nursing home, where he wound up after suffering a stroke on Palm Sunday in 1987. Wolcott goes to the nursing home and talks. Maglie doesn't respond, not to his own family, not to Wolcott. "I don't think he's getting any better," says Wolcott, who keeps in touch with Maglie's wife.

But he keeps returning because of what happened a couple of years ago, when Maglie's condition was so bad that Wolcott wondered if it made sense to visit. One night, at a time when he hadn't seen Sal in a while, Wolcott watched "Awakenings," a Robin Williams movie.

That film focused on encephalitis victims at a New York City hospital, patients who were unresponsive for decades. They abruptly revived after a physician treated them with an experimental drug.

It made Wolcott feel guilty. He kept recalling how one of the victims, a man played by Robert DeNiro, advised a young woman whose father was in a coma to talk to her bedridden dad. "He hears you," DeNiro said, and that made Wolcott remember Maglie.

So Wolcott returned to the nursing home, sat down next to the immobile Maglie, and simply started to talk, about their city, about the great days of the Dodgers and Giants.

Wolcott looked on the hospital wall and saw a banner for the Niagara Falls Rapids, a team in the New York-Penn League, and—feeling sillier all the time—he rambled on about Maglie's days as president of a minor-league team.

Sal Maglie, with the New York Giants. (National Baseball Hall of Fame Library, Cooperstown, N.Y.)

Suddenly, Maglie jerked up his arm. He pointed at the pennant, the arm hanging there, rigid and fixed. Then his arm dropped. Maglie said nothing. His expression remained blank.

"You could tell, you knew, that he understood," Wolcott says. "I still get the chills just thinking about it."

Wolcott is not sure anymore if Maglie can hear him. The days pass by, and Sal is 75, and the man in the bed seems far removed from the world. But Wolcott still goes there to sit and to talk, repaying some debt he can't quite put into words.

Sal Maglie died barely a month after this column appeared. Bill Wolcott is still writing, in Niagara Falls.

◆ ◆ ◆

16 Finding Peace in Images of War

Anna Jovanovich remembers Murry Dickson as a guy who made her laugh.

She remembers him going on and on about baseball. She remembers him being very proud of his family. And she vividly remembers his funny stories about World War II.

But she does not recall Dickson describing the core of what he saw, even though his war experience was so compelling that it is being featured in baseball's Hall of Fame in Cooperstown.

"The only time he ever talked about the war, at least beyond his own family, it was all a joke," said Jovanovich, an attorney in California. "He was like so many of the World War II veterans. He kept so much inside."

Dickson was a pitcher, a pretty good one, who spent most of his career with the St. Louis Cardinals. He won 172 games and lost 181. His earned run average over 18 years was 3.66. And he played on a couple of world champions, although he never won a World Series game.

The *Post-Standard*, Monday, June 5, 1995

He was also an amateur photographer who served in the infantry during World War II. Ted Spencer, curator of the Hall of Fame in Cooperstown, refers to Dickson as "our Forrest Gump."

Like Gump, Spencer said, Dickson always seemed to show up where things were getting hot. He took part in the Normandy invasion. He saw combat in the Battle of the Bulge.

And he was one of the first Americans to pass through the gates of the German concentration camp at Dachau, which is as close as you can come to descending into hell.

The photographs he brought home are central to a Hall of Fame exhibit called "Baseball Enlists." It commemorates the 50th anniversary of the end of World War II, and the role many baseball stars played in the conflict. It is well-known baseball lore, for instance, that Ted Williams sacrificed what could have been his greatest years to fight in the war. But Jovanovich sees Dickson as a symbol for tens of thousands of everyday U.S. heroes.

It is her belief that many veterans of the war are finally being forced to confront 50-year-old nightmares. She maintains that Baby Boomers often share the same image of war veteran fathers: quiet, hard-working men who were somehow distant and removed. Jovanovich contends that is no coincidence. She said those soldiers saw unspeakable things, and then pushed down those memories in order to lead "normal" lives.

Now, she said, many veterans are in their 70s, and abruptly alone. They have lost their wives, and their children have moved away, and they walk around empty houses where they can't lock out the war. She describes a documentary in which a U.S. veteran who helped liberate the concentration camps—a veteran who never told his own family what he saw—abruptly broke down and started weeping on camera.

That is why Jovanovich feels Dickson's photos are so important. As a high school kid in New York City, she used to go to the Polo Grounds to watch big-league games. She actually met Dickson, and it got to the point where he recognized her. She would brag to her friends about knowing a ballplayer. Decades later, as a grown woman, she decided to find out what happened to him.

That was three or four years ago. Both Murry and his wife had died. But their children invited Jovanovich to see Dickson's scrapbooks and photographs, which were powerful and troubling. She was particularly moved by a videotaped interview in which Dickson spoke of using retirement as a way of getting "peace from the war."

She was stunned. Dickson had never acted like a man haunted by the past. But once she saw the photographs, Jovanovich understood.

Dickson had seen combat, which was horrible enough. Then he had walked with the survivors of Dachau, human beings reduced to skin sagging from bone. Dickson watched as local townspeople, under order from Allied Commander Dwight Eisenhower, were forced to tour the camp and witness what had happened. Dickson was there when the Army had to deal with the remains.

"I think it had a tremendous effect on him," she said. "But like the rest of them, he kept it inside."

It was Jovanovich who suggested loaning the photos to the Hall of Fame. Dickson would be pleased, she said, that his name is being mentioned in Cooperstown. And she figures his photos serve a much larger role, reaching out to anyone who needs "peace from the war."

Murry Dickson, veteran of World War II, late in his baseball career, with the Pittsburgh Pirates. (National Baseball Hall of Fame Library, Cooperstown, N.Y.)

◆ ◆ ◆

17 Old Syracuse Buddies Remember Luciano

In those years, there was no Interstate 81. What Gerry Skonieczki remembers best of playing football at Syracuse University are the long

The *Post-Standard*, Friday, January 20, 1995

weekend rides, winding those back roads home to Binghamton, with conversation so good he was never in a rush.

They'd have three or four football players in the car, one of them a big guy named Ron Luciano. The stories were terrific, often gut-aching funny, by a grizzly of a man with this little piping voice.

That's what came back to Skonieczki Thursday, when he heard the news.

"Surprisingly, when you think about (Luciano's) image, he was a very brilliant guy," said Skonieczki, who works in pharmaceutical sales. "He was very articulate, and he knew a lot of trivia, a lot about movies and the arts. We'd go to the movies together downtown in Syracuse, and it was always for the classics—'Love in the Afternoon,' or 'A Farewell to Arms.'"

Luciano, 57, the All-American college tackle turned celebrity umpire, was found dead in his garage Wednesday. The coroner is calling it a suicide, which does not come as a complete shock. Dave Fisher, another SU graduate who co-authored Luciano's successful books after baseball, said the retired umpire was caught in a severe depression.

"He admitted to me it was really bad," Fisher said. Luciano, Fisher said, had stopped returning phone calls. His mother was in a nursing home, suffering from Alzheimer's disease, and Fisher wonders about the toll each visit took on his old friend.

"The person that I knew was very different from the baseball legend," Fisher said. "Ronnie was basically a shy person whom I always felt was born into the wrong kind of body. But he tried hard to be what others wanted him to be. He was happy if he could make other people smile."

The description fits, according to Skonieczki, who was a skilled end for the Syracuse teams on which Luciano starred. Both of them were from Binghamton, so they regularly drove those two-lane highways that connected the two towns.

Skonieczki said Luciano adored his mother, who raised three children by herself after her husband died young. Almost always, on the ride back, everyone in the car would tear into home-cooked food sent along by Mrs. Luciano, "finishing it off by the time we got to Cortland."

Bob Velie, who spent a year playing quarterback for Syracuse, was another regular. He recalls Luciano sitting in the back seat on one of those drives, helping a girlfriend work through difficult pre-med equations. "A very smart guy," Velie said.

Still, Luciano was always a showman, always a comic. As teammate Chuck Zimmerman got the news Wednesday on late-night television, he thought back to the 1956 arrival in Texas of SU's first Sugar Bowl team. A group of young women waited on the runway to present the Orangemen with 10-gallon hats.

Zimmerman has a vivid picture of the 300-pound Luciano pushing his way down the narrow aisle, bodies flying around the plane, while he screamed in his high-pitched voice, "Let's go, guys!"

None of them expected he would become an umpire. An actor, yes. Fisher said Luciano was not even a baseball disciple. He understood the sport, mastered the complex nature of its rules. But Fisher always laughed when Luciano, on some radio talk show, would be asked to make a prediction on the pennant.

"In my mind, I could see him flipping through a magazine to get the information," Fisher said.

What Luciano loved about umpiring, Fisher said, was the chance to perform. "He liked the players and admired their skills," Fisher said. "But he was never a big baseball fan. He couldn't care less who won."

Even in football, Luciano made good through his mind, not out of anger. "He was a big gentle guy with a little squeaky voice," Zimmerman said. "But when he got out on the field, he just went out there and did it."

Over the last couple of years, sensing Luciano's emotional retreat, Fisher said he kept urging a move from Endicott to New York or Hollywood, hoping the energy of those places might snap his friend out of it. Luciano retained a big name. He was a guy who easily could have gotten lots of work.

But he wanted to stay in a smaller town, with his hunting, his bird-watching, his long walks in the woods. Most of all, apparently, he couldn't leave his ailing mother.

During that time, Skonieczki rarely saw Luciano. So he found himself reflecting Thursday on those trips they took to downtown movies. Luciano always admired a bit actor by the name of Hans Conreid, a guy known for playing eccentric supporting parts.

In a sense, Luciano's billing exceeded that of his idol. Fisher summed it up, in a sentence that may serve as a one-line epitaph: "He was the only umpire in baseball history that people came out just to see."

◆ ◆ ◆

18 Chiefs Fan Grins, Bears Pain

It would be a stretch to say that Carlos Delgado broke Nancy Caruso's thumb. Nancy is 9 years old. When she went to see the Syracuse Chiefs play Tuesday, she wanted a foul ball. Delgado simply gave her a chance to go for it.

It was in the seventh inning. The Chiefs catcher had fouled off a bunch of pitches. Nancy was prepared to give chase. Delgado was obliging. He ripped a shot off a light standard. The kid played the bounce like she was in Fenway. She got a hand on it. It broke her thumb.

She started crying, while the ball skipped away. Nancy, amid her tears, crawled after it. A teen-ager in front of her picked it up, but he was so impressed by the effort he flipped it back to the girl.

"What a nice kid," said her mom, Sharon Caruso, who still feels bad she didn't get the teen's name.

Nancy went home and saw Carlos in her sleep. She dreamed he came to her house and told her he was sorry. Her parents smiled patiently when they heard the story.

Delgado, they knew, has plenty on his mind. Here he is, a hard-hitting major-league prospect, and all of a sudden the big leagues have gone out on strike. Big Mac, for now, is as good as it can get. On top of that, the Chiefs are in a race for a playoff spot. The Carusos weren't sure Delgado even knew what had happened.

Still, the family was invited back to the ballpark Wednesday, as guests of the club. General manager Tex Simone gave them prime seats, right behind home plate. "Least we could do," said assistant G.M. John Simone, who went in the clubhouse and told Delgado about Nancy.

When Carlos came out, he had his cap pulled down across his face. He pretended to slink past the family in shame. Then he smiled.

"I'm sorry! Did I hurt you?" he asked Nancy, reaching out to pat her cast. Nancy, who normally has the words for any occasion, kept quiet. "I didn't want to overdo it," she explained later to her folks.

Delgado told her it was the first time he'd signed a ball after bouncing it off a fan. "Usually, they're mad," he said. He signed another ball for

Nancy's brother, Matt. Then he wrote a get-well message on her cast. As he walked onto the field, he turned repeatedly to say, "Goodbye! Hope you feel better! Sorry! Goodbye!"

This was all observed with some amazement by Nancy's dad, Rick Caruso, who would have been happy with an autograph and a grunt.

The family went back to sit down. Nancy tucked the ball tightly under her arm, and it stayed there for the rest of the game. She plans to keep it hidden among the stuffed bears in her room, secret evidence that baseball can still be the stuff of dreams.

Nancy Caruso has grown into a 17-year-old. The ball no longer rests among her stuffed animals. It has made its way into the basement, where it holds a prized place among the family's collection of sports memorabilia. As for her cast, Nancy keeps it in a box, a prize to someday show off to her own children.

◆ ◆ ◆

II

BLACK CAT

19 The Worst of Being First

MacArthur Stadium was built in 1934, and it has withstood flood and fire and endless tinkering. Old-timers say the dugouts are the only things that haven't changed. They look about the same as when Jackie Robinson walked past them, never looking down.

The image remains fresh to Garton DelSavio. He lives in retirement along the lower Hudson River, but he was a second baseman in 1946 for the Syracuse Chiefs. That was the year Robinson signed with the Montreal Royals and sent a tremor through a racially divided America, an African American integrating the "white" International League. Everyone knew the next stop would be the majors.

The Chiefs had some players who did not want to see it happen. They savagely heckled Robinson, insults that were both foul and personal. "Abuse," is the way DelSavio describes it. On one road trip to Montreal, a Syracuse pitcher rubbed on blackface and tried to take the mound. DelSavio said the pitcher had to be ordered not to do it by Manager Jewel Ens.

Robinson never showed any reaction. His teammates, however, rose up in his support. When Montreal won a bitter playoff series over Syracuse, the games were marred by a beanball war triggered at least in part by racial taunts. Montreal general manager Mel Jones publicly accused Syracuse of giving Robinson the harshest punishment in the entire league, of threatening to bean him "almost every time he comes up."

DelSavio had played with Robinson on barnstorming tours. He knew Robinson's temper only intensified his skills. DelSavio used to tell the Chief bench jockeys they'd be smarter to shut up.

They didn't. After every at-bat against Syracuse, all season long, Robinson would go as close as possible to the Chiefs dugout as he jogged back to his bench, regal and aloof above all the bile.

"He'd just defy them," DelSavio recalls of Robinson.

This is the 50th anniversary of Robinson joining the Royals. A year later, he changed American culture forever when he signed with the Brooklyn Dodgers.

"Just remember, that was right after the Second World War," said

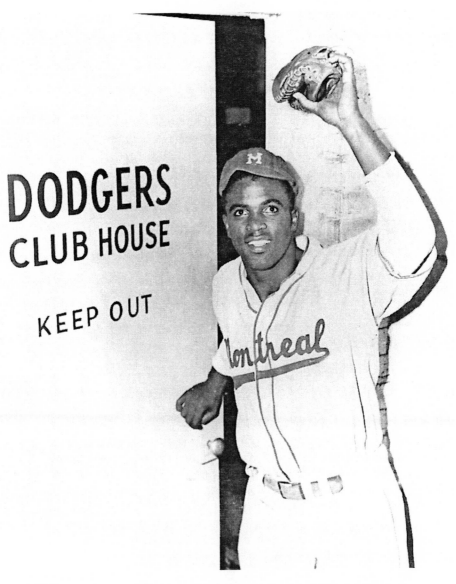

Jackie Robinson, not long after enduring savage racial taunts in Syracuse, prepares to break the Major League color line. (National Baseball Hall of Fame Library, Cooperstown, N.Y.)

historian Randolph Hawkins. "That was a war in which Americans fought for freedom and democracy, then came home to a country that did not offer those things to everyone." Those simmering emotions among blacks kindled the civil rights movement, and Robinson's courage and success became an early beacon.

In the International League, the Chiefs gave him perhaps the worst time of any team.

Some witnesses maintain that a black cat was thrown from the Big Mac stands onto the field in an attempt to shake him up. The harassment from the Chiefs dugout began in April on Robinson's first at-bat, according to Dick West, the Chiefs catcher in that era.

"I remember the first time he came up to bat, our whole bench was hollering at him, and he looked down at me and said, 'You got some players from the South,'" said West, who was born in Kentucky.

"I looked up and said, 'I don't feel sorry for you. You can go to hell,'" West recalls. He said he would say the same thing again today, noting that Robinson came across as what West describes as "cocky."

Like most Northern cities, Syracuse had an up-and-down history in its treatment of black athletes. One of the earliest examples was Moses Fleetwood Walker, who played with the Syracuse Stars in the 1880s after most teams would no longer sign a black man. By 1889, Walker was forced out of the International League, leaving it all-white until Robinson finally broke through.

Wilmeth Sidat-Singh was a legend for SU in the 1930s in both basketball and football, but the school identified him as Hindu. Earl Lloyd, the first African American to play in an NBA game, spent most of the 1950s with the Syracuse Nationals. He loved his teammates and felt accepted by the fans, but he also felt socially confined to black neighborhoods in the old 15th Ward. Sometimes he'd try to rent an apartment beyond those borders. By some mystery, once the landlord got a look at him, it would turn out the place had always just been taken.

Beyond even that, because of his enormous place in U.S. history, Robinson's reception left the city with a permanent bruise. Robinson often described Syracuse as one of the cruelest Northern towns in which he played. That perspective will be recalled many times in the next two seasons, as the nation remembers how Robinson broke baseball's color line.

Over 50 years, some things have changed. The Chiefs failed as a franchise in the 1950s and were later revived as a community-owned team. Hundreds of African American and Latino players have passed uneventfully through the same ballpark where Robinson was reviled. And this is the last season for that stadium, which is being replaced by a $30 million showplace.

Avery Brooks, founder of the new Syracuse Inner-City Little League, was 11 years old when Robinson joined the Brooklyn Dodgers. Brooks was a kid on a Southern farm, playing weekend baseball in a cow pasture. He remembers sitting with adults gathered around the radio, remembers the way they spoke of Robinson in reverent terms.

Robinson's arrival changed Brooks' view of his own potential. He still refers warmly to his childhood hero as "Jackie," and Brooks to this day remains a Dodger fan.

Ten years ago, the Chiefs held a small ceremony to recall the 40th anniversary of Robinson breaking through. The team is considering another ceremony this spring, which after 50 years could be a quiet means of making peace. Brooks wants to bring hundreds of his Little Leaguers to that game. There is a lesson in Robinson's courage, he said, and a reminder in the hatred that once spilled from the Chiefs dugout.

"This a story," Brooks said, "these kids can't learn enough about."

At the age of 67, Avery Brooks is still running a youth baseball league in Syracuse. His season extends into late July and early August, bringing baseball back to long-abandoned diamonds in the city. Those games are not affiliated with Little League Baseball. The official area Little Leagues close up shop and focus on All-Star games before summer hits its peak, Brooks says. Many everyday Little Leaguers are finished playing ball before school even lets out.

It is during the long days of summer that the children Brooks works with need baseball the most.

Brooks continues to be driven and inspired by his childhood hero. He speaks with reverence of Jackie Robinson, whose memory lingers in a city where he had such a hard time. Debate continues among Syracuse fans and baseball scholars as to whether the black cat incident — immortalized on film in "The Jackie Robinson Story"— actually happened at MacArthur Stadium.

Over the years, at least two witnesses have told Post-Standard *sportswriters that they saw the incident when it happened at Big Mac, and that it was over too quickly to register with most fans or reporters. Ron Gersbacher, a Syracuse baseball historian, remains doubtful. He notes that local newspapers in 1946 never made reference to any cat being thrown onto the field, at a time when Robinson was the subject of extensive coverage.*

Gersbacher believes the story is based on a similar incident that occurred when the Syracuse team visited Montreal, and several of the Chiefs brought a black cat into the dugout. The location was different, the intent the same. Gersbacher wonders if Robinson, in memory, confused the locations in his mind.

What is beyond dispute is that the 1946 Syracuse Chiefs treated Robinson with extraordinary cruelty and contempt from the beginning of the season until the playoffs in the fall, as evidenced by an accompanying essay in this book.

Horace Morris, one of the first African Americans to play football at Syracuse University, carries a particularly vivid memory of Robinson, in Syracuse. After college, Morris would go on to serve as an executive with the United Way. But he was a nervous and homesick freshman lineman in 1946, struggling to make his own cultural adjustment, when he met Robinson at the old New York Central train station.

Robinson sat alone on one bench, Morris recalled, while the rest of the Montreal Royals — a long line of white faces — huddled together on the far side of the lobby.

"I went over and told him who I was, and about my situation," Morris said. "He looked up and said to me, 'Kid, I'm going to make it, and you're going to make it, too.'"

◆ ◆ ◆

20 Syracuse Faces an Ugly Legacy from the Robinson Era

Fifty years ago this spring, Jackie Robinson broke into major-league baseball. He was African American, and he remains a vivid symbol of equality. Our teachers are celebrating his courage in our schools. His number — 42 — has been retired from the game.

Fifty years ago this spring, in singling out a minor league city that treated him the worst in all of baseball, Jackie Robinson chose Syracuse.

He had played in 1946 for the Montreal Royals of the International League. The Royals often played against the old Chiefs, and Montreal defeated Syracuse in the league playoffs. This is history. These are the words and quotes of the times:

Sept. 24, 1946, Dink Carroll's column in the Montreal *Gazette*: "(Mel Jones), the Royals general manager, had a brisk conversation with (Chiefs president) Leo Miller at the ballpark here Sunday:

"You've got the worst bunch of jockeys in the league on your club,"

The *Post-Standard*, Monday, April 21, 1997

Jones said to the Syracuse president. "You've been hollering at Robinson all season. He had to take a worse ride from your club than any other. Somebody in your dugout has been yelling at your pitchers to throw at him almost every time he comes up."

March 31, 1947, Robinson speaking in a Associated Press story in the Syracuse *Post-Standard*: "I had no trouble at all with Montreal last year. There was just one player on the club who rode me a little hard but not too much. On the road, they were fine. In Syracuse they got on me pretty good, but that didn't bother me."

It was the only city he brought up as a rough place.

April 1, 1947, Bill Reddy column, Syracuse *Post-Standard*: "Jackie Robinson put his finger on Syracuse as the only city in the International League where he was ridden hard. ... It was during the Royals first visit to Syracuse, when Jackie made a nuisance of himself at bat. Robinson had swung at a pitch, then claimed that the ball had hit him in the arm ...

"Robinson either didn't understand the rule, or wouldn't abide by the decision. Anyway, he did everything but get down on his knees as he implored the umpire to look at his arm ... No city in the league has fans who can take that sort of action from a visiting player and remain silent."

April 5, 1947, letter to Bill Reddy from Blair Henderson, an African American writer and reporter who still lives in our town: "I had the pleasure of talking to Jackie Robinson after one of the games here, and he told me he had been subjected to humiliating remarks that very game. He was not talking about the fans but about the players on the Syracuse ball club. They called him names that had a reflection on his color and his race. Robinson also said that this was the only club that continued to ride him up until the end of the season.

"The fans here were very fair and showed true sporting spirit," Henderson wrote.

Reddy, on Henderson's letter: "Any Syracuse players who participated in such a 'riding' are deserving of thorough condemnation, not only because they were hitting below the belt, but also because it gave the fans of this city an undeserved bad name."

Feb. 1, 1996, former Chiefs catcher Dick West, in the *Post-Standard*, acknowledging the racial taunts from the Chiefs bench during Robinson's first game in Syracuse: "I remember the first time he came up to bat, our whole bench was hollering at him, and he looked down at me and said, 'You got some players from the South,'" said West, who was born in Kentucky.

"I looked up and said, 'I don't feel sorry for you. You can go to hell.'"

That was Robinson's welcome to Big Mac. That Chiefs team, at least once during a visit to Montreal, brought a black cat into the clubhouse to

Jackie Robinson, 1951 Hall of Fame game at Doubleday Field in Cooperstown, batting against the Philadelphia Athletics. (National Baseball Hall of Fame Library, Cooperstown, N.Y.)

taunt Robinson. That Chiefs team had several players who rubbed on blackface and planned to take the field and had to be talked out of it by Manager Jewel Ens.

The second baseman for those Chiefs was Garton DelSavio, a New Yorker who knew and respected Robinson. He said his teammates called Robinson some of the foulest names he'd ever heard, the "worst things" you can scream at another man.

DelSavio recalled how Robinson, regal and aloof, would jog within inches of the Chiefs dugout every time he made an out, which would cause the Chiefs to explode and hurl more poison from the bench.

This is history. For the rest of his life, when Jackie Robinson thought of playing ball in our city, he thought of foul insults and the worst racist bile. It is in his biographies. It is all part of the record.

The question now, after 50 years, is what we do about it.

◆ ◆ ◆

21 The Fight Continues, But Some Players Stay in the Dugout

When Chuck Connors died this year, he was eulogized by the national press for his role as television's "The Rifleman."

Yet Don Newcombe chose to remember a heated day at MacArthur Stadium in Syracuse, and the way Connors saved him from a fight he couldn't win.

Newcombe, a 6-foot-4, 220-pound right-handed pitcher, was known for his speed and ferocity. He and Connors, a first baseman, came to Syracuse on Sept. 27, 1948, with the Montreal Royals. There was already an ugly mood in the stands at Big Mac, when Chiefs catcher Dick West charged at Newcombe, on the mound.

Newcombe was black. West was white. Newcombe stepped away.

It is something Newcombe still thinks about during this ongoing uproar about Marge Schott, the Cincinnati Reds owner who allegedly made frequent use of some racial slurs.

"If she said those things, if she said those words, if that's how she feels, then she's got no place in baseball," says Newcombe, 66, now a community relations specialist with the Los Angeles Dodgers.

But the feared pitcher for the great Brooklyn teams of the 1950s is not a hanging judge. He wants to hear Schott's explanation. And he knows she is not alone.

"There are thousands and thousands of people," he says, "who are just like her."

For real change, he looks to the young black men now playing the game. Still, Newcombe isn't expecting much. He often speaks with other black baseball pioneers, such as Willie Mays and Larry Doby. They would love to hear from today's players, simply to talk about nuances of the game, but the phone doesn't ring.

The young men, Newcombe says, are counting their money.

Yet he can't forget what he heard from opposing International League teams and crowds during that 1948 season, which climaxed in a bitter series with Syracuse for the Governor's Cup.

The *Post-Standard*, Tuesday, December 15, 1992

When the taunting got to be too much, he'd put the ball under some batter's chin.

"Jackie (Robinson) couldn't retaliate," Newcombe says of his close friend, a second baseman, who had been called up to the Dodgers in 1947. "I could. I did. I had the ball in my hand."

In that September game in Syracuse, Newcombe says, he wasn't trying to throw at West. Montreal was leading 2-1, and Newcombe had injured the Chiefs catcher with a pitch earlier that season. When the ninth inning fastball came in tight, West went for the mound.

Newcombe could have met him, could have drained his fury on the infield dirt. That would have made national news, especially if the "Negro giant," as white reporters liked to call him, got the better of a smaller white man.

He stepped away. Connors, instead, ran up and made the fight.

Newcombe was fuming that night when the phone rang in his Syracuse hotel room. It was Bill Robinson, the famous dancer known as "Mr. Bojangles," who was doing a gig at the Three Rivers Inn, near Syracuse.

"He had been in the stands, and he told me he was so happy I didn't hit that man," Newcombe says. "The next morning I met him in the dining room for breakfast, him and his wife, and he said if I had (hit West) it might have set us back in baseball 20, 25 years."

That moment is vivid in Newcombe's mind. Before Connors' death, whenever the two friends saw each other in LA, Connors would laugh about the day in Syracuse when he saved Newcombe's life. But they both knew that it had been no joke.

Nearly 50 years later, Marge Schott is accused of using words best left in the past, and other white owners volunteer to police her. Newcombe waits, with little hope, for a response from baseball's young black stars, who were handed the right to fight back without fear.

Don Newcombe continues to serve as a director of community relations with the Los Angeles Dodgers. A look back at the notes from this 1992 interview is a reminder of one of the inherent difficulties of column-writing: Due to space, an awful lot of good material doesn't get into the paper.

A situation, fortunately, that can be remedied here:

"Syracuse wasn't that nice a place for Jackie in 1946, and it wasn't nice for me and Roy (Campanella) when we came," Newcombe said. "It wasn't the worst town, either. That was the way people were. They don't do those things now, in a large part. But they might think them. I don't know what's on a guy's mind.

"We used to hear vicious racial epithets about your mother or your father

Don Newcombe of the Brooklyn Dodgers. (National Baseball Hall of Fame Library, Cooperstown, N.Y.)

from players who were pretty rough. All we wanted to do was play baseball. We just wanted a chance to play baseball in this fucking country. It ain't that long ago, either. Branch Rickey thought it was right that men born and raised in this country, people who fought and died and lived their whole lives here, why the hell couldn't they play baseball?

"I have no prescription for a cure as far as racism in the United States is concerned. There'll be racism in this country as long as there is a country. I take umbrage to the fact that a white woman like Marge Schott can make the statements that she's made. But she probably had that feeling because it was nurtured and fertilized in her. There are thousands and thousands of people who are just like her. You do what the law allows you to do about it.

"Rodney King? You don't even need to use his name. He's a black man beaten by a number of white men, and that's the history of black men in this country, just as it was with Don Newcombe, just as it is with Sam Jethroe (who complained about the lack of a pension fund for the old Negro League players).

"People ask me about Al Campanis (the long-time Dodger player and executive who created a furor when he said, on national television, that blacks lack the 'necessities' to be baseball managers). He's a fine man. I was supposed to do that show, but I got grounded at the airport, and Al went on. I watched it on television and I thought, 'Oh, no, Al. Don't!' If you know Al, you know how hard he worked for Jackie Robinson. He just didn't know (in the interview) what the hell he was talking about.

"But racism (back in the 1940s), you just had that engrained in a lot of people. And if you stood before me and spoke that way, then I was going to knock you on your ass. I had the ball."

◆ ◆ ◆

22 The Trials of Fleet Walker

He was a ballplayer, on trial for murder. That was enough in itself to grab the attention of Syracuse. But there was a more volatile element to the case against Moses Fleetwood Walker. District Attorney T.E. Hancock characterized it as the defendant's "peculiar disposition."

The *Post-Standard*, Monday, February 28, 1994

Walker was an African American, the first to ever play major league baseball. That is acknowledged by historians at the National Baseball Hall of Fame in Cooperstown. But he finished his playing days in the International League with the Syracuse Stars, where his career ended under the spike of the game's new color line.

Within two years, in the spring of 1891, he was thrown in jail in Syracuse, accused of murdering an ex-convict called "Curly" in a street fight. It was a killing, Walker maintained, set off by racial taunts and performed in self-defense. But one of baseball's pioneers was hurtled into a dramatic trial.

Moses Fleetwood Walker, the last African American before Jackie Robinson to play in the Major Leagues. (National Baseball Hall of Fame Library, Cooperstown, N.Y.)

A century later, his life takes on remarkable dimensions. He was a bare-handed catcher who spent the 1884 season with a major-league team in Toledo, where he batted .263. But not all crowds were glad to see a black player coming. According to historian Jerry Malloy, Walker — while with the Stars — was once arrested in Toronto for carrying a gun to protect himself from an angry, baiting crowd.

In a game dominated by products of the working poor, Fleet Walker was a college-educated man who had spent a year in law school. In 1889, after the Syracuse Stars let him go and no other team would pick him up, he quickly found a good job handling registered letters on the New York Central Railroad.

But it was hard to surrender his devotion to baseball. On the afternoon of April 9, 1891, Walker was searching for "Icewater" Joe Simmons, his former Syracuse manager, among the barrooms of the old Seventh Ward. Walker had a "baseball matter" to discuss, although it remains unclear if he still hoped to get back into the game.

A group of idlers, standing outside the Crouse Saloon at the corner of Monroe and Orange streets, demanded to know what brought Walker into their neighborhood. A rock was thrown. A couple of men moved toward Walker, who drew a knife. Within hours, Patrick "Curly" Murray was dead of a stab wound, and Walker was in prison.

"In those days," says Phil Dixon, a baseball historian who has researched Walker's career, "a black man charged with murder usually ended up buried deeper than the bottom of the jail."

A Baseball Rarity

Riding home from Rochester on a fall day in 1888, Walker, like the rest of the Syracuse team, had no idea what kind of welcome was waiting at the old Central station.

The Stars were coming back from their last road trip of the season, winners of the International League championship. Their train pulled in at 9 p.m., and the players were greeted by flares and fireworks, illuminating a crowd that spilled over the platform.

Team president Thomas O'Neill introduced the fans to every player on the roster, telling them, "We consider each one of you a Star in his place."

Walker's presence originally made it easier for Syracuse to carry Robert Higgins, a black pitcher. Dixon says many white catchers refused to share a battery with Higgins. Indeed, the rest of the Stars, in 1887, had been accused of throwing a game to Toronto to make Higgins look bad. Two players, says Malloy, refused to pose with Higgins in a team picture.

It didn't stop Higgins from contributing in the early drive for the '88 pennant. But by mid-season, Dixon says, Higgins grew weary of racial trouble and returned to his Memphis barber shop.

Walker remained the team's starting catcher. The pounding on his bare hands, says Malloy, affected his hitting. His average that year was .170, although he stole 30 bases, and his home run to left field at the old Star Park was the high point in a pennant-clinching victory over Albany.

It was a time of brief opportunity for black baseball players. While some popular sentiment, and some pragmatic owners, favored integrated baseball, America was already shoving blacks into the long twilight of Jim Crow. Baseball's progressive element would soon be overwhelmed by reactionaries, who held sway until Jackie Robinson joined Montreal in 1946.

Walker was among a handful of blacks in the 1880s playing in "white" leagues. Before joining the Stars, he did time with Toledo, Cleveland, Waterbury and Newark. He was talented enough that Newark fans were angry when he left. In Toledo, in 1884, he spent one year in the majors.

"The ease, grace and celerity through which he caught and threw to bases was admired by everybody," remarked the old Syracuse *Courier*.

No matter. His talent was unrelated to his prospects. By 1887, the International League agreed in principle to stop signing new black players, although the few active blacks were not barred from competing. When the Stars released Walker in August 1889, he represented the last black in the league.

No African American would play again in the International League until Robinson joined Montreal. As for Walker, he settled into his job on the railroad, and led a quiet life until the day he walked past the Crouse Saloon.

Unwelcome Climate

Walker's troubles were magnified by the racial tenor of the times. His attorneys fretted about finding an unbiased jury. Two days before the trial began, the *Standard* reported on Page One how Tump Hampton, a black man in New Orleans, had been "incinerated" by a lynch mob.

That animosity was not reserved to the South. Two weeks after the arrest of Walker, the Colored Knights of Pythias asked Syracuse Mayor William Cowle if they could raise the flag on the Liberty Pole during a convention.

According to the *Standard*, the mayor refused to respond. Finally, Jonas Johnson of the Knights approached Cowle on the street. The mayor, Johnson later complained to a reporter, "was in a hurry to raise the flag on every holiday imaginable," including such feasts as St. Vitus' Day.

But not for the Colored Knights. Cowle "dismissed the matter with a word and moved on," the *Standard* said.

It illustrates why ballplayers were such heroes to the African American community. Malloy says black leaders in the city sent a community letter of support to Stars officers in 1887, thanking them for their fight against the ban on black players. Throughout the three-day trial, local papers noted how a large group of blacks kept patient vigil at the courthouse.

The Case

Some things were working in Walker's favor. He had a skilled defense team, led by Harrison Hoyt of Syracuse and reinforced by A.C. Lewis, an Ohio attorney who had once tutored Walker in the study of the law.

Each day, as he entered the courtroom, Walker was greeted by his little son, who would offer his dad a bouquet of flowers. The boy or his young sister would crawl into their father's lap, while Walker would sit and clasp the hand of his wife, whose name was never identified in accounts of the trial. That scene was repeatedly described in the papers, and it had an effect.

"Public sympathy seems to be strong for Walker," remarked the *Standard*.

The trial itself was a muddle. The key issue of provocation was hard for either side to establish. It was difficult to tell whether Walker, who received a severe blow in the head during the incident, pulled his knife before or after he was struck with the stone.

The prosecution maintained Murray, a notorious drinker who had spent three years in state prison, only wanted to shake Walker's hand. That was tough to swallow, although Murray's cronies all swore under oath it was true, and Hancock tried to prove Walker was drunk.

The trial boiled down to Walker himself, who took the stand with "quiet demeanor," according to the *Standard*.

He recounted how he had been searching for Simmons throughout the Seventh Ward, before he stopped to have a few beers with a friend. They talked about that year's version of the Stars. A couple of hours later, Walker said, he walked past the group of men on the street corner.

Walker was wearing a derby hat and a nice suit. He testified the men asked why he was in their neighborhood. The exchange became increasingly hostile. He said one of the men accused him of putting on airs "for a damn nigger." The men said Walker cursed them. Walker said he left.

"I turned across the street when I was hit in the back of the head with a stone," Walker testified. He said he turned to defend himself, and was charged by two attackers coming off the barroom stoop. One held something in his hand. So Walker drew his knife and struck. Murray, cousin of a city councilman, died less than a day later.

If the question of race had only simmered throughout testimony, it flared up when Hancock offered his fiery summation. "If Walker, with his peculiar disposition and the blood that flows in his veins, is put in such a state that he magnifies every trivial incident into a cause for crime, then he ought not to touch the stuff," Hancock declared.

That attempt to win over the skeptical jury backfired when Walker's little daughter — frightened by the anger and volume of Hancock's voice — started crying while seated on her father's lap.

The all-white jury needed less than three hours to make a decision. Walker was called back, and he sat down and gave his wife a kiss. The courtroom was packed when foreman James Hill, an Eighth Ward farmer, stood and declared Walker to be innocent.

"The announcement of the verdict," said the *Standard*, "was followed by one of the most remarkable demonstrations of approval ever witnessed in a courtroom in this city."

The crowd let out a roar of jubilation and headed for the Walkers. Court officers slammed long rods on the floor to try and restore order. Judge George Kennedy demanded the arrest of anyone making excessive noise. "I would have to arrest them all," replied an overwhelmed sheriff.

Kennedy banged his gavel so hard that the head flew off. Peace was eventually restored to the courtroom. But even the judge seemed pleased with the verdict. He made a point of warning Walker to stop drinking, and then the judge shook hands with Walker's wife. Walker himself thanked each of the jurors, before his family left through a side exit, avoiding well-wishers and the curious jammed around the front door.

Walker's Sentence

It is difficult to say how much effect the trial had on the Walkers. They soon moved back to Ohio. No longer entertaining dreams about baseball, Walker became a theater owner, a journalist and an author. He despaired of any chance for an integrated America. In a 47-page book, "Our Home Colony," he warned blacks of potential genocide and urged them to strive to return to Africa.

Dixon, the historian, speculates that baseball and the trial may have helped to shape that view. Considering the times, it is remarkable — and a testimony to the bonding power of baseball — that Walker even won acquittal.

But he still spent two months of that year in jail, and he was reminded how some neighborhoods, and minds, remained closed to his people. In 1924, the man once called "a Star in his place" died convinced that place would never be the nation of his birth.

◆ ◆ ◆

23 Tested in Triple-A, Campanella Stood Tall

He got his first Triple-A hit in Syracuse. It was in 1947, on a raw April day with a few flakes of snow, and Roy Campanella singled hard in the first inning at MacArthur Stadium off a Chiefs pitcher by the name of Jim Prendergast.

Campanella singled again his next time up, and then he drove a couple of long outs to the fence. All in all he lived up to some high expectations. The Montreal Royals beat Syracuse, 11-10, behind a catcher pointed toward the big leagues and Cooperstown.

That is something to remember, amid the plans for ripping down Big Mac. You can finger the dust around home plate, where people like Campanella dug in their spikes en route to history, and when the whole place is gone, those ghosts will go with it.

The Royals played Syracuse 22 times that season and won 16, and then Syracuse turned around to sweep Montreal in the playoffs.

Campanella was always in the thick of the rivalry. In the final regular-season series between the two teams, his dropped ball at home had Syracuse fans screaming "protest" when Al Rubeling slid in and was still called out.

And in the last playoff game, his last minor-league appearance in Syracuse, Campanella got banged up when he plunged into the dugout chasing a Hank Sauer foul ball.

With his team down three games, he was still going hard. "I think he started that season at 220 (pounds) and finished at 180," said Walt Sessi, a Royals teammate. "He was catching double-headers, catching all the time."

Although Campanella himself couldn't believe it, Montreal was his fast-track training for the major leagues. He was 26 years old, an African American veteran of segregated baseball, while Jackie Robinson was breaking the color line that year with the Dodgers. "Campy" would join Robinson in Brooklyn the following season.

After the playoff loss to Syracuse, Campanella scanned a Dodgers roster thick with experienced catchers and fired off a letter to Al Cam-

The *Post-Standard*, Saturday, July 3, 1993

panis, his teammate on the Royals who was tight with Dodgers management.

Campanella wanted to know if he should switch to playing outfield.

Surprised, Campanis quickly wrote back: "Dear Campy ... We recently had a meeting with Mr. (Branch) Rickey and he agreed you are the best catcher of all the catchers we have. I don't know why you shouldn't be confident. Don't throw away your catcher's mitt."

Yet Campanella had trouble accepting his potential, particularly in a nation that still embraced segregation. Ed Stevens, another teammate in Montreal, said Campanella showed up in camp with his own soap and washcloth, assuming his teammates wouldn't allow him in their shower.

Stevens said some of the older players around the International League hated blacks, and they'd take cheap shots on close plays at the plate, trying to knock Campanella out of the game.

"We'd tell him to pick up his mask and give 'em a slap, and that would stop it," Stevens said. "But he'd always say, 'As long as I can get up, it'll be OK.'"

It was his nature to play hard and to live gentle. Campanis remembers Campanella being "quick as a cat" behind the plate, how he got off his throw to second so fast that you had to hustle from either side to cover in time.

"I told 'em once (in Brooklyn) that when he retired he'd make a great coach," Campanis said, "and he told me, 'They'll have to tear the uniform off me.'"

A couple of years later, an automobile accident put Campanella in a wheelchair for the rest of his life, although it had no effect on his sense of humor.

Campanis tells the story of a day when Don Newcombe's fastball was getting pounded in Brooklyn, how Campanella walked to the mound, shook his head and said in his distinct, high-pitched voice, "I keep calling the express, and you keep throwing the local."

Newcombe broke up, and then settled down.

And Stevens remembered a night late in that '47 season when his wife was alone at the Montreal airport, weighed down with her bags and their infant son, and Campanella appeared out of nowhere to help her to the plane, to offer a quick smile before vanishing in the crowd.

"That's the kind of person we're talking about," Stevens said.

Campanella would go on to be a Hall of Fame catcher and a tragic hero. But the years have not diminished the way the guy played ball.

Late in that 1947 campaign, in his last regular-season game in

The two great catchers of their era: Roy Campanella batting, Yogi Berra behind the plate, 1953 World Series. (National Baseball Hall of Fame Library, Cooperstown, N.Y.)

Syracuse, Campanella took off from first base on a Campanis hit and never stopped when the ball fell in the right-center field hole. Like Enos Slaughter, Campanella scored from first on a single, and Montreal went on to win, 7-1.

No one is talking about those old times at Big Mac, at least not with a new ballpark going up, just to the west. But on summer nights those basepaths seem crowded with the past, including a catcher who never let up.

◆ ◆ ◆

24 Imagine Life as a Cartoon's Descendant

Kenneth Paul is learning to duck the media, a skill the old man never figured he'd need. Until a few short months ago, he was happily obscure on an island in Maine.

He is an American Indian, a Penobscot. He works nights as a police dispatcher for his Indian nation, and he pretty much tries to mind his own business. He also happens to be a great-nephew of Louis Sockalexis, which has placed Paul amid a furor he had no wish to stir up.

Almost a century ago, Sockalexis played three seasons of professional baseball in Cleveland. That brief career remains the shaky rationale for the nickname, and bizarre mascot, of the only major-league team that calls itself the Indians.

The official team logo portrays Chief Wahoo, a big-nosed, grinning Indian stereotype. In defiance of visual logic, club management insists the point is honoring Sockalexis, whom they identify in their media guide as "The Cleveland Indian."

Yet the media guide photograph bears no resemblance to the manic Chief Wahoo. Sockalexis, who went to college at Holy Cross, is somber, almost wary, in a high-collared shirt. The expression is appropriate, according to Paul.

"The way I heard the story, he got messed up down in Cleveland because he was good, and some of the white men were jealous of him," Paul said. "They got him drinking."

In his first season, 1897, Sockalexis batted .338 in 68 games. He played in only 28 games over the following two years, and by 1900 he was out of the majors. He died in 1913, at the age of 42. Two years later, a Cleveland newspaper held a contest to rename the baseball team, and the winning entry was "Indians," supposedly to honor the first Indian in the majors.

But the mascot quickly became an Indian caricature, which evolved by the early 1950s into Chief Wahoo.

The rise of Indian activism brought growing pressure for dumping the nickname, or at least the mascot —calls that reached a crescendo this year, with the impending arrival of a new Cleveland stadium.

Team officials are unmoved. They are keeping the name, and the grinning face, which they maintain is a means of paying cultural homage.

Louis Sockalexis had no children. His sister was Kenneth Paul's grandmother. Decades after the ballplayer's death, when the Indians finally won an American League pennant, the team asked Paul's mother and grandmother to attend the World Series.

They turned down the invitation, Paul said. The women remembered the sentiments of Sockalexis' father, who had opposed Louis going off to play ball, afraid of what it might do to his son. The family blamed baseball for Sockalexis' early death.

Beyond that, inquiries about the family's baseball background were rare, until the debate flared up over the nickname. Kenneth Paul, as the oldest surviving relative, wound up taking the brunt of it.

He feels the new burst of media attention has falsely portrayed him as a bumpkin. He was photographed in an Indians cap, and he's been swamped by fiery mail both from proponents and foes of the Chief Wahoo logo.

"They made me look like a fool," he said. "Now everybody's writing to me, and calling me, and I try to duck them. One radio station wanted an interview, and I had my son Kenneth do it, and they didn't know the difference."

He is a 65-year-old man, living on the island of his birth in the Penobscot River, which is so polluted by paper mills you can no longer eat the fish. To Kenneth Paul, that is really something to worry about. Still, he doesn't hide his feelings on the Cleveland situation.

"Wahoo or Yahoo, it's more insulting than anything," he said. "I think they should just change the whole thing to something else. It won't break my heart. It won't break anybody's."

Louis Sockalexis is buried with his ancestors, Paul said, and the Penobscots have their own ways for honoring the dead. "We have our memories here," he said, "and that's all that counts to us."

Kenneth Paul is now 76, retired from his job as a dispatcher. "He's doing pretty well," says his son, Kenneth Jr. "He's got diabetes and some other problems, but on the whole he's well."

As for that baseball team in Cleveland, Kenneth Jr. says, "The name doesn't bother me. The word 'Indians,' to me, doesn't necessarily mean any disrespect. But yeah, I wish they'd get rid of that smiling Indian head."

◆ ◆ ◆

25   Dropping "Chiefs" Would Heal Old Sore

Oren Lyons wakes up each day to deal with major worries. He is a faithkeeper for the Onondaga Nation, one of the six Indian nations of the Iroquois Confederacy. His people are struggling with gambling and taxes and sovereign rights. The nickname of a local baseball team is not high on the trouble list at the Onondaga longhouse.

Just the same, Lyons wishes the Syracuse Chiefs—as a nickname—would cease to exist.

"It's one of those things... a little sore that doesn't heal," Lyons said. "You can go on, but it bothers you, and you always come back to it."

The baseball team is moving next year into a new ballpark. As part of the fresh start, a public contest is being held to pick a name for the team. The first phase whittled the list to five choices, including "Stars," "Thunder," "Dragons" and "Salty Dogs." But retaining the name "Chiefs" was an overwhelming leader.

That leaves the Onondagas and team officials in a box. Lyons hoped to stay out of such an inflammatory issue, hoped the fans would simply decide to make a change. If the team's board of directors supports the name "Chiefs," general manager Tex Simone will do what he has quietly done for years. He will play down the theme in order to avoid insulting the Onondagas.

Yet you're supposed to market the daylights out of a nickname. You're supposed to have fun with it. You're supposed to make stuffed toys and posters and funky, off-beat hats. That is not so easy to do with human beings, which is why the Onondagas want to see the nickname changed.

"We don't feel good about things like this," Lyons said. "We understand the Syracuse Chiefs are revered. We don't like being forced into these kind of positions."

But if you ask Lyons his opinion, he makes it very clear. Among the chiefs of the Onondaga Nation — the group of men our Triple-A team is supposed to honor — there is agreement that it's time for the old nickname to go.

"It's pretty standard with us," Lyons said. "What we have said is that logos and mascots should not be human beings. You know, you have

---

The *Post-Standard*, Monday, June 3, 1996

the Army mule and the Navy goat and the Yale bulldog and the Cleveland Indians. The Chiefs run in the same category. Their logo has changed, grown more respectful, from the time when it was a cartoon character.

"Still, it doesn't meet the principled position."

Lyons has traveled the world, and he has given talks on global problems at the United Nations, but he is sensitive to the dilemma faced by team management. He knows Simone is dealing with many fans who get emotional about change.

"After a long time (with an Indian nickname), people get to thinking they own the idea," Lyons said.

The Onondaga leadership rejects that reasoning. Within the spectrum of American history, amid an avalanche of symbols that insult Indians, Lyons maintains the logo of a Chiefs head simply cannot work. "It's a continuation of a myth," he said.

To Lyons, a chief is someone like Onondaga high chief, or tadadaho, Leon Shenandoah — a wise man, a holy man, a kind of religious figure. It is not an emblem you wave above a baseball field.

He was reminded that some sports teams—the Boston Celtics, the San Diego Padres— use ethnic or religious figures as their mascots. There are differences, Lyons said. Those mascots come from groups in the larger culture. The fans themselves are often tied to those groups. If the fans don't mind being used as mascots, that's their business, Lyons said.

The Onondagas mind.

That's because of history, Lyons said. That's because so many Indian mascots mock Native American speech or facial features or traditional Indian clothing.

"I want to ask these teams, 'Don't you have your own heroes? You must have heroes! Use some of your own!'" Lyons said. "You try to educate people about our sacred or social dances. They're done for reasons. We understand that it's hard to change a logo. It's very difficult. I have a lot of sympathy for that."

But he wants to see it happen.

Simone plans to meet with the Onondagas, wants to hear first-hand what they think about the nickname. Lyons welcomes the offer. But he wants the meeting to focus on "a real graceful transition" to a new logo, rather than finding some way for the team to remain the Chiefs.

As for the muscle behind his argument, Lyons has only his appeal to conscience. He said if the nickname stays the same, you won't see Onondaga pickets at the doors of the new ballpark. "We're embattled on so many fronts, and that's a lot of energy we can't expend," Lyons said.

Then he sighs. Lyons doesn't say it, but maybe one question should precede the big decision. A sports logo represents the whole community. Yet, would a casual fan be reluctant to wear a baseball hat or a baseball jacket onto Onondaga land?

Not if the logo was a Salty Dog.

After heated debate in Central New York, the Syracuse Chiefs were renamed the "SkyChiefs" in 1996, an attempt by team president Tex Simone to both honor the contest results and to respect the Onondagas. The logo became a fierce-looking fighter plane with shark's teeth. Some fans were delighted, while others argued the team should have either stuck with "Chiefs," or gone to something entirely new.

◆ ◆ ◆

26 Baseball Settles a Deep Debt

Milton Flowers loves baseball. He has taken overnight drives to watch its greatest players. He can speak in detail of pitching rotations, of infield precision, of the stylistic differences between hitting for power and spraying the field.

Yet the 86-year-old retired custodian from Hamilton, Ohio, didn't feel the urge to visit the game's most hallowed shrine until Monday, when he found himself in Cooperstown — shaking hands and slapping shoulders with the heroes of his youth.

"I never thought I'd see this day," said Flowers — a black man, who grew up watching black ballplayers.

For almost half his life, within both the white-skinned world of major league baseball and the hushed chamber of its Hall of Fame, those "colored ballplayers" did not exist.

Over the weekend, however, they found their peace in Cooperstown.

The Hall of Fame doors swung open for a general reunion of survivors from the old Negro Leagues — segregated circuits that began a slide into oblivion in 1945, when Jackie Robinson signed with the Dodgers' system and crossed the color line.

"There was a time when we didn't think we'd ever see integrated baseball," said Flowers, a long-time fan who spent long hours on the interstate this week with his son, Harold, in order to greet the old-timers.

"We thought we'd develop our own baseball," Flowers said, "and we hoped maybe we could draw the way the white players did."

It never happened. Robinson's carefully navigated entrance into the big leagues created a quick demand for black talent, particularly when such stars as Willie Mays, Henry Aaron and Ernie Banks moved over from the Negro leagues to light up the majors.

But there were hundreds of players—worthy in skill but burned by the fates—who fell short.

The Cooperstown reunion, which attracted about half of the 150 Negro League ballplayers still believed to be alive, was as much for those whose renown was only in the black community as for the luminaries, like Aaron—who is attending the packed schedule of receptions and banquets that end this morning.

But among those players—who displayed obvious jubilance as fans flocked to them in the streets, begging autographs—there was a remarkable absence of bitterness.

"I was angry (about segregation) before I ever got started," said Joe Scott, 73—a hard-hitting first baseman for the Birmingham Black Barons who was "a little too old" for the big leagues when the color line finally dissolved.

"But then it got to be, who you going to be angry at?"

Indeed, Scott said, he can claim a footnote in history. In 1948, at the age of 30, he was among the Negro League leaders in home runs when the old New York Giants of the National League decided to scout his talents.

They noticed, instead, an exuberant teen-age teammate by the name of Willie Mays.

Scott played from 1939 to 1950 with the Black Barons, the squad on which Mays broke in. "For a while, he was my roommate," said Scott, who still meets Mays—the man he insists was the best of all time—for occasional games of golf in Los Angeles.

Scott's best friend, however, is Merle Porter, 70, a retired L.A. factory worker who spent three years in the Negro League. The two men met while playing 1950s semi-pro ball in California.

While Porter is quick with a handshake and a smile, his stories recall the essence of those times.

He remembers an afternoon bus ride along the Gulf of Mexico, when some Alabama police officers noticed the players admiring women on a nearby beach. In the 1940s, Porter said, it was not wise for a black man to look at a white woman.

The police pulled the bus over. "They told us if they saw us take one more look, they'd throw us in jail," he said. "They got behind us and followed us for 10, 11 miles, and we all sat there, looking straight ahead."

On another occasion he waited with his teammates outside an Alabama gas station — all of them in new suits and shined shoes — while a mechanic repaired their bus.

The police drove up and made the players wait behind the building.

"This one guy, a white guy with a big belly, says, 'You niggers ought to be home in the field,'" Porter said — laughing once, and then shaking his head.

The veterans also told tales impossible to prove — how Satchel Paige and his fabled "hesitation pitch" could make a hitter swing around twice in one cut, how Luke Easter once hit a ball so hard and far that its cover flew off.

Today's players, the veterans said, fall short of Olympus.

"These guys … are basically playing dead," Scott said. "You got .214 hitters making a million dollars."

Scott, in turn, never made more than $650 a month playing baseball.

Yet it was not the salaries, but the achievements, of the black ballplayers that earned the attention of the faithful at Cooperstown — where 11 of the league's veterans have already been enshrined.

"This means everything, man," said Norman Lumpkin, veteran of the old Atlanta Black Crackers, as children pushed up scraps of paper. "It's been a long time in coming."

Matt Moore, 11, whose California family was visiting the hall, said he understands the significance of Lumpkin's signature.

"I know that if he did something in the Negro League," Moore said, "that he could have been a major leaguer."

Norman Lumpkin is now 83 and living in Atlanta, Ga. He often goes to a nearby locksmith shop to "just sit around, run errands, just spend time." The conversation usually touches on his beloved Braves.

The Negro League veteran has not returned to Cooperstown since the reunion, although he hopes to someday get there, one more time.

"It was one of the high points of my life," says Lumpkin, who keeps his

Hall of Fame photographs in an album, close at hand. "I had been there once before, but this time I was there because of my participation in the game. To be there, in the company of those ballplayers, you felt elevated."

◆ ◆ ◆

27 Clear Voices from the Past

Steve Carlton's Hall of Fame acceptance speech was very simple, very conciliatory. But he said one thing that explained it all, the reason the fans come back to Cooperstown each year.

"Memory," said Carlton, "is baseball's fourth dimension."

He could have been speaking of Josh Gibson Jr., whose father was among the greatest home-run hitters of all-time. But young Josh's mother died in childbirth, leaving behind a pair of infant twins. Josh Jr. and his sister went to live with their grandmother. Their father went on the road, year-round, hitting long balls to support them.

Josh Jr. is now 63, and he was seated Sunday in a room beneath a Cooperstown book store, signing photographs that sold for $5 a pop. He was flanked by six or seven old Negro League stars who see the impending major league strike with incredulous humor.

Million-dollar ballplayers and million-dollar owners? They understand why anyone would fight for a buck, because to this day nothing comes easy for them

Still, they wonder when that fight gets out of hand.

"Back then, you played for fun. That was it. That's all you had to play for," said Sam Jethroe. "This time, somebody's going to get hurt. Maybe the owners, maybe the players. This time, I think they're going too far."

Baseball has always been full of contract disputes, haggling, holdouts, angry words. The difference now is the overwhelming nature of the feud, which threatens to ruin a season full of vibrant baseball stories.

One of them, at least, got in under the wire. Beneath green hills that made him think about the minor leagues—anything Phil Rizzuto looks at touches off a different thought—the Yankee shortstop finally joined the Hall of Fame.

The *Post-Standard*, Monday, August 1, 1994

His acceptance speech was a pinball shot of memories and dialogue. Some New York fan kept hollering in a foghorn voice, "No strike!" Rizzuto must have heard it. He didn't respond directly about the walkout. But he did offer a little piece of his romance with the game.

His mother, he said, may have saved his career. As a kid in Brooklyn, he played baseball with the boys in the street. Windows were getting broken. The neighbors grew weary of fixing shattered glass. "Look," said Rizzuto's mom. "Bring me the cover off a ball, and I'll see what I can do."

So a ball wore out and they brought her the cover. She filled it with rags and other soft packing, and then sewed it shut. It was a ball that broke nothing, a ball that did crazy things in the air. They kept playing, and it helped the boys learn to hit the curve, which Rizzuto remembered as happily as any World Series.

The strike is supposed to come down within two weeks. Alice Deschaines laughed about it, her face hot from signing autographs in the open sun. Forty-five years ago she was a Rockford Peach, a shortstop and third baseman on the pioneer women's team that inspired "A League of Their Own." She quit to raise her kids, and now she is getting a chance to do card shows.

"Why strike?" she asked. "What are they going to go for? What do they want? What's left to get?"

Millions, the owners and players contend. The Negro Leaguers, behind their tables at the bottom of the stairs, agree there's plenty of money out there. Nap Gulley had a suggestion. He played for Negro League teams in Cleveland and Kansas City. If those profits are causing so many hard feelings, he has an idea for what to do with the cash.

There's 100 or so Negro League veterans still kicking around, Gulley said. They are survivors of a system that produced Jackie Robinson and Willie Mays and Henry Aaron. Many of them live in bare-bones retirement. "We made a contribution," Gulley said. He thinks a little pension would be a fair return.

"We go to plenty of reunions," said Edsall Walker, a teammate of Josh Gibson's on the great Homestead Grays. "We get plenty of caps, plenty of jackets. What all (that) is, it's plenty of nothing. What we never get is plenty of money."

He retired from baseball to a life of hard work. Financially, his life was never an easy thing. But when he talks about the game, the hard lines soften in his face and a smile breaks out. Josh Gibson? "He hit a ball out of Yankee Stadium! He hit a ball so hard at the Polo Grounds it broke the back of the seat! He could hit! He could throw! He was the best!"

Josh Gibson, Jr., spent his summers traveling with his storied father.

He remembers how the whole team hung wet clothes out bus windows to dry them in a hurry. He remembers the lousy food, the humid bus rides that went on forever.

Gibson's father died young, when his namesake was 16, but young Josh soon realized his dad hadn't gone away.

He is still out there, still swinging hard in baseball's fourth dimension, and the fans seek his touch in the handshake of his son. "They never stopped playing," Gibson said, of his father and his friends. It was a choice they never had, but a choice they helped create.

Sam Jethroe, one of the Negro League stars who signed autographs in Cooperstown, died in 2001, at the age of 83. His career epitomized the frustration and injustice of his youth. He batted a league-leading .393 for the old Cleveland Buckeyes in 1946, and he had a lifetime Negro Leagues batting average of .342.

Yet he was born a few years too early to get a fair shot in the Major Leagues. He was National League Rookie of the Year in 1950, batting .273, scoring 100 runs and stealing 35 bases for the Boston Braves. By 1952, his average had dropped to .232, and Jethroe endured some withering criticism from the Boston media and fans.

Except for one more Major League at-bat, he spent the rest of his career in the minor leagues.

Jethroe's last great triumph came in the 1990s, when he helped to lead a campaign that finally convinced Major League Baseball to offer small pensions to the surviving veterans of the Negro Leagues.

◆ ◆ ◆

28 Baseball Celebrates; Something's Missing

To Jim Wilkes, the symmetry couldn't get much better.

He is a 69-year-old veteran of the old Negro Leagues, a guy who barnstormed his way through the worst days of Jim Crow. On Sunday, he and

The *Post-Standard*, Saturday, July 29, 1995

Leon Day (left) during his Negro League career, and (right) as a soon-to-be Hall of Famer. (National Baseball Hall of Fame Library, Cooperstown, N.Y.)

about 20 other veterans of segregated baseball will go to Cooperstown, where the late Leon Day will be inducted into the National Baseball Hall of Fame.

The old ballplayers will come in from Albany, on the same bus.

"Riding the bus again!" said Wilkes, voice cracking with mirth. "I love it. Now, that brings back memories."

Not that he really minds the long ride. It turns out the hotels in Cooperstown are packed, and Albany is as close as the old Negro League stars could stay. The bus will give them some more time for reminiscing, for thinking back on the skills and dignity of Day.

He died last March, just a few days after learning he had finally made the hall. "When he heard the news, he was shining like a star," said Day's widow, Geraldine. But it will be Geraldine who stands in front of the crowd, accepting a great accolade that comes four months too late.

Wilkes played with Day on the old Newark Eagles, where Leon was a fast and dominating right-handed pitcher. In 1946, the final year before

Jackie Robinson broke the big-league color line, Day returned from World War II to open the Negro League season with a no-hitter.

That magic stayed with the Eagles to the end, when they won a dramatic Negro League World Series. They outdueled the Kansas City Monarchs, who featured Satchel Paige.

It makes for great memories. But for today's Negro League survivors, memories don't pay the bills or the rent.

To Max Manning, who pitched with Day on the Newark Eagles, the induction has an almost bitter taste. He understands that for Mike Schmidt and maybe even for Richie Ashburn, earning a plaque in Cooperstown is mainly about prestige and bragging rights.

But Manning, a retired schoolteacher from New Jersey, said induction into the hall means something more concrete to aging Negro League stars.

"What it means," Manning said, "is $50,000 or $60,000 a year."

That is what Manning estimates Day could have made off card shows and promotions. Instead, Day eked out a day-to-day living, even after baseball. He labored in the Jim Crow anonymity of the Negro Leagues, where all black ballplayers wound up until Robinson broke through. Their statistics were often lost, their glory obscured.

Manning is intrigued by the cultural aspects of the modern baseball fan. He notes how the whole memorabilia and nostalgia market is a primarily "white thing." African Americans, he said, don't seem that interested in autographs and relics. "Even when we were playing, it was that way," Manning said. "Black fans came to games, and they liked to be around us. But they weren't so caught up in all these other things."

That may be, he theorized, because baseball nostalgia invokes the good old days. And there weren't many good old days within Jim Crow.

Day's fame, as a player, was primarily reserved to black culture. Then he spent his entire life after baseball working as a bartender or a security guard, living in a series of small apartments, always wondering where his next dollar would come from. He was finally inducted into the hall last March, at the age of 78, after years of false rumors that he was about to get in.

He got the news in his hospital bed. A few days after his election, Day died of heart failure in his native Baltimore.

"I'm excited about (the induction) now, but when Leon died I was angry," said Ida Bolden, Day's 81-year-old sister. "His greatest ambition for years was to get in, and all those years they just didn't do it. When it finally happened, he was on his deathbed."

Manning was with Day at the moment the call came about his induction. As an example of Day's character, Manning said his old friend promptly signed a pile of baseballs for the hospital staff. Within a week, Day was dead. It grieved Manning, who wanted to see Leon get some time on easy street.

"It's good that he knew before he died," Manning said. "But he had a real financial need. I wish it had happened at least a year earlier."

Even now, almost 50 years after Major League Baseball finally opened up to blacks, Negro League veterans veer between joy and anger at what they achieved and what they missed.

Wilkes, for instance, was a speedy center fielder. He was nicknamed "Seabiscuit," after the race horse. And no one can take away the memory of a catch he made in Yankee Stadium.

"Josh Gibson was batting, for the Homestead Grays," Wilkes said. "He hit a line drive to deep center field. That was in the old Yankee Stadium, where it went a long ways back. I turned my back and started running. I reached up and stuck my mitt out and there was the ball. I was way back there. I turned around and there were the monuments for Babe Ruth and for Lou Gehrig. It's been called one of the greatest catches ever in Yankee Stadium."

But it is not exactly carved into the pantheon of baseball's famous plays.

Wilkes has an equally vivid story of how ugly things could get. He recalled one barnstorming trip down South, when the players could not eat in "white" restaurants, or use "white" public restrooms, or sleep in "white" hotels.

"I was batting in some little ballpark down there and I fouled the ball off my ankle," Wilkes said. "Now, you know how that feels. I went down and I heard this voice from the stands, 'Get up now, you nigger. You ain't hurt.'"

The voice was all business. Wilkes got up, in scorching pain, and kept his mouth shut. It is among the scars he'll carry Sunday, when Day goes in the hall. But it will also be Wilkes' first visit to Cooperstown, a place he hardly dreamed would someday treat him as an honored guest.

"Feels like cloud nine," Wilkes said. "It means all the world." He just wishes Day could be there, for that last ride on the bus.

◆ ◆ ◆

29 No Barrier on
the Basepaths

Lazaro Diaz knows the stereotype. He has heard how Latino ballplayers can be an umpire's nightmare. They supposedly kick the dirt, throw their helmets, wave their arms, curse out loud.

But Diaz contends many stories about Latinos lashing out are really stories about ballplayers who hit a language wall.

He has that perspective because he knows both sides so well.

"I remember one time, a brawl in (Vero Beach), when I threw a guy out of the game for throwing his helmet," Diaz said. "He walked off, waving his arms, shouting in Spanish, 'It wasn't me!' So I said to him, 'Well, who was it, then?'"

The player stopped and cooled off, stunned by an umpire who could answer in Spanish.

Diaz, who has worked at games in Syracuse twice this season, is the only Latino ump in the International League. He is 32 years old, races the basepaths at a full-bore sprint, and seems on a direct course for the major leagues.

"Laz is a prospect," said Edwin Lawrence, executive director of umpire development for Major League Baseball. "He's very intelligent, he's very smooth in handling players and he gets along with everyone. He's high on our list."

Lawrence said there are only two Latino umpires in the big leagues, despite the growing number of Spanish-speaking players. That is why Lawrence sees it as a priority to recruit bilingual umpires.

"If you're upset with a call, and the umpire can't answer, the only way to express yourself is with anger," Lawrence said.

The barrier can also cause strategic problems for a player. Carlos Delgado, the star first baseman for the Chiefs, spent most of his professional career as a catcher. Delgado said his conversation with an umpire was always crucial behind the plate, particularly early in a game.

"If he calls a (close) strike, you want to know if that's how he'll call them the whole game," Delgado said.

Most umpires, he said, are willing to reply. The catcher can then tell a pitcher to adjust. Delgado, who has lived through the challenge of mastering good English, said a Latino catcher faces a big disadvantage if he can't talk with the ump.

While Diaz agrees, he prides himself on umpiring skills beyond speaking Spanish. He grew up in Miami playing ball, the son of refugees from Castro's Cuba, and he was good enough to spend a season playing in Class A. That was as far as he got. Diaz, a fierce competitor, never guessed he might get a second baseball life by calling balls and strikes.

"I was never very friendly to the umpires at all," he said.

He returned to Miami, where he worked nine hours a day laying brick alongside his father. It was his dad who encouraged him to try umpiring. Diaz loved it. He went to umpire's training school and soon began what has been a fast rise through the minors.

"The good calls feel good, even if (players) argue," Diaz said. "But you remember the bad calls. You know you've blown one as soon as you do it. I think about it in my mind, between innings, and I think it helps me make sure I don't do it again."

No matter what happens, Diaz already has a classic story for his two children. A year ago, he was handling the plate in a Southern League game when Michael Jordan came to bat. Jordan was with Birmingham, where Steve Sax was doing a rehab assignment. As a major-leaguer, Sax was granted the right to wear a helmet with one ear flap. Jordan walked up wearing that helmet. Diaz told him to change it.

"Michael said, 'If Sax can wear it, why can't I?'" Diaz recalls. The fans, seeing their idol jawing with the ump, began shouting at Diaz. Diaz dug in. Jordan, grumbling, finally backed down. The next day, many papers in Central America ran pictures of this Cuban-American ump who stood up to Air Jordan.

Diaz dreams about the moment when he makes the majors. But he will need to perform at a high level for a long time in Triple-A. Lawrence said turnover among major league umpires is slow. There are good umpires in the International League with 10 years of experience still awaiting that permanent call.

So Diaz runs and works out to kill time on the road. He figures he needs to be in great shape, since he sprints back and forth when making calls on the basepaths. He always wants to feel weary at the end of a game.

"I give my players my best," he said. "No matter how long I do this, I don't ever want to be known as a lazy umpire."

As for the language barrier, Diaz takes satisfaction in his treatment by Latinos. They'll sometimes talk with him before a game or between innings, sharing a joke or a story in Spanish, and he can sense the players are reassured by that.

"They don't get as upset," Diaz said, "when they know you speak their language."

In 1999, Lazaro Diaz achieved his goal and became a Major League ump. In April 2003, Diaz found himself with an unwanted and unexpected burst of national attention after he was attacked by an angry fan during a game at Comiskey Park in Chicago.

◆ ◆ ◆

30 Team Leader Accepts No Excuses

Michele McAnany wasn't smiling. Little girls rushed toward her, little girls like Lauren Rodriguez and Stacy Taddio and Michele Broeker and dozens of lookalikes with ponytails hanging out of baseball caps, and McAnany dutifully kept signing autographs.

But you could almost see the steam coming out of her ears.

"We stank," she told the kids. "We were terrible. That wasn't us."

It was important to her that she leveled with them. McAnany, 31, stands 5-foot-1 and weighs 115 pounds, and she is the soul of the Colorado Silver Bullets. The women's baseball team lost Monday night at MacArthur Stadium, falling 6-1 to some all-stars from a senior men's league. The crowd gave the Bullets a standing ovation, but McAnany didn't think they deserved it.

"We had more errors than hits," she said. "Anytime that happens, you know you were terrible."

An excuse, a good one, was there for the taking. In the first inning, a pitch got away from Steve Grilli, a former big-leaguer pitching for the Syracuse team. It caught Stacy Sunny in the head. Grilli turned away, horrified. Sunny, the hottest Bullet hitter, went down hard. An ambulance took her away.

The *Post-Standard*, Tuesday, July 4, 1995

She was all right, but things like that can rattle major-league teams. McAnany, however, didn't want to hear it.

"If I used that as a reason, I'd be wrong," she said. "We had chances to make things happen. I popped out with people on base. This one isn't going away until I redeem myself. Before our next game, in our next city, I'm getting out the tee and getting down my stroke."

That is how she is. "What she brings to us," said pitcher Gina Satriano, "is intensity." McAnany is cut from the same mold as a player like Lenny Dykstra. She leads off for the Bullets. A year ago, when the Bullets were brand-new and a lot of people thought they were a joke, she was the team's first-ever hitter. She faced Oil Can Boyd, who gained his fame with the Red Sox.

McAnany singled.

"She's a gamer," said hitting coach Johnny Grubb, another former major-leaguer, as he watched McAnany chase a teammate from the batting cage who dared to take an extra stroke.

Her father, Jim, spent five years in the majors with the White Sox and the Cubs. McAnany was born in California in 1963, making her the oldest player on the Bullets roster. She played Little League baseball with boys, and then she played a year of Babe Ruth, where she got roughed up in a collision on the field. Her parents decided it was time for girls softball.

"My baseball career wasn't over," she said. "It never ended. It just wasn't happening. There weren't any opportunities."

McAnany was a fine softball player, a two-time All-American and a member of several adult national championship teams. But she defines baseball and softball as very distinct games. Women, she said, at least deserve the choice. When she heard about the Silver Bullets, when she heard Phil Niekro was coaching the team, she gave it a shot.

"She called me up (before the tryout) and said, 'Look. I'm going to make this team,'" said Kevin Lewis, the Bullets operations manager. "I was like 'Yeah, yeah, yeah, I've heard that before.'" But he hadn't seen any player give off sparks like McAnany.

Her decision to play was a monumental gamble. She quit a teaching job of six years, sold her car, left her apartment. Her parents wondered if she'd lost her mind. Now, she said, they're thrilled that she's playing. But her existence, during the season, is all buses and hotels. There are games every other day for 3 1/2 months, and the Bullets play from coast-to-coast.

McAnany paused, swept her arm across the vista of MacArthur Stadium, where little girls called out for Bullet autographs, where groundskeepers watered and packed the infield dirt.

"Sure, it's a job," she said quietly. "But what else could you ask for?"

Michele McAnany competed with the Silver Bullets until Coors pulled its funding for the team in 1997. McAnany now lives in Culver City, Calif., where she holds a full-time construction job.

"I miss playing," she says. "I miss Phil Niekro. I remember we were playing once on the Fourth of July, at Coors Field in Colorado, and I hit a double down the left-field line. My mom and dad were there, and the noise was incredible."

No job, she says, could ever be the same.

◆ ◆ ◆

III

VANISHED FROM THE GAME

31 A One-of-a-Kind
Collector Gets His Due

Jefferson Burdick was of slight build, his body twisted by severe arthritis, the pain so bad he often struggled to lift his arms off a table.

He worked as a parts assembler at Crouse-Hinds, in Syracuse. To the best knowledge of his surviving friends, he never attended a professional baseball game. He spent much of his life in a small Crouse Avenue apartment, where he devoted his energy to perpetuating what he always called his "hobby."

Burdick was a card collector. The greatest ever. The undisputed father of baseball card collecting in America. Thirty years after his death, in a time when that avocation has turned into a billion-dollar industry, the masters themselves defer to Jeff Burdick.

"He was the No. 1 guy," said Frank Nagy of Detroit, a titan among baseball card collectors. "He was bigger than life. Everyone looked up to him."

"My idol," said Alan Rosen, the self-described "Mr. Mint" of New Jersey, who lays claim to being the world's largest dealer of old sports memorabilia. "He's a legend. He literally wrote the book. All our library classifications, our way of cataloging, that came straight from Burdick."

Yet until an unprecedented museum opening Tuesday in New York, Burdick's legacy was understood primarily by collectors— even if every kid who loves collecting owes Burdick some thanks.

When the lifetime bachelor died in New York City in 1963, neither of the daily newspapers in Syracuse ran an obituary. For 30 years after Burdick's passing, his staggering collection of 300,000 postcards, hat cards, tobacco cards, military cards and baseball cards was kept locked away in New York's Metropolitan Museum of Art, available for viewing only on special request.

That all ended Tuesday, when the museum finally opened an exhibit of Burdick's elite cards.

It includes Wee Willie Keeler. Honus Wagner. Babe Ruth. Willie Mays. Jackie Robinson. Their cards are all on the museum wall, a few minutes away from the works of Rembrandt and Van Gogh.

The *Post-Standard*, Wednesday, June 30, 1993

The display consists of 80 baseball cards. It is a tiny fraction of Burdick's total baseball collection, which experts say is worth millions of dollars. The cards are mounted in a corridor of the American wing, which was jammed with visitors for Tuesday's opening. Yankee great Phil Rizzuto was the guest of honor. Reporters and photographers bounced off each other in the crowded hallway.

Burdick's best friend, John DeFlores, wasn't there. He was back in Syracuse, and he wishes it hadn't taken so long for a public exhibit. But DeFlores knows Burdick would be happy with the display.

"He was a very generous man," said DeFlores, who worked with Burdick on the factory floor at Crouse-Hinds. "Sometimes I'd ask him what one card was worth, and (he'd say) that card might be worth a fortune. But he didn't want to sell them. He said he'd rather leave them for posterity."

The only card hanging alone on the museum wall is a 1910 Honus Wagner, taken from a Sweet Caporal tobacco series. Wagner, a Hall of Fame shortstop, hated smoking. He demanded that his card be withdrawn from that pioneer release. Only 36 to 40 of the cards are believed to survive.

A mint copy has sold for $250,000. Burdick had one. In 1955, he estimated its value at about 50 bucks. The chance to see it up close was one big reason for the Metropolitan being packed.

"One long-time museum official said this is the most media we've had for an opening since they brought in the Mona Lisa," said Harold Holzer, the Metropolitan's director of public relations.

He wasn't kidding. Curator Elliot Bostwick Davis said Burdick may have saved an "ephemeral" art form, even though the backs of many of his cards were ruined when he pasted them into scrapbooks. Others remain pristine. They are all part of the first permanent exhibit of baseball cards at a major American art museum.

"It's a big deal because it acknowledges baseball cards for what they really are — an American art form," said Bruce Dorskind of Manhattan, who describes himself as "a serious collector."

Despite the enormity of Burdick's role, museum researchers struggled to gather detailed information on the life of the reclusive collector. They learned too late of DeFlores, 85, another retired Crouse-Hinds assembler.

He worked "back to back" with Burdick for years. They sat on the same bench inside the plant, piecing together detonators and intricate electrical parts.

On Saturdays, DeFlores often visited Burdick's Crouse Avenue apartment to help prepare the vast collection for donation to the museum.

A rare photograph of Jefferson Burdick, father of modern baseball card collecting, Syracuse, 1955. (*Post-Standard.*)

According to the writings of the late A. Hyatt Mayor, a former Metropolitan curator of prints and illustrations, Burdick first came to New York in 1947 to propose the donation. Mayor was unsure of how the museum would handle such a daunting task, but he decided to accept it.

He grew to admire Burdick, "this racked, frail man with black-lashed eyes of a haunting gray violet." The process of donating the collection would become, for Burdick, a race against death.

Weighed down by the pain of arthritis and by sickening doses of cortisone, Burdick retired from Crouse-Hinds in 1959. He moved from Syracuse to New York, where he continued cataloging and filing the massive collection.

"The mounting piles of scrapbooks drove him to work at a ... desperate pace," Mayor wrote. "From time to time he would say quite impersonally, as if he were talking about a horse race, 'I might not make it.'"

Burdick finished the job on Jan. 10, 1963. It was the last time he saw his cards. The next day, Mayor recalled, Burdick admitted himself to New York's University Hospital, where he died two months later.

For 30 years, as baseball cards exploded into a national obsession of finance and nostalgia, the Burdick collection was sequestered at the Metropolitan, available for viewing on a case-by-case request, known only to baseball card devotees.

"I asked (Burdick) once what good they'd do at a museum," DeFlores said. "He said he had collections of women's hats, military uniforms, baseball cards. He said if someone wanted to get information about that (American) period of time, they'd just go to the museum and check up on it."

That is the importance of what happened Tuesday.

Burdick was never able to drive, DeFlores said. He used the trolleys, and later the bus, to get to work. Milton Juengel, another retired worker from Crouse-Hinds, remembers Burdick's Crouse Avenue apartment as a single mass of organized cards, many of them stored in a dry attic space.

Neither Juengel nor DeFlores can recall Burdick attending a single baseball game, even though Crouse-Hinds is a few blocks away from the long-time home of the International League's Syracuse Chiefs. After Burdick donated his collection to the Met, he moved into a smaller Wolf Street apartment. It allowed him to walk across the street to his job. Throughout all the years of their friendship, DeFlores said, Burdick refused to ever use a cane.

That was in defiance of arthritis so severe, DeFlores said, that Burdick couldn't open his mouth wide enough to put in a ball of hard candy. "All he was interested in was cards," DeFlores said. "He was a bachelor, and that hobby was his life's work."

Nagy, a 71-year-old Detroit collector, is considered the man who elevated baseball cards into a profit-driven passion. But Nagy credits Burdick with establishing the entire hobby, particularly through his 1939 bible of collection, "The American Card Catalog."

The book outlined checklists and library systems, which grew into the complicated sorting and evaluating process used today.

Burdick's role, Nagy said, can be compared to what legend says Abner Doubleday did for baseball. The dogged tenacity of the Syracuse man established the hobby, and inspired myths among other collectors. "He'd go all over," Nagy said, searching for a single card.

Since baseball cards were of little value, museum researchers say, many collectors gladly gave them to Burdick. There were stories about Burdick finding treasures in trash cans.

Bill Mastro, another prominent American collector, said the rare

Wagner card was given to Burdick by a Pennsylvania enthusiast named Charles Bray, simply because Bray had two Wagners and Burdick had none.

"You have to understand, those guys were like a fraternity," Mastro said. "It's not anything like it is today. It was a group of older men who wrote letters and sent the cards to each other. They'd travel around the country in station wagons, and the thrill was in getting (each card). If you didn't need a Ty Cobb, you didn't take an extra one."

DeFlores said Burdick was the child of a farming couple. But his only sister died, and he had no direct survivors. That may explain Burdick's decision, late in life, against selling his collection. Burdick chose instead to leave a gift for all his descendants. They include anyone who ever kept a card-filled shoebox in the closet, anyone who knows the sheer joy of filling out a baseball checklist. Burdick died in obscurity, with millions of heirs.

◆ ◆ ◆

32 Scooter's Memories on Display at the Met

NEW YORK — Even when he was the finest shortstop in all of major-league baseball, Phil Rizzuto never had a year like this.

A few months ago, the worlds of baseball and literature were joined by a book, "O Holy Cow! The Selected Verse of Phil Rizzuto," co-written by Syracuse author Hart Seely.

And on Tuesday, Rizzuto—a fast-talking institution on New York Yankee broadcasts—was dogged by dozens of reporters in the Metropolitan Museum of Art, all of them hanging on his thoughts about culture.

As Rizzuto would say, that was something.

"Cracker Jack!" he exclaimed, looking at an ancient collection of Cracker Jack baseball cards. "They've been great to me ... Cracker Jack! Just like Granola! It's roughage! You need a lot of roughage to keep yourself healthy!"

The *Post-Standard*, Wednesday, June 30, 1993

He turned to smile as his young listeners suddenly understood what he meant.

Rizzuto was the guest of honor at the opening of a baseball card display donated by the late Jefferson Burdick, a Syracuse man considered the father of the hobby.

Within a crowd whose focus was often the priceless nature of the cards, Rizzuto saw them as a poignant family album.

They threw a museum cap on his head and he went through the exhibit, describing each face more to himself than to the crowd packed around him.

He called Roger Maris "the most misunderstood player in the annals of baseball." He spoke with reverence of the young Mickey Mantle, who could "outrun a rabbit, could hit the ball over the moon."

Rizzuto defended the integrity of "Shoeless Joe" Jackson, barred from the Hall of Fame by the Black Sox scandal. And the Scooter flipped around a question about his own omission from Cooperstown.

"These guys are immortals," he said, nodding at Willie Mays, Mantle, Warren Spahn. "You know what they did to the Hall of Fame? They lowered their standards, and they never should have."

There was another young man inside the same frame, who carried a dark growth of beard. "To think I was that young," Rizzuto said.

Among the pack trailing him was Joe Aponte, a museum maintenance man. Aponte had already brought his own son, Eric, to see the cards. It was Eric's first trip to the museum, which fulfills an administrative hope that Burdick's collection will attract a new working-class audience.

"That voice," Aponte said, hypnotized by Rizzuto's stream of description. "It never changes. What a unique voice!"

Rizzuto said he never saved his own cards. They weren't such a big deal when he was playing. But he does have regrets about the lost romance of baseball. Looking at the once-young giants of his era made Rizzuto kind of sad.

"It'll never be like it was before," he said.

As he walked away from the display he spoke of Roy Campanella, the great Brooklyn catcher who died Saturday. They were friends. On the night Campanella had the car accident that put him in a wheelchair, Rizzuto rushed to be by his side.

And he was there when the doctors forced a terrified Campanella into an iron lung. "He was claustrophobic," Rizzuto said. The horror of that scene still haunts Rizzuto.

"To be in that (wheelchair) that long and to be that cheerful ..." He shook his head, not even noticing that he had entered a vast and quiet gallery called the American Garden Court.

But Phil Rizzuto doesn't stay downcast for long. He reached up to touch his scalp, realizing his complimentary cap was gone. "HEY!" he shouted, like he was screaming for a popup. "WHERE'S MY HAT!" Who had ever done such a thing in that hallowed place?

Everyone turned and stared at the source.

It was baseball, inside the Metropolitan Museum.

◆ ◆ ◆

33 Decades Later, a Friendship Has Been Chiseled in Stone

John DeFlores wouldn't go. We wanted to drive him to Central Square. We wanted his photograph with the new monument he purchased for the Hillside Cemetery, the little piece of history he guaranteed a friend.

DeFlores refused. He is 89 years old, and he lives in quiet retirement on the north side. He didn't feel he deserved to be in the photo with the stone.

"This is about Burdick," said DeFlores. "He's the one who's been neglected."

Maybe so, but this is also about friendship. Jefferson Burdick, a Syracuse man, was the undisputed father of baseball card collecting. Today's most famous collectors speak his name in awe. He was a lifetime bachelor whose passion was accumulating 300,000 hat cards, tobacco cards and classic baseball cards.

He worked on an assembly line at Crouse Hinds. He suffered from arthritis so severe he could not open his mouth wide enough to slip in a ball of candy. To the best knowledge of DeFlores, Burdick never attended a single professional baseball game.

The *Post-Standard*, Friday, November 14, 1997

What he did — at a time when baseball card collecting was a child's passion, at a time when priceless cards were often trashed by grumpy mothers — was to hunt down rarities. He filed them and he wrote books about his cataloging system, a system which the best collectors still use today.

Burdick died in 1963. He died in such obscurity the Syracuse newspapers didn't run an obituary. His ashes were returned to Central Square, where his parents once owned a dairy farm. He was buried between his mother and his father.

There was not enough money left over for a tombstone.

"Thirty-five or 40 years dead, and all that time neglected," DeFlores said. "He's been a friend of mine my whole life. I hated to see it. People going there didn't even know who he was."

For all that time, DeFlores was unaware Burdick had no marker. He learned about it a few months ago, through a newspaper article. As DeFlores went through his day-to-day routine, he found himself thinking back to his old friend.

DeFlores had a brother, Rocky, born with disabilities. He couldn't walk. The doctors wanted Rocky placed in an institution. DeFlores' parents refused. They raised Rocky to be tough. He got around town on a little rolling board, and he ignored the teasing and the taunts from other kids.

He became a successful printer. When DeFlores met Burdick on a workbench at Crouse Hinds, he sensed a spirit similar to Rocky's.

"He was picked on his whole life," DeFlores said of Burdick. "He always kept to himself."

Burdick was thin, quiet, meticulous. Gruff factory workers found him peculiar. But DeFlores liked him. Burdick trusted DeFlores enough to show him his treasure, the cards that dominated Burdick's small apartment.

In the 1950s, Burdick realized he was dying a slow death. He decided to donate his cards to the Metropolitan Museum of Art. The collection, today, is on permanent display. It is worth millions. DeFlores helped Burdick package up the cards. They spent a Saturday driving boxes to the U.S. post office.

Burdick moved to New York City to help sort and file his cards at the museum. He finished the job a few weeks before he died in 1963. "A collection worth a fortune," DeFlores said, "and he left it to posterity."

Thirty-four years later, DeFlores was stunned to learn Burdick had no marker on his grave. DeFlores lives a simple, modest life. Yet, he took $500 from his savings to buy Burdick a stone from the Oswego County Monument Co. "I would have bought him a bigger one," DeFlores said, "but I didn't want to overshadow his parents."

The stone reads, "Jefferson Burdick — One of the greatest card collectors of all times."

It went up last month. DeFlores refused to be photographed at the cemetery. The stone, DeFlores said, did not go up for him.

"It's for Burdick," he said. "For me and Jeff, this is the end."

John DeFlores died in October 1998, less than a year after he bought a tombstone for Burdick's gave.

◆ ◆ ◆

34 Patches of the Past

It does not start as a quest. It starts out as a quick drive to the mall, where you figure you will find it in the first children's store. Time after time, the clerks hear your question and walk straight to a rack. Then they stand there, hands on hips, puzzled and surprised.

"We just had them," each clerk says. "I was sure we did."

So were you. That is the problem. From the malls, you roam to the thrift stores. You struggle to believe no one sells what you want. This is something every kid used to have!

Frustrated, you start making phone calls to collectors and historians. In the end you find Bill Perskin, the one guy with the answer.

You want a patch jacket. You want it for your kids, who are now in school. You grew up in the '50s or '60s. Your big brother had the jacket. When he outgrew the thing, it came down to you. It was made of soft blue cotton, cotton that smelled good when baked by the hot sun. It was covered by little round patches, patches for all the major-league baseball teams.

Most of your friends had those jackets. It was not a fashion statement, made of gleaming silk. No one hollered at you if you spilled jelly on it. It was the jacket you wore home from school, the jacket your mom threw in the machine when it got dirty, the jacket you loved until your arms just grew too long.

You remember that jacket. You remember the way you could fold it into a ball, like a pillow. You could sprawl on the ground, stare up at the sky on a beautiful June day, your head buried in the soft give of the jacket. You remember sitting on your porch steps, studying the logos. A Cub or a Tiger or that Yankee hat and bat, logos that led you to a favorite lifetime team.

Your own kids walk to school now, and you want them to understand. You want the patch jacket. You want it so bad for them you drive all the way to Cooperstown, where you go through every specialty shop in the village, the shops where they treat baseball like some fine imported wine. They show you sleek and expensive children's jackets, made in the style of whatever team you want. They don't understand. You want the patch jacket.

Nobody has it. You can't even find a snapshot to show the clerks, because your mother never took your picture in the jacket. You never wore it on the kind of days when she got out the camera. It was a walk-home-from-school jacket, a play-in-the-yard jacket, a throw-it-on-the-floor jacket.

It bothers you enough that you start making calls. You telephone the corporate headquarters of Sears. The public relations people dig into the archives. One day—Eureka!—they find evidence. It is a catalog ad from 1963, the year Kennedy was shot, the year Sandy Koufax and his Dodgers blanked the Yankees in four straight. The jacket sold for $4.87. Exactly.

"Perfect for young baseball fans," reads the catalog. "Each jacket has 10 emblems of the American League and National League teams. Cotton poplin body is lined with cotton flannel. Two slash pockets. Knit collar, cuffs and waistband."

You read that, and it's like you slid your arms into the jacket, like school has just ended and you can't wait to zip it up. The jacket came in red for the AL, blue for the NL. Sears sends the catalog page by facsimile. The guy waiting behind you at the fax machine happens to get a look. "Hey!" he says. "I had that jacket!"

You keep making calls. You reach Starter, maker of chic sports jackets in the '90s. They never heard of any patch jacket. You call Major League Baseball, where you get transferred and put on hold too many times to count. Finally, a decent guy in licensing spends some time with you. He digs out a folder, and that is where he finds it.

Genuine Sportswear made the patch jackets. It is a Brooklyn company. It still is listed in the directory. When you call, the phone is answered by this man named Bill Perskin.

His father, he tells you, invented the patch jacket.

Hy Perskin was a sales rep with many clothing firms after World War

Small fry favorites

3 **Big League styling** for young baseball fans. Each jacket has ten emblems of the American League and National League teams. Cotton flannel-lined cotton poplin. Raglan shoulders, slash pockets, knit collar, cuffs, waistband. Neat sleeve trim. Water-repellent treated. Machine washable, medium temperature.
State size 4, 6, 8, 10, 12 or 14. Shpg. wt. 1 lb. 1 oz.
40 A 76100F—Navy
40 A 76101F—Red......**$4.87**

4 **Plaid reversible.** 100% cotton woven plaids reverse to harmonizing solid colors in 100% cotton poplin. Matching rib-knit cuffs and waistband. Slash pockets. Machine washable, medium temperature.
State size 4, 6, 8, or 10.
40 A 76200F—Med. olive plaid; reverses to medium olive solid
40 A 76201F—Med. blue plaid; reverses to medium blue solid
40 A 76202F—Med. brown plaid; reverses to medium brown solid
Shpg. wt. 1 lb. 1 oz......**$3.97**

480 SEARS CPBKM

4 $**3**97
Sizes 4 to 10

3 $**4**87
Sizes 4 to 14

A Sears catalog description of the patch jacket, from 1963.

II. In 1954, the year the New York Giants won the World Series, young Bill asked his father for a "real Giants jacket." Hy went looking and could not find one for kids.

Baseball at the time ruled the sporting world. Hy started thinking about this untapped market. He wanted to put little baseball patches on cheap cotton jackets, jackets a working family could afford. He pitched the concept to Genuine Sportswear. The jackets took off.

"We used to sell 12 of them to a store for $22," says Bill Perskin, who went into his dad's business. "We'd sell 400,000 or 500,000 of them a year."

The jackets sold from the 1950s into the late '70s. They became a springtime ritual amid the Baby Boom.

"Times changed," Perskin says. Kids wanted designer clothes, and costs were going up. At the beginning, his company paid nothing for licensing rights. Pretty soon, the major leagues wanted big fees. Today, he would pay at least a buck for every patch on every jacket.

By 1980, the patch jacket was gone.

It is a hard thing to hear. You wanted your kids to have their own patch jackets, just in case they needed pillows to watch clouds in the sky. And you wanted the jackets for some deeper reason, for all those times when your kids have a rough or rocky day.

Because the jacket is warm and giving, and today that's hard to find.

"Sometimes," Perskin tells you, "simple things are the best." He wishes it made sense for him to bring the jackets back. But it costs a buck a patch, and they don't make them anymore.

Not long after this column appeared, Genuine Sportswear officially went out of business.

◆ ◆ ◆

35 After 27 Summers, Suddenly It Will Become Fall

We are the Baby Boom children of World War II, a generation whose youth drains away between our closed fingers.

We try to hold on. When our music gets outdated, we wrap it up in radio cellophane and call it classic rock.

And when our childhood sports heroes start to retire, we turn for solace to whoever we have left.

Nolan Ryan is the end of the line.

Each year takes us closer to a strange millennium. We get our money from talking machines, set in a wall. We heat our food in whirring boxes. We use laser beams to listen to music. We send letters through cables plugged into the phone.

And we sometimes stop, as life careens like a train wreck toward some dark tunnel, to remember the slow click of time on a childhood day, the way we'd check box scores each morning to see who hit home runs ...

The *Post-Standard*, Wednesday, February 17, 1993

Off some pitcher named Nolan Ryan.

When he broke into the big leagues, we kept baseball cards in a box, not a vault.

When he broke into the big leagues, there were active ballplayers who had been Brooklyn Dodgers.

When he broke into the big leagues, we still huddled in our classrooms to listen on fall days to World Series games.

But only if some kid was lucky enough to own a transistor radio.

Nolan Ryan first tasted major-league baseball in 1966, before many of us were fully aware the game even existed, which means he has been around as long as we measure our lives.

Now Nolan Ryan is retiring, although he promises one last, precious year.

Maybe it will seem like a very long summer.

Nolan Ryan threw fastballs to such ballplayers as Willie Mays and Henry Aaron and Roberto Clemente. People who played with such ballplayers as Ted Williams and Satchel Paige and Bob Feller. Who played with such ballplayers as Lou Gehrig and Lefty Grove and Josh Gibson.

Who were the immortals.

Nolan Ryan is a link. In so many sports we understand, instinctively, that teams of the '90s would crush and embarrass teams of the '50s. Sheer size, speed and conditioning ensure it. Linebackers run today like elite sprinters. Men who stand 6-foot-9 can handle a basketball.

Nolan Ryan threw fastballs past Willie McCovey. He threw fastballs past Rod Carew. He throws fastballs past Cecil Fielder. He remains a yardstick, a human bridge, between eras that seem impossibly estranged.

He was in big-league baseball before the first comeback of Richard Nixon. Before My Lai. Before crack cocaine.

Now he will retire, after one last triumphant tour. We can show up in the ballpark hoping for that implausible no-hitter (and his last three or four have all been implausible). We can hope he is rewarded with a Walter Johnson scenario, the aging fire-thrower with a chance for a final World Series.

Ryan will go out with most of the major strikeout records, and then he will take a quick cab to Cooperstown. Swell. That town already has enough Hall of Famers. It is, in a way, a baseball cemetery. We go there to look at the pretty bronze tombstones, and to wish we'd been alive when those men played ball.

We will make a point this summer of showing Nolan Ryan to our own sons and daughters. They will nod, but they won't understand. It is asking too much. They cannot imagine life without childhood. Neither can we, and the last piece of ours is about to call it quits.

36 Cut from a Family Tree

Perhaps once a week during the summer, the old man climbs onto a Centro bus and goes to a Chiefs game. He often sits alone in MacArthur Stadium, as lost in the crowd as he has been to baseball lore. But it is likely that some of the most famous blasts by Babe Ruth and other immortals came off bats polished by the hands of Joe Kren.

The great shame is that no one really knows.

"We made the best bats there were," says Kren, 88. "We didn't use any black stain to cover up knots and problems. My father told his ballplayers, 'I'll give you the best bat I can make.' He didn't want any runaround. If he gave them a bat, they'd know it would be a good one."

In the old days, Kren says, a bat was an appendage. A player would sit for hours spitting tobacco juice onto the barrel while rubbing it relentlessly with an old meat bone. The wood became impacted, almost rock hard.

"When they hit it," Kren says, "it sounded like a rifle shot."

Kren's only surviving brother, Walter, still owns the family home on Beecher Street. Before it burned in 1939, the factory that made Kren's Specials stood behind the house. Now Walter comes to the door and declines an interview, a decision his brother says is based on poor health.

Joe Kren, however, speaks for both of them. He remembers visits by great ballplayers, including Ruth and Honus Wagner. He remembers a busload of Negro Leaguers who bought dozens of bats.

More than anything he remembers his father standing at a lathe, shaping down a block of turning wood with his chisels and his blades. "Hand-turned," said the label on every Kren's Special. Joe's father worked in a floppy hat and a long coat, an artist with no option except perfect results.

If there was the slightest mistake in length or weight, a player would

Joe Kren, as a child, at his father's Syracuse bat factory. (Courtesy of Joe Kren.)

throw the bat aside. "They can tell," Joe Kren says. "If it's wrong, they know as soon as they pick it up."

It is World Series week, and the games occupy his attention, just as they have for every October of his life. A 1932 article in The *Post-Standard* described the family working with the radio on, listening to the series and straining for the sound of every hit.

Sixty-three years later, Joe Kren is usually dressed in coat and tie. Sometimes he talks business while gripping a Kren's Special fungo bat, a bat he received from a friend who was stunned that Joe had kept none for himself.

Joe and Walter were "finishers," which means they shellacked and boxed at least 50,000 bats a year. Oldest brother Henry was plant manager. Brother Frank was a sander. The soul of the outfit was their father, born in Germany in 1868.

His name also was Joseph Kren. The story goes that he was working in the 1890s at an industrial lathe in Syracuse when he saw some kids trying to hit with a shard of wood. Kren made them a bat on his lunch break. Pretty soon he had gone into the business, manufacturing only bats and police billy clubs.

Syracuse natives Jimmy Walsh (left) and Bill Kelly of the Buffalo Bisons, with their Kren's Specials bats in the 1920s. (Courtesy of Joe Kren.)

"My father was always happy," Joe Kren says. "He loved what he did. Sometimes he was in there making bats on Sunday morning. When he'd give a bat to his ballplayers, he'd always say, 'There's some hits in this bat, I guarantee it. But only if you've got the eye to go with it.'"

The wood came from white ash trees in the North Country. Joe Kren's father would go for long drives in his truck, touring farms and pounding nails into trees. If it felt right, he bought it. Only Ruth, of all the players, would ask for a bat made from harder hickory.

Joe Kren says many of the greats who passed through Syracuse would visit the lathe. The old man always warned his boys to keep busy, so the ballplayers knew the family meant business. Young Joe would take a broom and start sweeping up sawdust, watching Ruth or Lou Gehrig from the corner of his eye.

Old newspaper accounts noted the Krens also made bats for Al Simmons, Pepper Martin, Wagner and other immortals. Joe Kren says Bill Kelly and Jimmy Walsh, Syracuse sandlot legends who reached the major leagues, were devoted customers. They'd spend long hours at the plant, trying bats and hanging around the yard.

The trouble with these stories, as Joe Kren readily admits, is finding documentary proof. The company gave away bats to major leaguers, happy for any business that came from word of mouth. Most players who used Krens did so on the sly, because they had exclusive contracts to use the famous bats of Hillerich and Bradsby. The payback from H&B was often a set of golf clubs, but it still restricted players from putting autographs on any other bat.

"They'd use our bats, but they couldn't say they did," Joe Kren says.

Still, Kren is a name known by historians. "They had that distinctive diamond label," says David Bushing, a collector and expert from Illinois. "They were handmade. They were as good a bat as anyone could make."

Barry Halper, a minority owner of the New York Yankees, is a renowned collector of memorabilia. He owns a Kren's Special, a Gehrig model, that was signed by Lou himself. Joe Kren, upon seeing a photograph of that bat, instantly remembered the stove the family used to burn in the label.

In the 1930s, Gehrig was called to testify in a lawsuit between H&B and a smaller rival. Asked to describe under oath any bats he'd seen used, Gehrig spoke of several major leaguers who preferred Krens. Indeed, one of the New York Giants mentioned by Gehrig — Emil "Irish" Meusel — used a 48-ounce bat, reportedly the largest Kren's Special ever made.

The Krens also had ties to the St. Louis Cardinals. Some players on the famous "Gas House Gang" started off with the Syracuse Stars, which for a time was the St. Louis farm club. Joe Kren, as a child, would shuttle bundles of bats on the trolley to the team at old Star Park.

All of that ended in 1953, with the death of the older Joseph Kren. None of his boys ever learned how to "turn" a bat from unshaped wood, which the younger Joe regrets to this day. A year after their father died, the surviving sons sold their rights to the business. They donated their dad's tools to the Hall of Fame.

Gradually, the company's renown has faded out. Adirondack became New York's premier maker of bats. The last Kren factory on Bear Street is now home to the Book Warehouse. And Joe Kren himself has little left from his family's heyday.

The 1932 article related how great hitters like Ruth would crack a bat, tape Kren's address to the barrel, and then throw it in the parcel post for Syracuse. The Krens would size up the bat for a replacement.

All those relics used by baseball's immortals were saved at the plant as "models" for making bats. At one point, Joe Kren says, they probably had 2,000 models stacked on shelves. When their father died, the Kren brothers got rid of them.

Today, with the memorabilia market booming, it hurts Joe Kren to even think about the worth of those cracked bats.

"We could have been millionaires," he says. "What if we had stayed open? What if my brothers had lived? What if we had found someone else who knew how to turn a bat?" He shrugs and drops into silence, because there is no point now in dwelling on all that.

He simply hopes you understand why the bats were called Kren's Specials, because the "sound like a rifle shot" has vanished from the game.

◆ ◆ ◆

37 Joe Kren Does One Last Job for His Dad

Joe Kren knew the fastest way, by heart, from his James Street home to MacArthur Stadium. You take Catherine Street to Lodi Street, then follow it all the way through the North Side, until you get to North Salina Street. Then you take Wolf Street to beat some of the traffic, and from there you pull into the Big Mac parking lot.

He was right, except the destination has changed into P&C Stadium, while Big Mac is a pile of dust and memory. Joe used to go to that ballpark all the time, sitting in the old blue seats not far from the dugout. He'd listen for the impact when the players hit the ball, because the sound could tell him a lot about a bat. Now he is 93, and his legs are so stiff with arthritis they don't bend, and he can't take the bus to the ballpark anymore.

Wednesday was his first trip to P&C since it was built. Joe's father, the famed bat maker, will be inducted this fall into the Greater Syracuse Sports Hall of Fame, and the organizers asked old Joe's only surviving son to step in at the reception when the new picks were announced. Joe agreed. He dragged himself from his walker into a car, and then he looked out the car window and spotted things that were long gone.

The "Eye-talian and German" neighborhoods of his youth, as he puts

The *Post-Standard*, Friday, June 16, 2000

it, are now African American, Asian and Latino, kids in the parks playing basketball and soccer. Roaming children don't play sandlot baseball anymore, and when they play Little League, their metal bats go "ping."

"My friend, he tells me he thinks the aluminum bats are better," Joe said. "Aluminum? I don't think it rings when you hit it. Wood rings. Maybe I'm wrong, but I think it does."

According to Ron Gersbacher, the historian of Syracuse baseball, the Kren Company reached its peak between 1910 and 1954. Kren bats were used by some of the greatest players of all time. A Kren made for Lou Gehrig recently sold for $40,000 at auction. Joe still gets three or four calls every week from collectors. There is a guy from Utah planning to visit Syracuse, just to meet Joe.

Yet Joe kept no Krens of any value. His father died in the early 1950s. So did the company. None of the Kren brothers ever learned to turn a bat on a lathe, and they sold the company and went into different trades. At 93, Joe worries that his dad's company might be forgotten. That is why it meant so much for him to show up Wednesday, to sit in a line with the other Hall of Fame inductees.

"My dad, he'd be so happy," Joe said. "He was always smiling. He said he came into the world honest and he was going out honest, so what was there to worry about? I lived at home with him for the longest. He used to say to me, 'Joe. You know what to do.'"

They draped a medal around Joe's neck —"Class of 2000"— and then he stood looking at a Kren bat behind glass in a P&C trophy case, a molasses-colored Bill Kelly model at least 70 years old, with a wood-burned label bragging of "creosote treatment." That was young Joe's job for his father. He was the "polisher," the guy who put protective coatings on the bats. "Boy, that's a nice bat," Joe said, and then he talked about Bill Kelly as if Kelly were still alive, a Syracuse kid who grew up to play for the Buffalo Bisons.

There was a little reception on a stadium patio. Joe got into the buffet line. He pointed at a bowl of bean and nacho dip with olives, and he asked with some concern, "What's that?" He took some celery, some cubes of cheese and some pizza. "They got a lot more here than they used to have," he said, and then he stretched out his legs and sat down to eat, staring out at the green turf of the stadium.

As a child, Joe rode the streetcar to deliver bats to the old Star Park, and then he was a regular inside Big Mac, and Wednesday, finally, he got to see P&C. For the first time all night, Joe fell into silence. Some of the other inductees stopped to shake his hand, but his attention kept drifting back to the field.

**Joe Kren, in his 90s, with a bat made by his father's company. (Dennis Nett,
Post-Standard.)**

The stands were still empty, while the SkyChiefs warmed up in a lazy
rhythm. Some took batting practice inside the cage, young men taking
cuts with their wooden bats.

Joe pulled himself up. His legs were bothering him. He did not stay
for the SkyChiefs game. Riding home, he pointed out his father's last factory, the building now occupied by the Book Warehouse. Wild trees, tall
grass and shrubs obscured the old ornate brick walls. "A guy comes up to
me just the other day," Joe said. "He says to me, you know, you look just
like your father."

*Joe Kren, at 95, is still talking baseball at his James Street apartment in
Syracuse. He is also happy to remind potential visitors to Cooperstown that
they can find a Kren bat on display at the National Baseball Hall of Fame
and Museum, a bat used by George "High Pockets" Kelly to hit three home
runs in a game for John McGraw's New York Giants.*

◆ ◆ ◆

38 Hobart Takes a Designated Hit

Maybe John L. Brown was the key. Maybe if he had been sitting in his lawn chair on the little hill, looking down across the baseball field in Geneva that he loves so much, maybe people could have tried to sugarcoat this with nostalgia.

But even Brown, an old man whose life has revolved around the game, couldn't bring himself to stay. Saturday afternoon was probably the last time varsity baseball — a victim of cost-cutting — will be played at Hobart College. Brown could only bear it for a few minutes, and then he turned his back on the field.

"I'm sick about this," he said.

Brown is 85 years old, and he used to coach the Statesmen. He moved to Geneva in 1919, after his father died in the great flu epidemic, and ever since then local baseball has been central to his life. He was a fixture at Hobart games, sitting in his lawn chair just behind the backstop, but on Saturday his absence said more than anything.

"I couldn't stand to stay," he said. "I was afraid I'd break down."

He spoke for pretty much everyone involved in Hobart baseball — the coaches and players, the parents and alumni. The game started at the school in 1860. On Saturday, the Statesmen took on Hamilton, a traditional foe, in a season-ending doubleheader. It was a bright spring day on a field carved from a natural amphitheater. Hobart's players built it themselves in the early 1950s, shoveling dirt and throwing down seed.

If you wanted to pretend, it seemed a sweet goodbye. But the real sentiment was decidedly more bitter.

"What would it cost to keep baseball going?" asked one Hobart educator, who requested that his name be withheld. "Maybe the cost of two tuitions? Playing baseball on campus, on a day like this.... This is what college sports is all about."

The anger was reflected by some young Hobart fans, fueled by beer from too many outdoor parties, whose heckling of the visitors went over the edge. Girlfriends, families, anything was fair game. One guy, for instance, graphically mocked a Hamilton fan who had a speech impediment, much to the loud amusement of his friends.

The *Post-Standard*, Monday, May 8, 1995

No, nostalgia was hardly the prevailing emotion.

"Some goofy people out there," said Hamilton assistant coach Richard Hunt. "This is not an easy place to play today."

All the tension spilled over in the second game, when the benches cleared for mayhem at home plate. Statesmen co-captain Todd Stirling, normally more of a card than a brawler, was ejected. "I can honestly say that's the first time that's ever happened to me," said Stirling, as he stood away from the field, looking a little stunned.

Rick Ferchen was hired eight years ago with a mandate to make Hobart baseball respectable. "I think we exceeded that," Ferchen said. Six times his teams played in the postseason. A year ago, Hobart was 27-10. But one day the coach was called in for a meeting and told baseball was being cut out. Period.

"I understand there are financial problems," he said. "But I don't understand why they couldn't have looked at cutting extras, maybe junior-varsity teams."

Hobart President Richard Hersh had no easy answer. "There's no good reason to get rid of any sport," he said. The college felt the pinch, and had to cut something. Baseball got hit, with men's swimming and diving. Still, Hersh said he is proud of how the baseball team went out. "A lot of class," he said.

Ferchen lost some fine young players who got the news and transferred. This was a lame-duck season. Hobart came into the doubleheader 15-17 overall and lost the first game 5-1. In the nightcap, the Statesmen went out with a win.

Hobart jumped to an 8-0 lead, although Hamilton rallied. In the last inning, Ferchen stayed with senior pitcher Rick Williams, waiting out the last-ditch Continental surge, wanting a senior to get the victory.

A 135-year-old program came to an end when Hamilton's John Kowalczik drove a grounder to shortstop Mike Mahoney, who made the throw to first baseman Bill Coggins. The team ran out and huddled on the infield, then the seniors hugged and posed for photos, while Williams bit his lip and tried to hold back the tears.

"This field, this beautiful field," he said. "How many guys played their hearts out on it?" Junior Mike Granata walked away, face down, wondering if he would play organized baseball again. His dad, Mike Sr., pulled him over and gave him a kiss.

The players were angry. Many agreed with senior pitcher Chris Seitz, who blamed Hobart's decision to elevate lacrosse to Division I. "That's where the money's going," Seitz said.

Assistant coach Marty Olmstead spoke of a rumor rolling through the stands that some alumni were turned down in an offer to finance the program for four years, if the college would take over once the money crunch eased.

Hersh denied it. He said Hobart would have embraced that funding. He said there had been some informal proposals from alumni, but nothing close to paying for baseball for four years. Hersh said it would have cost $70,000 to $75,000 a season. "I had actually hoped something would occur," Hersh said. And he wouldn't rule out baseball returning someday, although he didn't want to raise any hopes.

Hobart baseball began in 1860. John L. Brown, its greatest fan, did not stay to see it die. Saturday was the birthday of his wife, Louise. In 55 years of marriage, through all the years he worked as a scout and a coach, he rarely had a chance to celebrate with Louise. On this day, he was grateful for the reason to leave.

As for Ferchen, he stayed for a long time in the dugout after everyone else left, the wind blowing around plastic cups at his feet. He stared at the field, thick grass and brown dirt, until he was asked how the school will use the diamond.

"I don't know," Ferchen said. He only knew that it was no longer the home of Hobart baseball.

John L. Brown died in May 2001, at the age of 92. "Really, he's still here," says his wife, Louise. "Not a day that goes by when I don't run into someone who played for him or someone who remembers him."

It took Brown a while to get past the loss of Hobart baseball. "He missed it a great deal," Louise says. "But the thing that was very, very pleasing to him was that he still got phone calls from his old players, asking his advice. Johnny was a coach even when he wasn't a coach."

◆ ◆ ◆

39 Night Series Steals from Young

The little boy, a first-grader, is a baseball fan. He heard all the excited talk from the grownups about this Subway Series, and he wanted to stay up Saturday to watch the whole first game. He tried. He made it as long

The *Post-Standard*, Wednesday, October 25, 2000

as he could. He fell asleep face-down, spread-eagle on the floor, as the Yankees and the Mets battled on well after midnight.

In the morning, when the boy woke up, his first words were, "Who won?"

No one needed to ask that question 30 years ago, when Wilma Fessenden was school librarian in Tully. The World Series games were played in the afternoon, on fields where long shadows cut through golden sunlight. Fessenden would turn on a television in a room attached to the library, and she'd keep all the teachers and children updated on the score — at least the ones who weren't listening already on clandestine transistor radios.

"In those days," Fessenden said of the children, "they were really into it."

The memory is much the same for Pat Dwyer and John Young, pupils in the 1950s at St. Patrick's School on Tipperary Hill. The school was run by priests and nuns. Discipline was fierce. But every year, on autumn afternoons, the teachers cut the kids a break. They'd turn on a radio in the school's main office. They'd put it next to the public address microphone, wired into every classroom.

If the kids were good, they'd get a chance to follow the World Series.

Young, a retired probation worker, can vividly recall sitting at his desk, listening as he stared at the green paint on the walls. The game crackled from the brown box around a public address speaker. Young was spellbound in the classroom in 1956, as Don Larsen, inning by inning, set down the Brooklyn Dodgers — the Yankee pitcher on his way to a historic perfect game.

Above all else, Young remembers Sister Monica Hogan, a teacher feared by even the worst bullies in the school, a teacher who would tolerate nothing frivolous in her classroom.

Except for the World Series.

"I remember that very well," said Sister Monica, 79, retired now from teaching. "I think sports is very healthy for the children, and that was a space of time devoted to the game."

As for Dwyer, he became a teacher at Westhill. He's never had the classroom option of turning on a game.

Major League Baseball officials would argue that night games are better for the fans. Working people can sit and relax in their own homes. Sure, there's give-and-take. Yes, the night weather in late October is hostile to baseball. Yes, the players in the dugouts wear mittens and heavy jackets. Yes, the pitchers rub their hands and blow steam out on the mound.

But isn't it good to give more viewers a chance to watch the games? Hasn't World Series attendance continued to go up? Don't the cameras always manage to find wobbling children with sunken eyes in the stands for midnight games? Why go back to those old afternoon games in the World Series, when factory workers had to push radios against their ears, when whole offices had to squeeze around some black-and-white TV....

And when little kids got the chance to see Bill Mazeroski beating the Yankees with a homer, or Yogi Berra running to leap into Larsen's arms, or Brooks Robinson stealing a World Series with his glove.

Bill Fox, 51, teaches fifth grade in the Fayetteville-Manlius district. He remembers jumping off the school bus and sprinting into his house, where his father and his uncles surrounded the TV. Every year, they took vacation during World Series time. Fox would rush in, breathless, after pushing through the leaves, and his dad would quickly fill him in on what was happening.

Now, Fox allows his pupils to watch Syracuse University play basketball in March daytime tournament games, the closest he can come to recreating that old magic.

"It's terrible," Fox said of baseball games in the wee hours. "It's freezing for the players, and it's freezing for the fans."

A few idealists might even argue that afternoon World Series games sent out a subtle message, teaching children that baseball was part of some deep national fabric. Each tense game was like a rocket launch, or even a moon landing. The World Series was hard-wired into children's souls.

Nowadays, if we remember, we quickly tell the kids who won.

♦ ♦ ♦

40 Take Me Out of Prime Time

I came downstairs Friday morning to get the kids ready for school, making a quick detour to grab the paper from the porch. The headline on the sports page stopped me before I even got to the kitchen. I made a noise

The *Post-Standard*, Saturday, November 3, 2001

that was strange enough to cause my daughter to stop combing her 11-year-old head.

"What happened?" she asked.

"Unbelievable," I told her. "The Yankees won again."

Two nights in a row. I had stayed up past midnight Wednesday to watch this first World Series grand finale, when Tino Martinez and Derek Jeter delivered their back-to-the-wall home runs to beat the Arizona Diamondbacks in theatrical fashion.

Thursday night, dead tired, I fell asleep in front of the screen in the eighth inning, when the Yankees trailed 2-0 and seemed completely out of gas. No way, I thought, as I nodded off. No way this can happen twice in two nights.

It happened. Considering the big picture, one miracle was unforgettable enough:

New York City, grieving for thousands lost, still under siege from anthrax-tainted mail. Yankee Stadium, with tens of thousands of fans packed into baseball's grand cathedral. Great pitching, greater drama, a great team back from the dead.

But these games were played on school nights. Ninety percent of the children on the East Coast were fast asleep for some of the most moving and meaningful World Series games in our history.

I remember how it was when we were kids, when the games were played on crisp fall afternoons, when teachers would allow us to watch a few innings at school.

That is how baseball, for many of us, came to be part of our soul.

Today, we tell our kids about the games in the morning. Night World Series games are all about sponsors, beer commercials, prime time and money. Baseball officials bleat that they have no choice but to play at night.

Still, they had a chance with this World Series to do an extraordinary thing. Baseball is proudly recalling — and trumpeting — its link to the national spirit. The Yankees have become symbolic of a resilient New York.

And our children — the ones who bring home crayon drawings of burning towers and bomb-throwing terrorists, the ones who deserve a break from all the fear — are asleep before the drama even begins.

Yet imagine. Imagine if President Bush had thrown out the first pitch at 2 p.m. Eastern time, with every schoolroom television, coast to coast, tuned into the game.

Imagine if our children could have heard those stirring renditions of "God Bless America," which have replaced "Take Me Out to the Ball Game," during the seventh-inning stretch. Imagine if we could have shared the moment with our kids when Martinez and Jeter — and then Scott Brosius Thursday night — delivered those home runs.

Those are scenes that baseball-loving children, whether they cheer for or against the Yankees, would have remembered for the rest of their lives.

Friday morning, looking at the photograph of Brosius celebrating in the night, I thought about the nature of these terrorists, their whole twisted pathology. They build their murderous rationale around the idea that Americans have become an empty people, that we place money and consumer goods above everything else, that we are almost culturally incapable of turning down profit to do the best thing for our children.

In a sense, part of this war is the quest to prove them wrong, and the lords of baseball have a chance to take an obvious first step:

If there's a seventh game, it's scheduled to start at 7:55 p.m. Sunday, bedtime on a school night for the children of New York.

◆ ◆ ◆

IV

ONE OLD BALLPARK

41 An Era Comes to an End at Big Mac

There is serious talk in Syracuse about knocking down MacArthur Stadium, the rusty old ballpark on the city's North Side.

While that discussion continues, parts of MacArthur already are gone.

Johnny Russo, Mark Conti and Cliff Douglas, a trio of longtime groundskeepers with faces as familiar as any Syracuse Chief, all died within the last six months.

And on Tuesday morning there was a gospel funeral service for Cloyd "Fats" Hollinger, 67, the men's restroom attendant for about as long as anyone with the Chiefs can remember.

"He went with the stadium," said Tex Simone, the team's general manager, who sent roses down to the South Side wake.

On summer afternoons before Syracuse home games, Hollinger would drive into MacArthur's parking lot and nap for an hour in the shade of a tree.

Then he'd join in the amiable pregame routine — wiping down the restroom, opening the cigar box that he always used for tips and settling in on a bench by the door.

He worked near a sign that read "Cloyd the Porter." A crackling radio kept him up with each pitch for his beloved New York Yankees. In return for a few dollars, he would sell you a watch with a big-league design.

"Fats" did that for decades, game after game.

"He was one of the nicest guys down there," said David Lamb, 57, a plumber who holds a season ticket for the Chiefs. "I never heard him say a bad word about anyone, but he would talk about just about anything — baseball, or what was in the news that day."

Hollinger's companion of many years was Fannie Cunningham, who sat with hands folded Tuesday in the front row at the Antioch Missionary Baptist Church, listening to Sister Bessie Clinton nailing all the high notes in some perfect Gospel hymns.

At the end of the service they opened the casket and Cunningham

---

The *Post-Standard*, Wednesday, December 18, 1991

Opposite: MacArthur Stadium, Syracuse, 1996. Only eight batters in history cleared the stadium's 434-foot center-field fence. (Dennis Nett, *Post-Standard.*)

nodded goodbye. She went home to her Furman Avenue house, to a clock bearing the message, "Happy Mother's Day, From Fats." It hangs on the wall and the hands don't turn, but she doesn't have it up there to remember the time.

"He was a calm, nice, pleasant man," she said. "Every day when you saw him, you knew he'd be the same."

Hollinger was born in Arkansas, where he grew restless as a teen-ager and took off for California. He drove a fruit truck before coming East in search of a job in construction, a line of work that brought him to Syracuse.

Years later, after retiring from the building trade, he continued with his sideline — taking care of the restrooms at the stadium and some area speedways, as he'd done every summer for at least 30 years.

"He used to keep the place clean, and you could tell the difference when he was gone," Lamb said.

"Fats" died Thursday following several debilitating strokes. That was hard on Frank Ferretti, 88, another veteran ballpark employee.

"A very sociable guy, a beautiful person," Ferretti said, recalling hours spent on the bench near the men's room. He and Hollinger talked about baseball, their health — and about the plans to put up a new ballpark.

On Tuesday, instead, they buried part of the old one.

◆ ◆ ◆

42 Bloody Day Echoes in Beanball Wars

Dan Carnevale has spent a lifetime in baseball. He is 74 now, and he still scouts for the Cleveland Indians, after years of playing and managing in the minors.

But he finds no honor or tradition in beanball-triggered wars like this month's brawl between Syracuse and Scranton. "It's the worst thing that can happen," Carnevale says. "All the years I managed, I never told a pitcher to hit anybody."

The *Post-Standard*, Saturday, May 15, 1993

He could see too clearly the blood on home plate.

"The sound, you can't describe it," Carnevale says. "It was a 'thunk,' a sound like a marshmallow, a dead sound."

It was branded into memory in MacArthur Stadium on Aug. 6, 1938, a day of humid 84-degree heat. Carnevale was a teen-age shortstop with the Buffalo Bisons, as they played the Chiefs in the second game of an International League doubleheader.

Baseball comic Al Schacht, the sport's "clown prince," did his routine between games, and 12,000 fans jammed the grandstand and overflowed the bleachers.

In the third inning, Bison outfielder Woodley Abernathy, a 32-year-old Louisiana journeyman, dug in to face Chiefs ace "Long John" Gee. Abernathy was a former International league home-run king who used a peculiar, flat-footed stance. So the 6-foot-9 Gee, known for his speed, fooled Abernathy twice with sharp curves.

That strategy worked all too well. On his third pitch, Gee let go of a steaming fastball and immediately screamed, "Look out!" The lefty-hitting Abernathy, waiting for the curve, didn't budge. The pitch struck him above the right ear, cracking open his skull almost back to his spine.

It is the sound that stays with Carnevale, the crunch of bone that was clear to every fan in Big Mac. "I remember running up to the plate and there was blood all over," Carnevale said. The ballpark dropped into silence as Abernathy was rushed to St. Joseph's Hospital.

They kept playing the game, although no one cared. Gee, visibly shaken, didn't make it through the inning. The Bisons won, 8-2, and then Gee hurried to a hospital room, where Abernathy, his head covered in bandages, told the pitcher he knew it didn't happen on purpose.

Not long after midnight, once Abernathy's family had made it to town, surgeons went in and "decompressed" the fractured skull. Abernathy lingered while the community and the ballplayers maintained their vigil.

They were delighted when Abernathy rallied, although he remained too ill to leave St. Joseph's. Gee shook off the accident and regained his place as the Chiefs' stopper. He started an Aug. 23 benefit game in Buffalo that raised $4,000 for Abernathy.

On Sept. 3, nearly a month after he went down at home plate, Abernathy left Syracuse to the applause of 300 fans at the New York Central train station. By the next year, he was again a productive minor-league hitter. Gee went on to pitch in the majors and spent a few years playing pro basketball.

Carnevale settled in Buffalo. He still scouts for the Indians, and he has outlived Gee, Abernathy and most of the principals from that day at

Big Mac. But it remains with Carnevale whenever he reads about the latest brawl, or any of baseball's head-hunting injuries.

It's the sound, Carnevale says. The worst penance is forever hearing that sound.

◆ ◆ ◆

43 Bailes Takes the Final Ride

The perfect exit.

Babe Ruth couldn't do it. Neither could Willie Mays, or Mickey Mantle. Scott Bailes, however, knew when and how to quit.

The Syracuse Chiefs left-hander hadn't planned Wednesday on ending his career with a ninth-inning flourish, but he spotted the John Deere tractor by the shed at MacArthur Stadium, and the maintenance guys were agreeable, and it seemed like the thing to do.

Fresh off what was probably his last turn on the mound, Bailes slid into the seat and revved up the engine. There were possibly 300 warm bodies in the Big Mac stands, all of them bracing for another Chiefs loss.

Bailes surprised everyone. Beneath a perfect full moon, as the Toledo Mud Hens prepared to hang on for a 5-3 win, Bailes burst through the outfield gate on his growling John Deere, cap held high in the air, for one high-speed sweep of the warning track between halves of the ninth inning.

The players loved it. By magnificent coincidence, the P.A. system roared out a song called "Final Countdown."

"I never seen anything like that before," said groundskeeper Chuck Garbut, "but that's what baseball is all about."

Or should be. Early today, Bailes, 30, plans to fly home to Springfield, Mo., where he'll finish a semester of college and become a biology teacher.

He spent seven seasons in the big leagues. He remained effective in the minors, good enough to retire 23 of the 28 left-handed batters he faced in Syracuse. Still, Wednesday became a personal deadline — if Toronto didn't call him up, he was going home to school.

The *Post-Standard*, Thursday, June 3, 1993

"I'm going because of my family," Bailes said. "People ask me if I'm bitter or angry, and I say, 'Not at all.' I never expected to be here in the first place. I signed my first contract just to say I played professional baseball. There were a lot of guys more talented than me who never made it."

He has two daughters back in Springfield, 5-year-old Allison and 3-year-old Tara. Wednesday was Allison's final day of kindergarten. She was in a little pageant, and her dad couldn't be there. He sees that absence as an omen.

He recalled how the ancient Bert Blyleven only saw his own teen-age boy play high school baseball once. That price is too high, Bailes said.

When Bailes was with the Indians, he'd often seek out homeless people while the team was on the road. He'd take them to lunch and tape their stories.

It gave him some perspective. He considered writing a book from those accounts. It convinced him, more than ever, that disintegrating families are at the core of American problems.

He was watching his own little girls grow up from far away.

"He's a great guy," his wife, Joanne, said Wednesday by phone from Missouri. "He's always giving, he always wants to give, and sometimes I want to kick him because he tries to be so good."

She wished she could have been at Big Mac for Scott's final game. She feels for her husband. Like Chiefs manager Nick Leyva, Joanne knows Scott retains big-league abilities.

"He's pitched better than he has in a long, long time," she said. "It just seems so odd that somebody's not interested."

But even as she said that, she spoke of how much her daughters miss their father, how his return will ensure the kind of summer they've never enjoyed. For his part, Bailes seems ready to accept that kind of major change.

"I get out when I can and I talk to school groups about baseball and drug awareness and other things," Bailes said. "The teachers always come up to me and say how the kids seem to listen. I don't think it's because of me. It's because I played major league baseball. But I thought maybe teaching would let me make a difference in some lives."

He pitched to two batters Wednesday. He gave up a fly ball that was misplayed and two runs scored, and then he got the Chiefs out of the inning. The bullpen gave him a standing ovation. Bailes tipped his hat toward some guy with a baby, surrounded by empty seats in the stands.

Finally he grabbed his perch on the tractor, where he signed autographs for a couple of 12-year-olds named Brian Otis and Daniel Giamartino. They knew Bailes was retiring. They called it their "last chance."

In the locker room, Bailes stopped by to shake hands with Leyva, who said he'll miss Bailes' ability, but respects the decision. Unlike three-quarters of the Chiefs, Leyva said, the pitcher has forged a separate life outside the game. "Baseball's not his only thing," Leyva said.

Still, Bailes lingered a long time before he walked out the door.

Despite the perfect nature of his departure, Scott Bailes did not stay retired. "I started to screw around with some friends in semipro," he said, and that led to an appearance at a national tournament for players 30 years or older. He was impressive enough to capture the attention of the Texas Rangers, who brought Bailes back for two years of relief. "I pitched pretty well," Bailes said, and this time his children were old enough to appreciate their dad, the Major Leaguer.

In 1998, with a torn rotator cuff that made it painful to even lift his arm, Bailes retired for good. "It was a simple decision," he says. "This time, it wasn't emotional at all. A lot of players say they want to leave on their own terms, but you never do. You play until they say they don't want you, and another team won't sign you. For closure, maybe, that's the way it's got to be, and why it's been that way for 100 years. I left the way I wanted to leave, and then — by sheer luck — I got another chance."

◆ ◆ ◆

44 "Coroner" Captures Big Mac

In a sense, Jim Dow was serving as a coroner. He brought his camera Sunday evening to MacArthur Stadium. He set it up on the concrete concourse, above the seats. Then he patiently shot a panorama of the ballpark, trying to photograph every scar and tattoo upon Big Mac.

His work will soon be among the only ways to see the field.

Dow has visited roughly 150 ballparks across the nation, nearly all of them minor-league stadiums. He has gone to places like Great Falls, Mont., and El Paso, Texas. He has photographed stadiums that rise above the

Mississippi River and old stone ballparks in the heart of warm and quiet Southern towns.

Usually he photographs diamonds with a future. But sometimes, like a coroner, he makes a record of the doomed. That prospect weighed him down Sunday at Big Mac, where the Chiefs lost to Ottawa 6-1.

"I'm 54 years old," Dow said. "When I do a job like this, I feel like a little piece of me is going, too."

Dow is from Massachusetts. The Smithsonian Institution has organized a traveling exhibit of his stadium panoramas. As a way of commemorating the last days at MacArthur, the Onondaga Historical Association will feature that display, beginning Saturday, at its downtown museum.

The photographs range from the splendor of Camden Yards in Baltimore to splintered walls at a ballpark in Bakersfield, Calif. There are also shots of Rochester's soon-to-be-demolished Silver Stadium.

Dow calls Silver one of the 10 most beautiful ballparks in the country. "It's hard to believe," he said, "they would want to take it down."

He also has deep affection for Big Mac. During a conversation with local historian Dennis Connors, Dow learned how the new north-side stadium is going up next to the old one. That kind of structural pairing rarely happens.

Dow came to Syracuse on Sunday to capture that brief interval on film, the sleek new stadium and the 62-year-old baseball relic waiting for the wrecker's ball.

"Out of all the ballparks I've seen, this is one of my absolute favorites," Dow said of Big Mac. He had been to the stadium twice before. He understands the place just by looking it over, the way a veteran detective in a bar can size up every customer.

What he loves, he said, is Big Mac's ordinary nature. It has grand scope, but it also has its quirks and homeliness, which makes it an awful lot like all of us.

"This stadium here is exactly what it is," Dow said. "That new stadium is what it wishes that it was."

He laughed, even as he said it. He knew that sounded like a deep dive into romantic stadium hogwash. His point was simple. What is being lost, Dow said, is a ballpark that serves as the honest face of a town, replaced by a ballpark that's a face of what a town wants to be.

"Please don't take offense at this, but (Big Mac) offers that whole sense of a tank town," Dow said. "I mean that in a complimentary way. Bruce Springsteen sings about tank towns.

"The easiest way to put it is that most ballparks exist in their own landscape. You look out from this ballpark at that wonderful candle factory.

You have the whole sense here of a ballpark on the very edge of town. I wish they were saving this one and tearing the other one down."

Still, he understands why Big Mac will soon be gone. He knows Syracuse had no choice, at least if it wanted to keep Triple-A baseball. The major leagues have imposed tough new regulations on minor-league stadiums. MacArthur didn't cut it. But Dow has spent years traveling the nation, walking through ballparks peculiar to the souls of their towns.

Almost always, when they fall, what replaces them is clean and nice but not unique.

"One thing I've noticed in Syracuse," Dow said. "The people who come here really watch the game." It is not always that way, he said. In many towns, going to the stadium has become an event, a thing to do. It is not about watching baseball anymore. It is about economic development and prestige and being seen in the right place. That is why Big Mac is special, why you can't build it again once it falls into the dust.

Dow was glad for the chance to see MacArthur one last time. He planned to work throughout the game, until they turned off the lights.

Jim Dow's stadium photographs are now on permanent display at the FleetCenter in Boston. Ultimately, he says, he hopes to use them in a book. He still mourns the loss of both MacArthur Stadium in Syracuse and the old Silver Stadium in Rochester, both of them abandoned to make way for new municipal ballparks. "Those were two of the most atmospheric, wonderful places to watch a game," Dow says.

◆ ◆ ◆

45 Rochester's Stadium Passing into Memory

ROCHESTER — By the third inning Wednesday, Jim Schulz was getting worried. The seat in front of him at Silver Stadium remained empty. Every time he spotted some old friend in the crowd, Schulz would lean forward and call out, "Where's Carl?"

The *Post-Standard*, Thursday, August 15, 1996

Schulz is 69, a retiree from Eastman Kodak. Since 1957, he and his wife, Jean, have held the same two seats for every home game of the Rochester Red Wings. Throughout that time, Schulz has sat behind the same guy, Carl Desens. For many years, they all knew everyone else in their section. "The R-1 Gang," they called it.

They had big picnics. A Christmas party. They rarely missed a game. Snow in April? Heat in August? The R-1 Gang was there. "I had a rough year in 1993," Schulz said. "Heart trouble, an operation to get rid of the cancer. You should have seen the cards I got from these people."

But the years have eroded the original crew. "Died off," Schulz said. "Not too many left." He looked around, picked out one or two familiar old couples. For the most part, the stands around him were filled with new faces. That is why it troubled him when Carl did not show.

They both live for baseball, and they come no matter what.

Schulz was watching his beloved Red Wings take on the Syracuse Chiefs. Historians say it is the oldest continuing rivalry in minor-league baseball. They have gone at it since 1934, and before that — under different names— the baseball rivalry between the cities goes back deep into the 1800s.

But tonight's game will be the final meeting between the teams in Silver Stadium, which opened in 1929. Like the Chiefs, the Red Wings are moving into an elaborate new ballpark, a jewel on the expressway in the heart of the city.

"I don't see the need for it," Schulz said. "This is a beautiful place. It knocked the air out of me to find out they want to knock it down."

Silver Stadium is a time capsule sliding into memory. The grass is thick and green. A city neighborhood rolls out beyond the fence. A church steeple pokes out above the first-base line. It rises from Our Lady of Perpetual Help, a church that provides a patron saint for all batters.

Schulz was in Silver on the magic night when Monte Irvin burned the Wings with home runs to left, center and right. He saw Luke Easter and Specs Toporcer and Stan Musial and Bobby Grich. He saw more than 20,000 fans pack the place for a high school football game, in the days when the bleachers hugged the outfield fence.

He was a child in the Knothole Gang during the Great Depression, an era when baseball bordered on theology. The men in his neighborhood would circle their cars around a sandlot game and pop open the kegs, watching baseball and drinking beer until darkness drowned the field. Silver Stadium, in those days, was the highest shrine.

"The kids today have television," Schulz said. "One of my sons, I was so proud of him, he couldn't get his kids to do anything else. They'd sit there and always watch the TV. He got rid of it. Took it away. His kids now, they play sports, they go and play outside. The kids, with the television, they turn into little robots."

Schulz's mother was from Syracuse. She was a vaudeville dancer. She died when he was four. His dad raised the family. Still, those Syracuse roots are appropriate in Silver Stadium. In the 1920s, the St. Louis Cardinals had a farm team called the Syracuse Stars. Branch Rickey, the legendary baseball executive, demanded a new stadium. Syracuse wouldn't build it. Rochester did.

The team, the young nucleus for what became the great St. Louis "Gashouse Gang," moved to Rochester and turned into an International League dynasty. Syracuse, stung, regained a franchise in 1934. The city scrambled to build a ballpark in less than three months. The result, MacArthur Stadium, is also in its final summer.

Schulz has been to Big Mac a few times. He used to travel to other stadiums with his wife, Jean. "The greatest fan of them all," he said. "When she first came here with me, she knew nothing about baseball. Before long, at every game, she was always keeping score. At Christmas, a scorebook was always the first thing on her list."

Jean died of cancer 11 years ago. Schulz has a son, Eric, who lives in Cicero. Now, at Christmas, Eric buys his dad the same present. He sends in the check that reserves his mom's old seat at the stadium. It is empty, next to Schulz, for every Red Wings game. Jean retains her place.

"If baseball is in town, this is where I am," Schulz said. He comes out because he loves to talk with Carl, and Schulz yells at the Red Wings whenever they foul up. "Maybe if you turn and look for the ball, you'd catch it!" he shouted Wednesday when Wings catcher B.J. Waszgis couldn't grab a pop-up. The voice is clear and loud. You know Schulz is there.

The stadium, to Schulz, is more like his back yard, a place where he can squint and make out figures from the past. Used to be members of the R-1 Gang were masters of baseball trivia. It was a way to pass the gentle time in the middle innings. Then some young guy in the section brought a small baseball computer. "Can you imagine?" Schulz asked. "What fun is there in that?"

He doesn't like the idea of the new ballpark, although he has already reserved another season ticket. The sight lines are similar, not too far from home plate. "I didn't know if I'd be here this year, but I'm here," Schulz said. "I don't know if I'll be there next year, but I have my seat.

"I'm dying," Schulz said. He has cancer of the liver. He is in chemotherapy. He won't give in to the disease or to the treatment. Baseball is his passion, and that becomes his statement. He gets out to every home game, for at least three or four innings. How could he stay away?

He has been around Silver Stadium since 1938. He remembers the great days, when Buffalo, Rochester and Syracuse had the Thruway rivalry, when fans sometimes watched from the roofs of nearby houses. He remembers when hot dogs were a nickel, when a beer cost a dime. He remembers when there was no Sega, no Internet. Just baseball, only baseball.

"This is my favorite place," Schulz said. He looked around and wondered once again why Carl wasn't there.

Carl Desens, now 81, is still going to Red Wings games at Frontier Field, the new downtown stadium in Rochester. In the end, Desens came to love just about everything about the new ballpark—except for the absence of Jim Schulz, who died of cancer.

◆ ◆ ◆

46 Youngsters Have a Ball by Homer Heaven

Soaking wet sneakers. Water dripping from the brims of their caps. The two 13-year-olds waited outside MacArthur Stadium in the rain Tuesday, keeping their first drainage-ditch vigil of the season.

D.J. Goodson, at least, was rewarded. He and Nick Salerno shot out of school, raced home with their books, then hustled to Big Mac in time for the opener. They settled in near the ditch beyond the left-field fence. It was cold, but the wind was blowing their way, and no rivals showed up to challenge their turf.

Right away, they got lucky. Howard Battle of the Chiefs laid into a fourth-inning pitch, smashing it over the left-field wall. It sailed above a chain-link fence and then past the ditch, landing in the middle of a blacktop access road.

The *Post-Standard*, Wednesday, April 13, 1994

Big Mac was built 60 years ago, and kids ever since then have waited out beyond the fence. But Goodson had the advantage of wearing a Walkman. He heard the call as Battle's shot headed out of the park. Then it flew into vision, high over the wall.

Goodson jumped the drainage ditch and grabbed it on the roll, scuffed with tar from hitting the blacktop. The stamped signature of International League president Randy Mobley remained clear on the leather.

For a long time, in satisfaction, Goodson pounded the ball into his glove.

"It was great, but it's not the best," he said. "The best is at night, when you see that white ball come falling out of the black sky."

Only 13 years old, and the kid is a poet. He and Salerno are baseball buddies. They are eighth-graders, and they met at Grant Middle School about a year ago. The game drew them together. The talk in junior high these days isn't really about baseball. Their classmates, for the most part, are NBA fans.

"This is the national pastime," Salerno said, as if that said it all.

Goodson likes the White Sox, Salerno the Mets. They announce it with their caps. They know how to give that perfect bend to the brims, twisting them down for that hip, rounded look.

They are North Siders. When they first began traveling together to the ballpark, they'd walk a couple of blocks and pay their way in. Their big goal was coming up with an errant foul ball. Once, Goodson chased a ball to the railing and it skimmed off his mitt. It haunts him as much as any on-the-field error.

"A lot of good times and bad times inside that place," he grumbled.

Yet as they sat brooding and frustrated in the ballpark one day, it occurred to the boys that the area behind the fence is as high-percentage as it gets.

That is where you'll find them now, on any Chiefs homestand. The atmosphere is not any trip to the beach. It is a place of standing water and rusty metal. They cannot see the game. Last year, they came to regard the towering Marlboro Man as a kind of companion. They felt for him when Domingo Martinez slammed a homer that nailed the Marlboro Man between the legs. The thought of it makes them grunt in sympathetic pain.

But the Marlboro Man has been removed this year, because of the message his presence conveys.

The shredded stump of his legs is not far from the boys. "I still see him all the time," Goodson said defiantly, as if he was speaking of some friend kicked out of school.

The vigil, while lonely, retains exquisite thrills. They cannot see the game but they are right on top of it, separated from the playing field only by a metal fence. Occasionally, as they stood and waited Tuesday, a fair ball crashed into the wall with noisy violence.

"Oh, yeah," they'd both say, and then they'd start laughing.

Salerno got his home-run ball last year. He and Goodson were there with a couple of friends when a long blast soared into the cattails. Salerno and one of his buddies gave chase. They ran after the ball, tripping each other, wrestling until they tumbled into the ditch. Salerno won. He went in the murky water and came up with the ball.

"I still have it," he said. Sometimes he and Goodson play catch with that trophy, but for the most part he leaves it sitting in his room.

The two boys know Big Mac will be gone in two seasons. They've looked at drawings of the ballpark that will go up in its place. It will be bigger, fancier, which is how it has to be. But they don't see much room for kids by the fence.

The two boys were correct. A formidable chain-link fence separates young fans from the perimeter of the new ballpark in Syracuse. The days of standing beyond the fence and waiting for home run balls are over.

◆ ◆ ◆

47 Staring at the Barrel of a Smoking Gun

My mother's hands always shook. She was a strong person but exceptionally nervous, and cigarettes helped her sustain a balance. She began to smoke heavily when she was a girl, and it was impossible to envision her quitting.

It would have been almost like amputating a limb. Even after the cancer went from her lungs and took over her liver, she would hide in a hospital bathroom while my father slipped her a drag, and then she would emerge to face what was coming.

The *Post-Standard*, Friday, August 13, 1993

She smoked, and my dad smoked. It was their only bad habit, and it killed them both. His heart gave out. She descended into one final month that I block from my memory. Sometimes, long before they died, my parents would see a catchy ad, and they'd talk it over, and if it was good enough it would make them try a new brand.

It was all legal, perfectly legal, unlike crack or reefer or horse or all those drugs we warn our children about. But I can say this, and I imagine I speak for anyone who has watched a loved one disintegrate:

I wish my mother had died from a heroin overdose, or that crack had caused her heart to explode, or that someone had simply blown her away. Because I cannot imagine a worse way of dying than the last 30 days of that strong, decent woman.

Granted, that makes me emotionally unreliable when it comes to this whole fuss over whether the Marlboro Man belongs in municipal arenas, including our MacArthur Stadium. It makes me wonder, for instance, about the people who warned how "drug dealers" might frequent the new Syracuse ballpark, while the old one is host to that seductive cowboy. Folks, believe me. He's in the same business.

Yet smoking presents an evangelistic quandary. Most of the people I love have been smokers. I see them in memory with cigarettes in their mouths. I told all my secrets to ribbons of smoke. I've fought my own battles with all kinds of excess, and I try not to tinker with the habits of others.

Still, my respect for them does not extend to the Marlboro Man. He and his brethren help finance pro sports in the United States. He has control over numerous smaller corporations. He holds power by sustaining tens of thousands of jobs, and he would be impossible to render illegal — indeed, people would do the same crimes in his name that they now tend to do for their smack or their crack.

Many of his disciples who try to quit find that they can't.

Despite all that, his image stares out toward only one end, which is as bad as anything we find on the street. He stands for tubes and mucus and the loss of control. He represents the defeated apathy of a government that wages war against some kinds of addiction while subsidizing the well-being of others.

The numbers are so big they are hard to take in. The Centers for Disease Control and Prevention estimates 434,000 Americans die each year from using tobacco. That is more than 10 times the combined total of deaths caused by crack, heroin, morphine and AIDS.

We know those figures are true, because we all know the victims. They are our grandparents or our parents or the guy down the street. They make the sound so many of us remember from childhood, the gravel cough of a pilgrim on the long road to dying.

The Marlboro Man is a formidable salesman, pitching a fate that is absolutely legal. He's become an old chum by the wall at Big Mac, and I like what he does for my sense of nostalgia:

Whenever I see him, I remember my mother.

The Marlboro Man was removed from MacArthur Stadium in 1994.

◆ ◆ ◆

48 "Mr. Everything" Has Nothing Nice to Say About Big Mac

If anyone has a right to be sentimental about MacArthur Stadium, it's Frankie Ferretti.

Ferretti is 88. He's worked at the ballpark for 32 years as a self-described "Mr. Everything." He was driving a truck at the nearby public market in 1934 when the stadium was built in 48 days for $300,000.

Yet as he crouched last week on a dugout step, watching a mechanical pump suck freezing water six feet deep from an abandoned tunnel beneath the grandstand, Ferretti was hardly nostalgic.

The flooding occurs every April. One year, Ferretti found a carp swimming in the water.

As far as he's concerned, they can finish off "Big Mac" tomorrow.

"I don't mind a new stadium," said Ferretti. And he smiled when he said it.

The Syracuse Chiefs may have only one or two more seasons at MacArthur. The Metropolitan Development Association is seeking a consultant for a $50,000 study on a ballpark that would accommodate baseball and football.

The study will be finished in six months. If it identifies a need—

and you can bet it will — the Chiefs and the MDA will look for the dough to build a $15 million to $20 million stadium near MacArthur's present site. It would seat about 12,000, and would use — ugh — artificial turf.

Yes, as untraditional as it might seem (what is baseball without the aroma of clipped grass?), a carpet makes sense. Chiefs general manager Tex Simone emphasizes that a major function of the new park will be hosting high school football games, even in the snow.

"All you have to do is sweep it off," said Simone. He added — and he was only half-kidding — that they should name the new ballpark after Ferretti.

After all, Simone said, Ferretti is the guy who tapes "Big Mac" together.

Indeed, a walk through the stadium in early April quickly destroys any architectural sentiment. "Big Mac" is not Fenway Park, or even Silver Stadium, the quaint little Rochester ballpark that may also face the wrecking ball.

MacArthur went up fast and cheap in 1934. In February of that year, Jersey City owner Jack Corbett offered to move his International League team to Syracuse. He needed a stadium. The North Side landmark was built in two months.

Fifty-eight years later, Ferretti said, the only physical remnants of the original stadium are the structural steel and the actual dugouts. The old clubhouse is long gone. The original offices and the ornate facade were destroyed in a 1969 fire.

The drains are shot. They plug up each year, flooding the dugouts. The "new" clubhouse doesn't meet specifications set by the big leagues.

Simone walks the ballpark and points to all the little repairs done by Ferretti over the years, all the places where "Frankie" used brackets and nails to fix rotten metal.

Still, the park has undeniable history. It is where some witnesses claim Jackie Robinson endured the legendary 1946 incident in which one of the Chiefs, attempting to rattle the first black player in the modern minor leagues, threw a black cat onto the field.

It is where longtime Chief Hank Sauer spent the magic summer of 1947, blasting his way toward 50 home runs.

Fans can sit there in the summer, breathing in the mingled musk of

Opposite: The late Frank Ferretti, "Mr. Everything," groundskeeper and maintenance man at the old MacArthur Stadium. (Al Campanie, *Post-Standard.*)

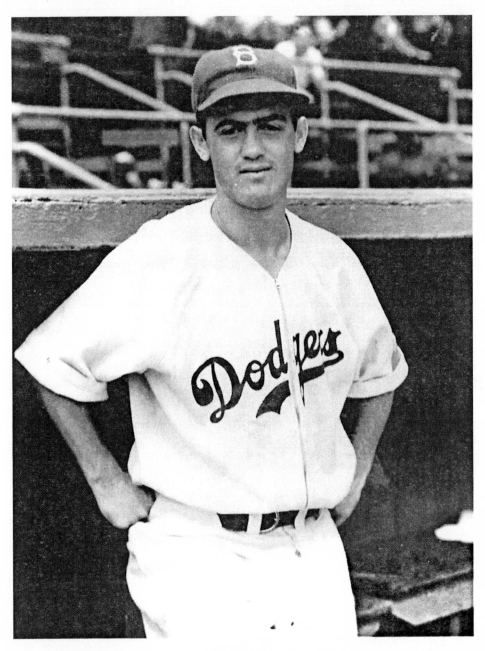

Goody Rosen, long-time center-fielder with the Syracuse Chiefs, during his time with the Brooklyn Dodgers. (National Baseball Hall of Fame Library, Cooperstown, N.Y.)

cigar smoke and coffee, watching the game while a warm breeze ripples through the nearby neighborhoods. At those moments, it is easy to forget Ferretti at the mud-stained dugout, knee-deep in ice water.

It is easy to forget that the place is a dump.

Ferretti died in February, 1995. He never set foot inside the new stadium, which was built near the same North Side site as "Big Mac," following a fierce community debate about the possibility of putting up the new ballpark in downtown Syracuse.

◆ ◆ ◆

49 Feisty Center Fielder Sparked Great Team

They will tear down MacArthur Stadium within a year or two, and with it will go that vast center field, one of the biggest yards to cover in baseball.

Few have played it as well as a little man named Goody Rosen.

He died Wednesday, in Toronto. He was 82 years old, and he had not seen Garton DelSavio since they shook hands and said goodbye 51 years ago. That was on a cool Ohio night after their Chiefs were defeated in the Little World Series and no one sure what World War II would soon do to their lives.

But they were starters on one of the finest Syracuse teams in history. DelSavio, 80, living in retirement near the Hudson River, mourned when he learned Rosen was gone.

"We had a good club in Syracuse, a club that could have beat some big-league clubs," DelSavio said. "Goody was a winner. He was a guy you wanted on your team."

Rosen had his share of fistfights. He would challenge any Chief who dogged it to first. Former Chiefs star Hank Sauer remembers Rosen brawling from the clubhouse to the field with a teammate who questioned his dedication to winning. "He gave 100 percent, and then a little extra," said Sauer.

Sauer, DelSavio, Dutch Mele, Frankie Kelleher. They made up a solid veteran core. Rosen and his wife, Molly, were close with those Chiefs, married guys who didn't always go out on the town. Before every game, all the couples would head for Snook's Pond, where they'd eat sandwiches and let the kids run until it was time to play.

The Chiefs came on strong toward the end of the year. In the International League playoffs they leveled Newark and Toronto to win the league. Syracuse was known for its ferocious bench jockeys, and in the playoffs Newark's Joe Page lost his edge when he was driven into a rage.

That didn't work in the Little World Series against Columbus, or Preacher Roe.

Rosen was a native Canadian. He stood maybe 5-foot-8. His sister, Fay, believes he was the first Jewish ballplayer to ever make the Brooklyn Dodgers. In 1945, he batted .325 for the Dodgers, but he held out the next year. His reward was a subway trade to the Giants, for whom he ran into a wall trying to make a catch in Forbes Field.

It jammed his shoulder. By 1947, he was back in Toronto, playing golf. When he was named to the Canadian Baseball Hall of Fame, Duke Snider — his Ebbets Field successor — introduced him.

Rosen made what might have been the greatest catch of his life for Syracuse in the '43 playoffs against Newark, a diving catch so stunning that his own teammates forgot to get ready for the throw. Before the Little World Series, DelSavio recalled, Rosen talked as if he already had the winning money spent. He taunted any player who expressed any doubts.

After the final loss to Columbus, the Chiefs' locker room took on a funereal silence. Many of the players would soon leave for the war. DelSavio and Sauer had enlisted together, causing something of a circus in Syracuse. The papers ran their pictures as they signed up for the Coast Guard. It was all very exciting, until the time came.

Rosen was older, already 29. He was called up to the Dodgers the following year, where he soon had a love-hate relationship with Leo Durocher. He retired to Canada, and he lived long enough to see the Blue Jays win the world championship. But Molly died in May. They had been married 59 years. Rosen's sister said Goody lost his will to keep going.

It was the only thing in his life big enough to make him quit.

◆ ◆ ◆

50 Phantom at Plate Awaits Call Up

MacArthur Stadium at midnight only seems an empty place. Even in the fall, when the leaves go swirling around the road circling the ballpark, the digital clock stays on all night in right-centerfield, throwing shards of yellow light out across the bleachers.

I went there, just before midnight, because I had heard the story. At first, sitting in those empty stands, looking out at the silent contours of the diamond, I thought the tale was a lie, because I saw nothing at all.

But pretty soon, just like they said, I could see him taking cuts.

Maybe he goes 5-8 or 5-9, 180-pounds, short and squat with a ton of line-drive power. He stood up to the plate in a gray uniform, socks pulled high, bat cocked, trembling all over, and then he would swing and get into the ball hard. When the ball hit the wall, it sounded like a cannon shot. He'd stand and watch for a while, and if there was an echo in the wind it would soon die into nothing, and then once again he'd dig in at the plate.

This went on for a while, until I wondered if perhaps I could sneak out without him seeing, which is exactly when he turned and saw me. That was the first time I was really afraid, the kind of fear that comes from your spine and flows down your back, but I stayed where I was as he walked over to the seats.

"You're from the paper, right?" he asked, nodding at the notebook, standing so close to the railing I could almost see his eyes. "You hear anything about when they're gonna call me up?"

"They're not calling anyone up," I replied, but my throat felt so tight I wasn't sure I made a sound. "They're all on strike."

He turned, spat toward third base, waved his arm out toward the field. "They gotta do it pretty soon," he said, voice harsh. "I never hit like this in my life. Anything they throw—anything this guy throws—I can put where I want it, all over the field. I got my eye, my eye, like I never had it before. They can't just leave me sitting here forever."

There was a long silence. "Yeah," he said, "they gotta call me up pretty soon."

So far I had played it all pretty well, but that was when I made my

The *Post-Standard*, Monday, October 31, 1994

mistake. It was enough just to see him, to know he was there, and that would have been the story you are reading. But I am a sportswriter, and a question came to my mind, and it was almost like I didn't have a choice.

"Who sent you down?"

He whirled, turned with such fury that for a second in the half-light I saw the hollows of his eyes. "You know that!" he screamed, clenching his fists. "You know who's got my rights, and you know damn well I oughta be up there! But no! What about those personal problems, they say! Playing the game ain't everything, they say! Syracuse, they say! You're going to Syracuse! And all of us here, we're in the same boat!"

Grabbing the bat in one hand, he made a vicious, sweeping gesture out toward the field, and suddenly I saw that we weren't alone, that the old park was filled with shortstops making great plays in the hole, long-armed pitchers heaving heat from the mound, outfielders stealing long shots deep in center. It was crazy, a baseball anthill, and then he called to them, waved one arm, and they all sprinted over to crowd around, asking the same question:

"Whaddya hear? Are they going to call me up?"

They surrounded me and I buried my face in my hands, until abruptly I could again hear the faint, welcome sound of steam leaking from some north side factory. When I looked up all of them were gone but him, the bat over his shoulder, his back to me from the on-deck circle.

"I never hit the ball like this in my life," he said again. "They need me. One of these days, pretty soon, they gotta call me up."

He stepped back in the box and started taking his cuts, angry swing after angry swing, the ball disappearing in the shadows at Big Mac. When I got up to leave he did not turn to watch, and by the time I reached the exit I could not see him at all.

◆ ◆ ◆

51 From Ashes to Ashes

Stacy MacDonald will be glad when they build the new ballpark in Syracuse. She will be glad for the Syracuse Chiefs, who will gain a new

The *Post-Standard*, Saturday, July 30, 1994

future. And she will be happy for herself, because old ballparks trap the past.

It has been only a few weeks since Stacy said goodbye. She took her husband's ashes and went alone to a beach near Kitty Hawk, N.C. She scattered them there, in the surf and the sand.

They were mixed with dust from the MacArthur Stadium infield.

"My husband was a huge Syracuse baseball fan," Stacy said. "We tried to make it to every home game, and we had been doing that for 17 years."

Thursday would have been John MacDonald's 48th birthday. He died last August of a massive heart attack, while they were preparing him for emergency surgery. The whole thing was a preposterous shock.

He was a professor of sociology at Onondaga Community College, near Syracuse. Stacy met him when she was a student. They stayed in touch after she graduated, and eventually they started dating. They were married in October 1978, the same month the Yankees won a World Series. It didn't take her long to join in John's mania for baseball.

The MacDonalds were the kind of fans whose loyalty kept the Chiefs in this town. John was happy that the team's survival would be ensured by a new stadium, but he liked the rusty comfort of Big Mac, the way it took on the same feel as a worn but well-loved chair.

He grew up in Westchester County. The Yankees were his great sports love. When he moved here the Chiefs were still a Yankee farm club, and he gave the franchise whole-hearted devotion. He was disappointed when the Chiefs switched to the Blue Jays, but it did not stop John from going out to Big Mac.

"It was what he cared about," Stacy said. He understood baseball. It drove him nuts when once-a-year fans would sit behind him, loudly trying to diagnose the whole team. "I remember the first time he ever saw Fred McGriff," Stacy said. "He turned and said, 'That man's going to make it big.'"

John also enjoyed Big Mac as a sociologist. He liked leaning back and watching the rhythm of the crowd — the parents and children, the old-timers and young couples.

Stacy remembers the night when Mark Fidrych pitched in Syracuse, and hundreds of fans pursued "The Bird's" autograph. Her husband somehow managed to wriggle down by the fence, and he was one of the few who prevailed on Fidrych to sign. To John, that was a unique lifetime thrill.

His absence, Stacy said, remains hard to believe. They had talked a little about dealing with death. Each July, they vacationed at the beach in North Carolina that her husband always loved. He told her to spread his ashes near the water. According to those wishes she had him cremated, but for months she put off that one last trip.

She told herself she was waiting for the weeks in July when they usually traveled south. Deep down, she knows it was all a delay. "I couldn't bear to part with what was left of him," Stacy said.

It was a friend, Meg Ksander, who suggested infield soil. Ksander had worked with John in social sciences at OCC, and she knew how much the Chiefs meant to him. She worried Stacy would see it as frivolity. Instead, to Stacy, it made profound sense.

Now, the ashes are scattered, although some farewells take much longer to end. Stacy still follows the Chiefs, but she will be glad when they get a new ballpark. The old one, to her, has known much better days.

◆ ◆ ◆

52 Simone Sees His Dream

Tex Simone doesn't drink. But he will find a liquor store this morning and stop to make a purchase, because he can't think of anything else to do the job.

Simone was at MacArthur Stadium Sunday evening, sitting in Seat 22 in Box 31. That's pretty much where he has sat every night since he started running the Syracuse Chiefs 25 years ago. You hear the sizzle from the fastball in Box 31, the thwack of the ball as it hits the catcher's mitt.

Tex has sat next to Bobby Thomson and Carl Yastrzemski and any number of baseball heroes. He has sat next to scouts with their radar guns and hotshot executives from both the Yankees and Blue Jays.

But on Sunday, as the booms of two cranes towered over the place, Simone wished he was sitting next to Frankie Ferretti.

Frankie was a maintenance guy who spent three decades gluing, nailing and taping the ballpark together, until he died last winter at the age of 91. The two of them would sit in the stands at lunchtime, alone in Big Mac, where Frankie would hand Tex a salami sandwich and then explain the latest leak.

Now the big cranes are out in the lot, and today they'll dig some holes to start building a new ballpark for the Chiefs.

The *Post-Standard*, Monday, July 10, 1995

"Some of the young guys used to wonder why Frankie was around," Simone said. "They know why now, every time somebody else has to fix a seat."

That is what Big Mac represents to Tex Simone. Broken seats and a drainage system so bad that water from the infield goes right into the dugouts, which means the game's brightest prospects better have some extra socks. Simone has seen breezy summer nights with 10,000 people in the place when abruptly all the toilets decided to back up. When you talk about nostalgia, Tex Simone sees that.

He is 67 years old. He started as a trainer, and step-by-step he moved up to run the Chiefs. He is gentle but persistent, as steady and unstoppable as Onondaga Creek. During the five-year stadium process, not everyone agreed with him. Many of us thought the new stadium would be better off downtown, and others argued any new stadium at all would waste the public's money.

Simone would rub his tired face and keep on plugging. He saw the ballpark as a North Side showcase, both for the Chiefs and for the region's high school teams. The whole thing took longer than he wanted. Many people he loved — including his brother Nicholas, who was buried last week — did not live to see the piles go into the ground. Today, Simone will witness what few of us achieve. He will know he's lived to see his greatest dream become the truth.

"There'll be baseball here now for another 60 years," he said.

He was in Seat 22, where you can see the low curve snap in at the knees. Nearby sat his son John, the assistant general manager, who will be the guy to lead the Chiefs into the new millenium. On Wednesday, Tex will go to an International League meeting in Scranton, and he will tell the rest of the league how Syracuse will be around for a long time.

Before that, however, he has something left to do.

On his way to work today, he will stop at a liquor store and buy a bottle of champagne. He will go to the stadium he has babied for a quarter-century, and he will watch them drive a pile deep into the ground. Then Simone will think of plugged toilets and flooded dugouts and all those broken seats, and he will smash the bottle against new steel into a million little bits.

In 1997, Tex Simone was honored with the dedication of a bust in his likeness. It was unveiled on the concourse of P & C Stadium, the new Syracuse ballpark.

◆ ◆ ◆

53 Creaky Old Ball Park Was Worthy of Our Affection

We have all known the feeling. The boxes are gone and the floors are bare. Your bags are packed and the moment comes when you cannot invent a reason to go back inside. You stand on the porch waiting for the door to slam behind you.

Maybe you are leaving the house where you grew up. Maybe you are walking away from the house where you raised your kids from babies. You know you are getting out for a good reason. You are going to a finer place, or you need more room, or you've transferred to a new job in a new town. Whatever the reason, it is a move you can't avoid.

But you stand on the porch, and you remember everything. The drowsy infant in your arms in the middle of the night. The place in the basement where you wrote your name in wet concrete. The corner of the room where you always put the Christmas tree.

You stand there, and you see all that, your packed bag in your hand.

Today, we all stand on the same porch at MacArthur Stadium.

The Syracuse Chiefs are moving out. They have no choice. Stay put and the International League leaves town. Stay put and the team is denying the future. The new stadium will be gorgeous, a great place to watch a game. And Big Mac, for all its history, is falling to pieces. The field won't drain. The sewer lines back up.

None of which means you cannot love what you are leaving.

Even now, in these final days at MacArthur, you half expect to bump into Frankie Ferretti underneath the grandstand. Gnomish figure, baggy work pants, constant stogy in his mouth. He was a maintenance guy. Some people called him the soul of MacArthur. At night he walked from gate to gate, keys jangling in the dark. He worked until he was 90 years old.

Frankie is gone now, dead last year, gone like "Fats" Hollinger the restroom attendant and Johnny Russo the groundskeeper and all the Big Mac faces that seemed so permanent. You see them all as you stand there on the porch, bag in hand.

For years you'd shake your head when you came to Big Mac. Plugged toilets, broken seats, a lumpy and wet field. But today, as you prepare to leave, the past takes you by the sleeve. Hank Sauer hitting another one out

The *Post-Standard*, Monday, September 2, 1996

of the big park. Babe Dahlgren cracking a single to drive in some runs for the Chiefs, three years before Dahlgren took over for Lou Gehrig when the "Iron Horse" sat down.

You remember the humming fastball of Johnny Vander Meer, who went upstairs to pitch two straight no-hitters for the Reds. The long blasts of Willie Horton, the famed Detroit Tiger. The acid wisecracks of pitcher Jim Bouton, who descended to the Chiefs after some fine years with the Yankees. He began his writing career in Syracuse, which resulted in a book that shook the baseball world.

All these ghosts, famous ghosts, in this homely house. Stan Musial. Roy Campanella. Reggie Jackson. Jackie Robinson. Mickey Mantle. Willie Mays. Those ballplayers, along with thousands of anonymous and weary minor leaguers, passed through town, climbed on the bus and turned their backs on Big Mac.

Not you. You are a waitress or an insurance guy or a General Electric retiree. You always came back. Your hands wore the paint off the railings. Your feet ground the steps into crumbling concrete.

You were the one begging your dad and mom for one more cotton candy, the one chasing your toddlers along the cement concourse, the one now begging your own grandchild to please sit still for one more inning.

As a teen-ager, you'd come here as a way to find some freedom, a safe place where you could go and hang out with your friends. Maybe you even came here on one of your first dates. Years later it became a place to flee the grind of daily life, a place that always seemed to look and feel the same way, a place where time moved at the same molasses pace.

That is the secret of why you pause on the porch, pause for this heap of rust and chipped blue paint. The ballpark does not belong to the players or the county or the city or the state. It belongs to you, the one who each year skipped school or work to come on opening day, the one who often made that abrupt decision, "Let's go see the Chiefs tonight."

It comes back in a cascade, these family memories. How the old stadium went up in three months in a swamp on the edge of town. How they renamed it for a general from a World War that took the lives of so many soldiers, who today — as old men — might have joined us at MacArthur.

Turn your head and you see the facade of the new ballpark. It is impressive, beautiful, all pillars and brick. It will have all the newest perks and fast-food sweets, and everyone says the view will be terrific. Before long, it will be hard to even conjure up Big Mac, that plumbing smell and rotten metal and restroom catacombs.

So conjure it up right now, while you have it spread before you. Remember every detail, every inning, every name. More than anything remember the first time you came here, a little kid with big eyes drinking in that wide green yard. You are standing on the porch, and this is your last chance. Batter up, nine more innings, and the door slams shut.

A few months later, MacArthur Stadium was razed. The site of the old ballpark is now covered by a blacktop parking lot.

V

THE YEAR WITH
NO OCTOBER

54 They're Not Having a Ball in the Hall

October in Cooperstown. The hills around the village have again turned scarlet. Dry leaves scrape across the sidewalks leading up to baseball's shrine. For 55 years, since the Hall of Fame opened, those autumn changes always signaled another sure thing.

Baseball would play its World Series, and then it would send some artifacts for display in Cooperstown.

The third floor of baseball's museum holds the most famous of postseason relics. The resin bag used by Don Larsen during his perfect game. The mitt opened wide by Willie Mays 40 years ago this month, when he made "The Catch." Bats used by Babe Ruth, Bobby Thomson and Bill Mazeroski to smash home runs that are still celebrated.

This year presents an obvious problem. No divisional playoffs, which would have started last week. No World Series. Museum managers are debating how to handle the void. Do they put up a display? Or do they simply note it and move on, as was done with the lost October of 1904, when the New York Giants refused to play in the Series?

"Anything that refers to the Series will include a line about the Series being canceled, due to a strike," said Ted Spencer, the museum curator, who adds with much cheer that he was named for Ted Williams. "But we're dickering with how to deal with the season as a whole."

The easy way out would be bypassing the strike year, and going on with business as usual. "Just paint it black," grumbled John Krukowski, a fan visiting from Florida.

But there is also a need to reflect what might have been. The Cleveland Indians most likely would have played in the postseason, for the first time in 40 years. Tony Gwynn was building toward a run at .400. Three ballplayers, particularly Matt Williams, were chasing the monumental record of 61 homers in a season.

"Because of the strike," Spencer said, "it guarantees that Roger Maris' (single-season) record will stand for at least as many years as Babe Ruth's did."

So Spencer is doing some serious thought about a "What if?" exhibit, about trying to get Gwynn's bat and Frank Thomas' jersey and a few other mementos, and then working out some figures on how they could have finished.

The *Post-Standard*, Thursday, October 13, 1994

None of that resolves the problem of the World Series room, which contains a time line describing each of baseball's October showdowns.

"The series was resumed in 1905 and has become THE American sports classic," huffs a passage on the wall. "It gets bigger — and some say even better — every year."

The point is supported with a powerful buffet: The mitt worn by Al Gionfriddo when he stole a Joe DiMaggio home run. A ball used in the very first Series, in 1903, between Pittsburgh and Boston. Pepper Martin's cap from the '31 World Series, when he dominated Connie Mack's Philadelphia Athletics. The ball Willie McCovey lined at Bobby Richardson to end the 1962 World Series.

The hall has some breathing room to figure out what to do, since the World Series room will be gutted — and improved — within the next few months. Spencer plans to install new electronic terminals, with more hands-on access to historic information.

Still, what fans want to see are the grass-stained artifacts. As Spencer looks at Mays' mitt, or Ruth's bat, or Larsen's cap, he often ponders what epic moment has been sacrificed this year. "You have to wonder," said baseball's curator. "How can you not wonder?"

In the end, Spencer says, the Hall of Fame — limited at the time by space and funds — elected to simply skip past the strike year, moving from the 1993 World Series directly to 1995. But Spencer says the World Series exhibit will soon be updated and expanded, and that some interpretative reference will be made to that sad year with no baseball in October.

"Good or bad," Spencer says, "you can't just ignore it."

55 Strike Puts Hearts on Hold

The three kids came strutting Thursday into the parking lot of the Toomey-Abbott Towers in Syracuse. Some of the elderly residents took wary notice, especially when the boys began kicking and pulling at a stop sign near the door.

The *Post-Standard*, Friday, August 12, 1994

Willie Gerideau put an end to that business. He had trouble enough on his mind. In a few hours, the baseball strike would begin.

"Excuse me," he called from his lawn chair, by the pavement. "I don't see that sign doing nothing to you."

One of the kids jerked up his head, spat out defiant words. "Excuse me," Gerideau said again. "How about you walk over here, so I can kick you in the butt?"

The boys looked him up and down, taking his measure, then decided to walk away. Good thing. Gerideau, 77, is a baseball fan. Every night, he watches his beloved New York Mets. He was getting ready to write a letter to Bobby Bonilla, telling him to move up closer to the plate.

That letter may need to wait until next spring.

Marjorie Lewis, 69, is already feeling the loss. She uses a wheelchair, the result of osteoporosis of the spine. A few times a week, she works the desk in the lobby of that Almond Street tower. Then she goes upstairs to catch the Yankees on TV. It is a ritual, like a warm cup of milk.

"I hate it during the winter," she said. She has a little gift shop. When there's no baseball, she crochets and makes dolls. That's all right, but she'd rather have the Yanks.

She gets by without many frills. She slid a calculator out of her purse, punched a few buttons. Her pension, all totaled, is less than $5,000 a year. She likes the Syracuse Chiefs, and she tries each year to see a few of their games. She can't do it unless the tenants get a chartered bus. That hasn't happened this year, so she finds her baseball in her living room.

"I love all the Yankees," she said. "I love the Old Timers games. I wanted to see that deal for Phil Rizzuto a couple of nights ago (he was honored at Yankee Stadium for his Hall of Fame induction.) I didn't make it upstairs in time, and they didn't do a replay."

Lewis' parents were farmers, who didn't care about sports. She fell in love with the game by herself. "It's the action," she said. "It's so exciting. Now the Yankees are going great, and it's just a shame this darn strike is going on."

Gerideau will wait it out by taking long walks. He grew up in New York City. He traveled to Ebbets Field all the time. He saw the 1941 World Series game when Brooklyn catcher Mickey Owen let a third strike slip by, breathing new life into Joe DiMaggio's Yanks.

A career as a welder eventually took him to Syracuse. Gerideau lost something in his gut when the Dodgers left Brooklyn, and he was glad for the day when the Mets filled the void.

Marge Lewis has never attended a big-league game. Gerideau has not been to one since 1950. The strike still carries a big sense of loss.

"The way I see it, the owners gave something to the players, and now they're trying to take it back," Gerideau said. "God bless 'em all." He said he is not angry. He will kill time taking long walks around town. When they bring back his baseball, he will be there to watch.

The options are more limited for George Willis, a 75-year-old patient at the nearby Veterans Administration Medical Center. He has been there five months. Last October, his wife of 50 years, Dorothy, died of a heart attack. "God, that hurt," Willis said. "It set me back."

Within two months of her death, he had two massive strokes.

It was therapy for him when baseball returned. He has cable in his room, and he watches at least one game every day. The Braves and the Yankees are frequent visitors. But he is always trying to search out his Phillies.

Willis is from Philadelphia. As a child, he often approached Connie Mack, the legendary manager of the old Athletics. "I'm a pushy guy," Willis said. "Connie (Mack) never drove. He always rode the elevated (train) to the park. I'd go up and start talking to him."

After more than a decade in the U.S. Army, Willis took a job selling machine parts. A promotion brought him to Syracuse in 1963. He lost the chance to watch big-league games live, but he remained a loyal student of the game.

His all-time team is not ruled by nostalgia. It includes Mike Schmidt and Ozzie Smith. Willis is a sharp and knowledgeable fan who finds baseball as fascinating as ever to watch, even more so while living in a hospital room.

During his first months of recovery from the stroke, he often burst from sleep calling out Dorothy's name. He would think, for an instant, the morning nurse was his wife. The hospital sent social workers to him, counselors who told him to let the past go. "It's hard," he said. "Fifty years, you know?"

But baseball, at least, still makes him sit up in bed. When his grown children come to visit, they often sit and watch a game.

"It's the strategy," Willis said. "I watch the pitchers, and I know when they should go up or down, or in and out. I love the Phillies, but I knew they couldn't win it with that Mitch (Williams) last year, because all he had was the fastball. God, the great hitters, they'll kill that stuff. They sit back and time it, and pretty soon, 'Boom!'"

Losing his wife, coupled with the back-to-back strokes, imposed a burden hard for anyone to bear. As a young man, Willis admired people who lived to be 90. Now, he wonders if old age is worth the price. But that mood passes, abruptly, when he starts talking about Ted Williams.

"Uncanny!" he said. "The greatest hitter I ever saw! And this year, the baseball, 'Boom!,' there it goes. You think they juiced it? Griffey, I think he could get Maris' record."

Old age is a blessing for a man who loves baseball. He is electrified until reality comes back, that whole weary prospect of a season-ending strike. "Yeah, that's it," he said, releasing his breath. "I'll just have to turn some other crazy thing on."

George Willis died in December, 1996, six years before his beloved Ozzie Smith made it into the Baseball Hall of Fame.

◆ ◆ ◆

56 There's a Place in History for Scabs

Baseball's holy book. In its earliest versions it was thick and black, just like the Bible. Its size alone seems to translate into some lofty meaning. All it needs are colored ribbons to help mark off the pages.

If you grew up as a child who loved baseball, there was probably a day, some lazy and sun-drenched summer afternoon, when you sprawled on the floor and ran your finger along the names, hoping to find one guy born in your hometown.

As you grew older, before that moment of harsh reality when you learn it just won't happen, perhaps you even fantasized about someday finding your own name in the book, next to the line that indicates whether you bat right or left.

The book is the living record of the game. The definitive version used to be known as the Baseball Encyclopedia. But the new king of baseball lore is the 2,700-page "Total Baseball," which includes a statistical biography of every human being who's made the Major Leagues.

In approximately 50 days, that book will become some 20 pages longer, due to the presence of 700 scabs, each of whom will require at least three lines of ink. And that is not sitting so well with rank-and-file fans, who somehow see the whole thing as a kind of desecration.

The *Post-Standard*, Monday, February 20, 1995

"Rag-tag," is what the replacements are called by John Thorn, the Kingston man who co-edits the expansive "Total Baseball." But if the season does indeed start with replacements, every one of their names will go in the book. "No question about it," Thorn said. "They're included."

Like it or not, he said, the Major League clubs define what is known as "big league." The book will certainly note in its baseball history that '95 was a strike year. But the scab players will appear without asterisks, their names on the same level as DiMaggio or Mays.

Thorn has heard from many fans who don't like that at all. But he said he's surprised at the sense of revulsion. The Major Leagues, he explained, hardly have a pristine past. In 1912, for instance, the Detroit Tigers went on a one-game strike, as a gesture of support for the suspended Ty Cobb. The American League threatened to seize the whole club, so Tiger management had to field a team of seminarians.

Every one of those players is listed in the book.

So is Eddie Gaedel, the midget who drew a walk for the St. Louis Browns in 1951. So is Clarence Dow, a sportswriter who played one game for Boston in 1884, when the team ran out of outfielders. Dow went 2-for-6, thus fulfilling, as Thorn said, "every sportswriter's dream."

And so is the name of every baby-faced teen or growling old man who managed to make the big-leagues during World War II.

Like them, each replacement player will go into the book.

Thorn likes to think that it is all a lot of smoke, that the issue will be resolved by Opening Day. He likes to think the threat of using scabs is the "ultimate suicide squeeze," that replacements in spring training won't suit up on opening day.

But he also has a theory on why people get upset. The practice of giving city names to local sports teams started centuries ago in England, he said. A victory for your team was equated as a community triumph. In a sense, that remains unchanged today.

Every city, Thorn said, wants to be equated with the best, wants its athletes to be fastest, renowned as most courageous. But if your heroes are suddenly overweight and middle-aged?

"I think we all feel substantially less heroic," said the guy who keeps the book.

Thorn's revisions were averted. Replacement players were never used in regulation games, although minor league players who seemed ready to cross the line carried the stigma for many years.

◆ ◆ ◆

57 Baseball Strike?
It Works for Us

This is a quick thank you to Mr. Fear and Mr. Ravage, or Mr. Fehr or Mr. Ravitch, or whatever they call themselves.

Please continue your strike, indefinitely. We here in Syracuse like it just fine.

Oh, maybe a few loyalists out there would disagree with me. But I became convinced of all this about 45 minutes before the Chiefs playoff game Monday.

I had just finished parking in some industrial parking lot, down by Hiawatha Boulevard, because the traffic was so thick. For a Chiefs game. In September. And then I hustled toward the ballpark, where I saw the most amazing thing.

A scalper.

Yes. It is true. The scalper was dickering with a man named Joe Pesner, who moves furniture for a living, back in Pawtucket. He and some friends had come here to watch Michael Bolton at the State Fair. By coincidence, the Chiefs and the Red Sox were also starting their series, so Pesner and friends went looking for tickets.

There weren't many left. "I'd be willing to pay $10 or $15 for (reserved) seats," Pesner said.

All I can say is thank God for the strike. Sure, I feel bad for the stars among the Chiefs and the Red Sox, who might be padding around now on plastic Major League grass.

Oh, that's a lie. I don't feel bad at all. It was a blast to see thousands of Chiefs fans, standing and stomping in top of the ninth, as Syracuse finished off stubborn Pawtucket. I loved seeing the happy woman with the sign that read, "Hail to the Chiefs!"

And it was a sheer pleasure to watch Carlos Delgado slicing three doubles, or Alex Gonzalez making a few improbable throws from out of the hole, or Randy St. Claire coming in to step on the PawSox toes.

Because these guys, quite simply, would have been gone.

"This is an exciting team, with a lot of talent," said Chiefs Manager Bob Didier. He described the strike as a tragic situation, but he also conceded some of his ballplayers might now be earning their pay in Toronto.

The *Post-Standard*, Tuesday, September 6, 1994

Instead, a terrific Chiefs team has stayed together into September, and might be playing — get this — the best professional baseball in the world.

Now, I am enough of a romantic to say that if you are ever going to show up and watch the Chiefs, tonight might be a good choice. See, an International League team with guys of Major League potential is playing top-flight baseball in an old ballpark that will be dust within two years.

You won't get that chance again. Ever.

The whole thing resolves what for years has seemed a paradox. Tens of thousands of people watch Syracuse University football and basketball, where in a good year one or two guys go on to the big leagues. But the Chiefs are often all but ignored, despite rosters that almost always have future Major Leaguers.

The answer, I think, is simple. SU plays for championships that mean something to the town, and no one comes around before the end and takes the stars from Orange rosters.

For once, that is the same thing we have in these Chiefs.

"This is the way it always should be," said Joe Caruso, a truck driver. He sat way back in the stands, glowing down on this big, electric noisy crowd. Unfortunately, due to the way baseball works, it can't always be this way.

So take our word for it. Unless you lead some amazing social life, there's no place better than Big Mac right now. For that I thank Mr. Fear, and I thank Mr. Ravage, for helping us remember why the Chiefs are still around.

◆ ◆ ◆

58 The Kid Likes
a Good Fight

Some parents might cringe at this situation. Some parents might not want their kid to come up to bat with two outs in the last of the ninth, his team trailing by a run, and a slick rain coming down.

Not Joe Lis, Sr. At the end of it all Tuesday, with the Syracuse Chiefs

The *Post-Standard*, Wednesday, September 7, 1994

trailing Pawtucket by a run and Joe Jr. standing on the muddy remains of the on-deck circle, Joe Sr. was kind of hoping they'd walk Carlos Delgado. "Got to pitch to him very carefully," he said out loud, as if it might influence the Red Sox strategy.

But Delgado went down swinging. Big Joe sighed and shook his head. "Takes a little sugar from the sweetness," he said.

Big Joe's son is Joe Lis, Jr., who on Tuesday knocked in four Syracuse runs with a double and a homer and was called out sliding hard into the plate when he sure looked like he was safe. That matters when you lose 7-6. But the old man was less proud of that pile of RBI than he was of what his kid did in the second inning.

When Lis came to bat, Pawtucket starter Frank Rodriguez tucked a whistling fastball right around his Adam's apple. Rodriguez had opened the game by planting another heater way up around the grandstand, leading some of us to theorize he was a wild man. Not Big Joe. "Just trying to get into their heads," he said.

Bang. On the next pitch, Little Joe rifled a shot over third base that scored two runs, and Big Joe was so happy he could hardly explain.

"When a guy puts it under your chin, tries to make you back out, and then he comes back with his best stuff and you take him for a double...."

Big Joe smiled, shook his head and lit up another cigarette. He had just defined what he means when he talks about tough.

He is a former major leaguer. He now sells insurance in Evansville, Ind., and he and his wife Susan made a spontaneous decision to drive like crazy to watch a couple of Chiefs playoff games. They were not completely without friends here.

Susan is a computer whiz. She had been corresponding for months over something called "Q-link" with a Central Square woman named Linda Priolo, who happens to be a big Chiefs fan. They bumped into each other electronically, and pretty soon Linda was shipping along all of Joe Jr.'s stats, and her 13-year-old daughter Victoria had become a devoted fan of Joe Jr.

The two families finally met at this week's playoffs, and they greeted each other with big hugs at Big Mac. That, however, is a story for '90s, about terminals and modems and high technology. The link between big and little Joe is more primal.

Big Joe remembers Syracuse well, because he hit two home runs in one game over the left-field wall when he was with the Toledo Mud Hens. He was still seeing the ball when he retired from the minors, but he wanted to spend more time with his family. Little Joe, at that point, was about 10 years old.

"The Cubs wanted me to be a batting instructor," Big Joe said. "I wasn't ready to divorce my own kids."

He had this theory. He is built like a cinderblock, and he had worked his way through baseball by being tough as nails. He hit .233 in the big leagues, but he dug in his feet and stayed there seven years. He wanted his own kids to be about as fragile as sandpaper. "Baseball is a tough game," he said, "and you play against tough people."

So he made them tough, not that they didn't already have the spark. Both of his sons, and his daughter, can hit the ball. At the age of two, little Joe smacked family friend Tommy Lasorda in the can with a plastic bat. It was not a love tap. Tommy jumped.

By the time the kid was 10, the old man had him out in a garage, hitting off a tee to the warmth of a kerosene heater. Sometimes it would leave the boy with sooty circles under his eyes. Those sessions would evolve into Big Joe's still-successful youth baseball school in Evansville.

Yet Big Joe never cut his kid a break on the field. Once he was at a high school game when his son came up to bat, and the kid bowed to baseball dogma by taking the first pitch. Big Joe stood up, right in the middle of the crowd, and started screaming at his son. "You swing at that pitch!" he shouted. "Next time up, you swing at that pitch!"

The old man figured the news was out among the pitchers (a word he uses as if speaking of some dark fraternity) that the kid would always take one for a strike. Little Joe yelled right back, but the next time up, he went for the first pitch. Easy out. He glared at his father, and they stared each other down for everyone to see.

"You do it again!" the old man boomed. Sure enough, next time up, the first pitch went for a double, and big Joe shouted at the top of his lungs, "Doing it my way, you're hitting .500."

Yeah, Big Joe said, his kid learned to be real tough.

This is for sure. No hitter for the Chiefs is any tougher right now. For the last two weeks, Joe Jr. has been pulling his team's fat out of the fire. When the Chiefs go to Pawtucket, he's the guy you want to see come up with men on base.

Both his double and home run Tuesday came at pressure points. Watching him in the on-deck circle, the way he paws at the ground like a 5-foot-10 bull, you can tell Joe Jr. wants to bat when it counts. This is not always the way, in sports or in life, and for that Big Joe thinks the kid came out all right.

◆ ◆ ◆

59 Baseball's Enduring Grip

You have played on this field, even if you've never been there. It is little more than a yard, a square of grass outside the Bayberry office building in Liverpool, a suburb of Syracuse. Beyond it, on the other side of a low brick wall, a river of cars fills four lanes along Route 57.

The kids, six or seven of them, show up to play every day after school. The oldest is 11, the littlest 6. They pick sides with two captains, who use their fists to "climb the bat." First pick means last ups. No field is closed, and a home run is anything over the wall.

Their parents forbid them from chasing balls into the road, which means a long homer becomes a kind of sacrifice. When that happens enough times, when their supply of balls is exhausted, they forage in the weeds at a nearby tennis court.

The place has no official name among the kids. It is simply the field. Jesse Wetmore and Ryan Kellogg pass each other at school, look at each other and mouth one word. "Baseball?" They nod their heads, although the nod is purely ritual. They both know they'll show up.

You have played on this field, even if you've never been there. No adults, no uniforms, rules made and kept by children. They are not old enough to know much about the Major League strike—"A bunch of babies," Kellogg says—but they are old enough to know what feels right about the game:

A hard swing that drives the ball far out into traffic. Backpedaling to the wall to stretch out and make the catch. Taking a grounder on one hop, pivoting off the old shingle that serves as second base, throwing under the tree limb to nail the double play.

They do those things and they go home. They eat supper, do their homework, brush their teeth, fall into bed. Then they lie awake, barely an hour removed from the field, still feeling sweet contact tingling in their palms.

Jesse, 11, lives next door. He brings along his little brother, Beau, the 6-year-old prodigy, who wears a hat far too big and lives for the day when he hits his first home run. It may have happened by the time you read this. Beau has already hit it off the wall.

The whole crew revolves around Jesse, a bright and cocky kid in a Tasmanian Devil neck chain. He chose the field because it is where his older brother, Jason, used to bang a rubber ball off the brick wall, where Jason would go to play catch with his friends.

Jason is now on the junior varsity team at Liverpool High School, a matter of some awe among the little ones. If you root around in the tall grass on the edge of the field, you will find ruined balls and other relics of the past. They were left behind by Jason, or by you and by me.

That is why the kids play there, every day after school. In the summer, they start in the morning, break for dinner, stay until front windows burn yellow in the dusk.

All four bases are scraps of wood. The children usually play with tennis balls, because Ryan Kellogg has hit a few blasts that drilled passing cars. Drivers might not be so forgiving of a hardball.

Kellogg, 10, is broad-shouldered, powerful, the Boomer of the group. He is a pleasant kid with a freckled face, but at the plate his lip curls in a confident sneer.

He has lifted balls across Route 57, where they roll four or five spots deep in the Hayden Jewelers parking lot. Last year, at the field, he hit 45 home runs. He kept count because each one feels just as good.

Eleven-year-old Aaron Richardson was introduced to baseball by "my grandpa," who took him out to MacArthur Stadium when Aaron didn't want to go. He liked it. He started playing. Hank Aaron is his favorite legend, for an 11-year-old's reason: "Same name."

Eight-year-old Kevin Sweeney specializes in stealing home runs, hanging his mitt over the brick wall to grab some Kellogg drive. Ten-year-old Chris Teller has a pierced ear and is a catcher in Little League. "I like the equipment," he explained, noting with pride that he is a teammate of the Boomer's. Teller's 13-year-old sister, Kelly, used to be a regular. But now she comes as often to watch as to play, growing into other interests like the school color guard.

Beau is the baby, the kid learning the game. Jesse is proud of the little guy, the way he can field and handle the bat, but brothers are brothers. "You better hit it," Jesse hisses, when Beau comes to the plate. More times than not, Beau does, although Kellogg grudgingly provides the kid with an occasional fourth strike.

While we've all walked that field, some things have changed. They have a boom box, and they listen to rap. At home, on rainy days, they play their Sega. They use aluminum bats, which Jesse gives names like "Young Blood" or "Black Thunder."

Still, much of it is familiar. Big kids pitch to big kids. Little kids get to pick their own pitcher. No stealing, just lead-offs. The team with its ups provides its own catcher. It leads to teasing and taunting between pitchers and runners, those cocky one-on-ones that stop the whole game, while the rest of the kids shriek, "Just pitch the ball!"

You watch them play, and you feel for what is going to happen. They will come back someday, beyond their childhood, and they will not believe just how much their field has shrunk. Wasn't it bigger than this? The wall higher? A home run farther?

But they have, right now, what we all want from baseball. They understand joy, and that joy is the game. They keep score, but no one bothers keeping track of innings, because the game only ends when they're forced to go inside.

They get home from school, dump their books and race to the field. They play for hours, until parents pull up and start honking their horns, until the sun falls down and shadows claim the grass. We played there, and they play there, and someone else will take their place.

Jesse Wetmore, now a high school graduate, can still see the field from his house. Not long after this piece appeared, he says, the owners of the lot did some rearranging. They made changes in the wall. They anchored a picnic table in the middle of the field. That put an end to the daily baseball games, and the group of childhood friends began to split apart.

"Two of the kids we played with moved out," Wetmore says. "Another kid we haven't seen. Some went to college, some went to work."

On spring days, in what all too quickly became an adult life, Wetmore sometimes glances at the wet grass near the field and recalls foraging for balls. And he remembers vividly how it felt to take one deep.

◆ ◆ ◆

VI

THEIR OWN
KIND OF VALHALLA

60 If Walls Could Talk, You'd Hear His Name

Jake Eastman has no regrets. That would be the wrong word. It is better to say that even now he sometimes wonders. He spent the whole winter hanging drywall at P&C Stadium. He saw the ballpark gradually take shape, saw the mud change to a diamond with a fine mound in the middle.

Jake could envision himself on that mound, young and thin and throwing smoke and then the knuckle curve, young and thin and watching yet another batter shake his head.

"From the time I was a kid," Jake said, "I knew I was going to wind up playing baseball."

He didn't. He hangs drywall. Sometimes— only sometimes— he signs his name on his work.

In the early 1960s, he was a right-handed pitcher at Madison High School in Madison County. He was fast, cocky and dominant. "I remember, during batting practice, he hit me in the arm," recalls Dick Engle, a teammate who is now Madison's basketball coach. "I could see the stitches of the ball in my skin for a couple of weeks."

Jake was the sixth of 10 Eastman children. He learned to play baseball from his older brother, Pepper. From the time Jake was tiny, the two of them would play catch in their yard.

When Jake was 8 or 9 years old, Pepper took a job as a mechanic. He'd put Jake on his lap as he drove away from work. He'd let his little brother hold the steering wheel as they went home.

"He was special to me," Jake said. Pepper, too, had a natural feel for sports. He became a stock car driver on area dirt tracks. Jake, every weekend, would go to watch him race. Pepper was his hero, his buddy, his best source of advice. Jake remembers only one thing he could not tell his brother.

Pepper, in the yard, had always been Jake's catcher. When Jake was small, his big brother caught his lobs in a stretched-out catcher's mitt. The lobs, as the years went on, turned into steam. A time came when Jake was so fast the ball burned through the thin padding. Pepper would grimace, in obvious pain.

The *Post-Standard*, Thursday, April 3, 1997

Jake turned down the heat. But only for his brother.

In high school, Jake used his fastball to set up timid and uncertain hitters. He'd throw the knuckle curve — "It came in slow, and dropped like Niagara Falls," he said — as his sure third strike. Sometimes, coach Jack Tenhope would pitch Jake on back-to-back days against good teams. Pro scouts showed up to watch.

During Jake's senior year, he ripped open a letter from the Los Angeles Dodgers. They invited him to a tryout at their Vero Beach, Fla., training camp. Eastman drove straight down in an old '53 Cadillac. There were 50 other pitchers at the same tryout. Jake was one of three who survived for one final look, a scrimmage against a local college team.

In the end, the Dodgers cut him. He went home, to live his life.

Jake did not give up his dream, but he had to make a living. Pepper, once again, stepped in to help. A few of Jake's older brothers, including Pepper, had a drywall business. They hired Jake. Pepper showed him the craft.

"It's all patience," Jake said. "You've got to have a knack for it. When you get done, you don't want to see a seam or a bump. Pepper was gentle, real easygoing. It took a while, but he taught me how."

Jake remembers, distinctly, when he let go of baseball. In the summer of '65, he'd been out of high school two years. He was still playing some adult league ball around Madison County. In the back of his mind, he wondered if maybe he could earn another chance with some pro team.

One Friday, Pepper went to the track while Jake went on a date. He was at a party with his girlfriend when he got the news. Pepper's car had rolled over at Fonda Speedway. Pepper broke his neck. He was killed. "It hurt me kind of bad," Jake says now.

Jake, too, would become a race car driver, although he raced on pavement instead of dirt. "I wanted to carry on the family name," he said.

And day by day, over the years, he mastered the art of drywall.

Yet he never completely forgot about baseball. In 1971, he was hired to hang drywall in Cooperstown. They were doing an expansion on baseball's Hall of Fame. One day, Jake pulled out a marking crayon and autographed the Sheetrock. Then he covered it up, so no one else knew it was there.

"Every baseball player wants his name in the Hall of Fame," Jake said. "Mine is."

Twenty-five years later, Jake, 51, found himself helping to put up a new Syracuse ballpark next to the ruins of MacArthur Stadium. Every day, he watched as the field took shape. He'd look down on the mound, and he'd again feel like a child, a kid who always thought he'd get his big-league chance.

"You just wonder, you know?" Eastman asked this week. "You look down and wonder what it'd be like to play on a field like that. This stadium, I was part of making it. I almost feel like a part of that stadium is mine."

It is. He hung his drywall, slow and patient, just the way Pepper taught him. You'll see his work today, when the SkyChiefs start their season. Walk the concourse, check the drywall, and you will find no bumps or seams.

But somewhere, behind those walls, Jake Eastman signed his name.

◆ ◆ ◆

61 Day Off Rates an A-Plus

Patty Green was in the office Thursday for maybe three hours. She kept looking outside, where the sun was beating down and a warm spring wind was blowing. Patty, abruptly, got up from her desk.

To their surprise, Rebecca and Justin Green soon were yanked from their classrooms in Parish. Rebecca is 10 and Justin is 8, and they had no idea of what brought their mom to the main office at school. Rebecca's teacher, worried, asked Patty why she needed both her kids.

"Opening day," Patty explained.

The teacher replied, "I wish I could go with you."

The Greens played hooky and went to P&C Stadium. Thursday's opener renewed the oldest rivalry in minor league baseball, the SkyChiefs against the Rochester Red Wings. For many parents, for this one day, baseball mattered more than school.

"My father was a teacher," said Nick Acquaviva, Jr., of Liverpool. "No way would he have ever gone for this." Yet Nick and his neighbor, Mike Gilbert, are opening-day regulars. A year ago, they put a challenge to their kids: If they kept their grades up, they could skip school and watch the SkyChiefs in their first home game.

The boys passed the test. The Gilbert brothers, 9-year-old Jeff and 12-year-old Tim, tailgated Thursday in the parking lot with 10-year-old Nick Acquaviva III. They were joined by Mike Pacini, 11, a schoolmate at the Roxboro Road Elementary School. They chattered about escaping a stuffy classroom and dodging science projects.

The *Post-Standard*, Friday, April 9, 1999

"What I like," said Jeff Gilbert, "is being with my dad."

Fifty or 60 years ago, skipping school for a baseball game carried a certain risk. Some teachers didn't celebrate the rituals. But this is a different America, where parents are working more hours than ever, where easy hours with your kids become a precious luxury.

Ed Cosentino, for instance, is a native north sider. He spent much of his childhood roaming the chipped aisles of MacArthur Stadium. In all that time, Ed never once snagged a foul ball.

A couple of years ago, he brought his own daughter, Ashley, to her first SkyChiefs game. A fan barehanded a foul ball, turned around, and gave the ball to Ashley. Now, like any regular, she shows up with her dad on opening day.

"This is better than school," said Ashley, 10.

That sentiment was embraced by 6-year-old Jake Files and his older brother, Ryan, who coyly gave his age as "just about 9." Jake and Ryan had the day off in Westhill because of a teachers' conference.

They were eating meatball sandwiches for lunch when their dad, Mike, burst into the house, tickets held high. He had rushed through an early-morning meeting in Albany, then pressed the gas pedal to make it home on time. He grabbed his startled boys and hurried to the ballpark.

"This girl in my class, her name is Melissa, she said she had tickets to this stupid game," Ryan said. "Stupid! I don't know how she could say that!"

For the Files family, opening day is a new tradition. For the Cupelo family, it goes back 70 years. In the 1920s, Bob Cupelo would climb the fence on opening day to watch the old Syracuse Stars at Star Park.

"Did my mother know?" Bob asked. "Sometimes she did."

Years later, Bob routinely pulled his own son, Robert, out of school for opening day. Parents, heed the lesson: Robert became a doctor.

Now Robert and his wife, Barbara, have five kids of their own. They were all there Thursday, three generations of hooky-playing Cupelos beneath the tower at the ballpark. Bob and his wife, Mary, kept embracing old friends, and the grandkids wore their mitts and dreamed about a home run ball, while Robert and Barbara — in the middle — tried to bronze it in their minds.

"We do it for memories," said Robert. That is worth one day of school.

This column may have celebrated that old-school feeling of innocence and escape, but it also evoked some Old Testament wrath. In a subsequent letter to the editor, a 69-year-old woman questioned the morals of any writer, or any parent, who might be "aiding and abetting" wayward children who play hooky to go to a baseball game.

"Add lying to the mix!" fumed the writer, who came to the devastating conclusion that many of the children at the Syracuse opener probably used deceptive notes about phantom colds and flu bugs, to hoodwink their gullible teachers.

"It has been over a week now since the beginning of baseball season, so I'm hoping that I have calmed down enough so that this newspaper will not burn up as I write!" the letter continued. "Does your newspaper support immorality and lawlessness? Is this what we should be teaching our children?"

The letter could just as well have been written in 1909 as in 1999, which is — in many ways — why playing hooky for an opener still feels absolutely great.

◆ ◆ ◆

62 A Pocket of Frustration: Foreigners in Our Mitts

By all logic, in an economy that routinely squashes little guys, the Nokona athletic goods company should not be producing baseball gloves.

Nokona operates in the Texas flatlands, two hours from Dallas. The company employs 65 people, whose average wage is about $6 an hour, and they go head-to-head with such titans as Rawlings and Spalding.

"We've always thought small," said Nokona president Robby Storey, whose grandfather was the company founder. "We're not giant-killers, or anything like that."

Yet Nokona manages to survive — maybe because of idealists like John Russo, a Central New York ironworker who lives out his philosophy about buying and selling.

Russo runs a small Canastota contracting company. A couple of years ago, he made a vow to stick with buying only American-made products, in order to help save American jobs.

It was nice in theory, until Russo went to buy his 4-year-old son a basketball. The closest he could come was Korea. "A lot of things are hard to find," Russo said. His frustration boiled over this spring when he tried to find an American-made glove for his daughter, Amy, who is playing modified high school softball.

A baseball glove. Symbol of the national pastime. Rich musk of leather, sweet smell of cut grass.

Fat chance, they told him, at store after store.

"You'd think you could find a ball glove made in this country," Russo said. "Everybody's crying jobs and this and that, but nothing's made here anymore. That's why there's no jobs."

So Russo dug in his feet. He called the Hall of Fame in Cooperstown, and he called the offices of Major League Baseball. He learned that 98 percent of all gloves are produced overseas. Not a single major-league ball-player, he found, is believed to use a glove made on the continent. A few U.S. outfits make tiny orders of specialty gloves, but that's pretty much it.

The only American company producing gloves from domestic materials, on U.S. soil, is Nokona.

The company makes a quality glove, which costs from $100 to $150. But it does not have the dollars to put into promotion. In the old days, the signatures of such ballplayers as Carl Erskine and Dick Williams appeared on the palm of Nokona products. In return, the players would get a couple of free gloves each year.

That was until the early 1960s, said Robby Storey, when the big man-ufacturers "went off-shore." Baseball players began demanding thousands of dollars in return for their signatures. Nokona was faced with cheaper competition. The company decided it could survive without celebrity endorsements.

Now, it produces 15,000 gloves each year, mainly for softball. It also does a solid trade in youth football helmets. And it refuses to go overseas for production.

Nokona is based in Nocona, Texas, population 2,992, where 65 jobs remain a big deal. "Maybe it's sheer stupidity," Storey said, "but we don't like the idea of sending our people home."

Stupidity? Hardly. This is the 1990s, when the great American game is played with balls made for peanuts in Costa Rica. Those balls are caught by gloves made for peanuts in Asia, while the games are watched by unem-ployed laborers living on peanuts throughout industrial America.

John Russo can't stand it. "We did it to ourselves," he said. "We sold ourselves out." He may only have one small finger in the dike, but his daughter has five fingers in an American-made glove.

John Russo's daughter grew up, joined the U.S. Marine Corps, had a daughter of her own — and still owns her Nokona glove. But her father eventually had to make some concessions. It became too difficult, and too expensive, to buy only American-made products. His son is now playing Babe Ruth baseball. If he stays with the game, Russo promises to buy him a Nokona.

"Right now, he doesn't wear an American-made glove," Russo says, "because I wasn't going to pay twice as much."

◆ ◆ ◆

63 Challenger Stars Light Up P&C Stadium

Bill Norton grew up in the Valley. With his buddies, he would spend long summer days playing ball at Meachem Field. Bill, like most kids, dreamed that big-league dream. He fancied himself in Yankee pinstripes in their great Bronx stadium.

Bill never made it. He went to work instead. But he allowed himself the same dream for each of his six kids—a cheering crowd, a big-time ballpark, the Norton name on the scoreboard.

Tuesday night, at P&C Stadium, Bill's youngest son arrived.

Chad Norton, 12, came to bat in the second inning. He made the usual choices in the on-deck circle. He decided to use an aluminum bat. And he chose to stand and bat, instead of batting from his wheelchair, which means Bill helped Chad walk to the batter's box.

Chad watched as pitcher Aldo Talarico, a parent, kept pitching outside. The fourth pitch was over the plate. Leaning against his father, Chad drilled a one-hop single to left. He advanced around the bases, finally scoring on a hit from teammate Chris Metcalfe. As they closed in on the plate, Chad quietly asked his dad to release his grip. Chad slid in, safe. Everyone went nuts.

"Awesome!" Chad said softly, sweat running down his face. "It was wild. It looks a lot bigger once you get out there!"

Chad lives with cerebral palsy. He cannot walk and he can only use

The *Post-Standard*, Wednesday, August 5, 1998

one hand when he plays ball. But he was at P&C as part of an all-star event for the 110 children in Onondaga County who compete in the Challenger Little League, a division for kids with disabilities. In this all-star game, everyone played and no one kept score.

Chad's story is powerful. It is not unique. All around him, children did extraordinary things. A kid named Eric Kisselstein, for instance, pulled himself to the plate on two metal crutches. He threw one crutch away to swing the bat with one hand. After one vicious cut, he fell hard to his knees. He picked himself up, pounded the next pitch, and beat the throw to first.

"When we started this, none of us could envision this moment," said Skip Soule of Syracuse, the league's founder and a national pioneer in the Challenger movement. The first game was played in 1982, on a field behind the Roberts School on Glenwood Avenue. The league took off. Last year, when P&C opened as an all-purpose stadium, Challenger president Bob Nelson knew he had found a perfect all-star showcase.

Only Yankee Stadium, to Chad Norton, could be a bigger thrill.

He sits up late each night to savor Yankee games with his father, who works 17-hour days to help finance his son's care. The payoff, for Chad, came when he watched Yankee David Wells pitch his perfect game. "I was shaking," Chad said. "I blew on my fingers every inning to give him luck."

Chad was the second and last child born to Bill and his wife, Doreen. Their first son, Adam, was four months premature. He died 30 minutes after he was born. Chad was born in the seventh month. He weighed 2 pounds and 10 ounces. "I knew about his spirit right away," said his father, who watched Chad — as an infant — battle past an infection.

Chad never crawled. By 4 months, the doctors diagnosed cerebral palsy. Bill had five children from an earlier marriage. Those kids were ballplayers. He remembers lying in bed, fighting off self-pity about his youngest son's condition, trying to accept that Chad might never swing a bat.

As for Chad, he found other goals to keep him busy. His mind works just fine. He learned to speak very early. He went to mainstream schools and nursed a passion for computers. He kills time by tooling around the Internet.

When Chad was in second grade, his parents learned about the Challenger league. "It was our chance," Bill said. Finally, the father had a way to teach his youngest son the game.

Tuesday, his pants still dirty from his slide into home, Chad began talking about the Yankees, how he loves Tino Martinez and the way he clears the bases. Chad is left with only one great childhood fantasy, a chance to someday swing a bat in Yankee Stadium.

"We'll get there," said his father, lifted up by his son's dream.

Chad Norton is now going into the 10th grade of high school in Syracuse, where he carries a 94.2 grade average and is on the honor roll. "He's a computer nut," his father says. Shortly after this column appeared in the Post-Standard, *Chad was invited to be a guest of the Colorado Rockies for 10 days, where he attended six games and got to meet the players in the lockerroom.*

He still loves baseball and the Yankees, and Chad made his first trip to Yankee Stadium in summer 2002.

◆ ◆ ◆

64 End of the Innocence Is in the Cards

Al Leary is a hopeless romantic. A few weeks ago, he wrote a column lamenting his loss of baseball-card innocence. He remembered how he would mow his neighbor's lawn for a couple of bucks, and then pedal to a drug store to spend it all on cards.

Many of us have similar memories, particularly if we're grizzled products of the postwar baby boom.

Leary, however, is 17 years old.

He penned his column for the monthly paper at Cortland Junior-Senior High School. It triggered an afternoon phone call to his classroom, where Leary was happy to discuss the matter at length — since it got him out of 11th-grade math. "I think it's algebra," Leary said.

Once he loved baseball cards. Now he's sick and tired of them. He cringed as friends evolved into fiscal analysts of each card's value. He saw children treating cards like rare and ancient scrolls. His breaking point occurred when faceless corporate executives yanked the bubble gum out of each pack. Collectors cheered, since the sugar in the gum was a threat to the longevity of the cards.

Heaven forbid. Never mind that the cards were intended for kids in the first place, and that kids enjoy gum — even dry pink slabs that are difficult to chew.

So Leary — news editor for his school paper — sat down and got a little nostalgic. He banged out a column recalling the days when he could get six packs of cards for $2, way back when in the early 1980s.

And then he would climb on his bike and chew the gum.

His classmates basically ignored his opinion. He got a lot of nice comments from whimsical adults, who recalled a time when baseball cards were valued primarily by kids — while their own parents often saw them as needless junk. Indeed, Leary's father — like so many of us — saw his own cards tossed out by an impatient mother.

But he was from a generation that shared those communal moments, when you'd walk into the corner stores that existed in every city in America, the ones with the aroma of very strong salami. The cards would be set on the counter, between the jar of pickles and the round bin of pretzels.

You'd drop your change into the cracked leather paw of some bored old man in an apron and T-shirt — who nonetheless watched every kid in the place. And once or twice in a childhood, you'd rip off the paper to find a Mantle or a Mays.

The sheer, joyous triumph fueled the bike ride home.

That was before adults, and their wallets, became very involved. Consider the case of one nationally known collectibles expert, who used his syndicated column this month to verbally paddle a youngster for daring to put a single pinhole in a Joe Montana card.

Imagine. The kid had the nerve to hang it on his bedroom wall.

That is why we can all thank goodness for Al Leary. He is both throwback and visionary. When he got a Dwight Gooden card in 1985, the heyday of "Doc's" career, Leary ogled it for a day or two and then threw it in a shoe box. He didn't go out and buy an airtight container.

"I started collecting when I was 12 years old, because these guys were my heroes," Leary said. "But I think it started to get to me when I went into junior high and everybody was keeping their cards wrapped up in plastic and carrying around price guides."

Now, it's off his chest. He wrote his column. He still hopes that someday, somehow, they'll bring back the gum.

Sorry, kid. That'll happen on the day Brooklyn gets back the Dodgers.

Al Leary, as might be expected, went on to journalism. He now works as a staff writer for the St. Petersburg Times.

◆ ◆ ◆

65 The Bear Beats the Odds

For two innings Tuesday, in the green hills of Fabius, the Bear took the mound and flirted with myth.

He was making his first start of the season for the Fabius-Pompey boys baseball team. He faced the cannons of Hannibal High School. His Falcons were 4-4. Hannibal had muscled out nine wins in 10 games.

But the Bear had his brother, Rob Golden, calling signals behind the plate, and for a while — in a field carved out of a dandelion pasture — the whole scene was a work of pure baseball lore.

The Bear, whose corkscrew windup is reminiscent of Luis Tiant, struck out the first kid he faced on a knee-high called strike. He set down the next five batters on high flies and true grounders, mixing in the curve with a knuckler and a changeup.

"He had us completely off-balance," said Hannibal coach Pete Rossi, whose team struggled even to bunt against the Bear.

The Bear is Barry Golden, 16. He has cerebral palsy, which visibly limits the use of the left side of his body. It doesn't stop him from pitching. "No one ever told me I couldn't do anything," he said.

He is normally a reliever, but he got the second start of his career when Fabius ran out of arms. The Falcons are making up a lot of early rainouts. All their pitchers are playing a role.

"If he has a limitation, he doesn't know it," said umpire Tom Holgate, who watched the Bear close out a recent Fabius victory over LaFayette, watched how the whole team stayed with him when he gave up a few runs.

Tuesday began like an improbable drama. An eighth-grade shortstop named Dennis TenEyck drove in four quick runs, and Fabius grabbed a 5-0 lead.

It didn't last. The Bear tired, and left, in the third inning. By the end of the game, Fabius went though four pitchers and Hannibal had a 10-5 victory, behind hard-throwing relief by a prospect named Leon Havlik.

The Bear, a junior, joined the varsity last year. It was the first season for head coach Shawn May, whose posted team rule is, "Never say never." He is a true believer in the romance of baseball.

May was driving through the hills of Fabius, for instance, when he saw a kid named Josh Sipfle running in a horse pasture, throwing a baseball in the air. "I decided that any kid who caught a ball in a horse pasture was going to be on my team," said May, who played a year of pro ball at the game's lowest rung.

So he talked Sipfle into trying out, and Josh showed up with a bat he found in his barn, an ancient piece of wood carrying the signature of Hack Wilson.

A Hack Wilson model? The bat, honed and varnished by the coach, now hangs in Josh's bedroom. Like Wilson, the Cubs great, Josh was made into an outfielder. The whole team has taken to calling him "Hack."

"This is a special team," said May, 27. His first season ended at 2-13. This year's Falcons are playing .500 baseball.

Yet even May, at first, lacked faith in Barry Golden. The coach met the kid in a school corridor, saw how his weakened arm and leg affected his gait. May didn't know about the workouts the Bear put himself through, how school therapists helped him learn to deal with hot line drives.

May gave up his doubts when he shook the Bear's right hand — the strong grip of a kid who does chores on a farm. The coach, on the spot, came up with the nickname.

The Bear has played baseball since the fourth grade. Rob, two years his elder, joined a Fabius youth league, and Barry asked to give it a try. Pretty soon Rob and the Bear wore a mound and basepaths into a field by their house. They still play catch, almost every night.

"We're like this," Rob said, folding two of his fingers together.

That will end soon. Rob leaves in a month to join the Marines. Hannibal may have been the last opponent they ever start against as a battery. The Bear, lost in thought on a half-empty field, wondered aloud if anyone can fill that void.

He didn't have time to worry about it. "Great game!" screamed Alan Hathaway, a sophomore right-fielder, who jumped up to pound the Bear on the back. "Next year we'll be back, and we're going to do it!"

The Bear flashed a quick smile and pumped his right fist. He cannot replace his brother, but his team needs him back.

Shawn May quickly established a baseball powerhouse at Fabius-Pompey. In 2000, he led the school to its first New York state baseball championship, in its small school classification. His team repeated that feat in 2003.

As for Barry Golden, he is now a manager at a Burger King in suburban Syracuse. He often drives to work past the field where, for a few precious innings as a teen-ager, he held Hannibal at bay.

Does he think about it? Golden laughs.

"Almost every day," he says.

◆ ◆ ◆

66 Auburn's Foul Balls Land in Forbidden Territory

AUBURN, N.Y.—Thursday offered the first night of baseball ever at the new Falcon Park, and Patrick Waldron, Nick Wiwsianyk and Nathan Cockrell—a trio of newly graduated eighth-graders—were scouting out the best places to grab a foul ball.

Even with a new stadium, one thing hasn't changed. The boys gestured with some awe beyond the fence behind first base, where a stocky guy in a lawn chair sat beneath a weeping willow. Baseball may have a new era in Auburn, but it remains risky to chase foul balls into the yard of Stanley Roche.

"We don't even try it," Wiwsianyk said. "Some kids, they'll go into his yard to get the ball."

"But only at night," Cockrell added. "The only chance they've got with Mr. Roche is at night."

Roche, 74, is a classic baseball figure. He is the old guy next door who doesn't want you in his yard. For his entire life, professional ballplayers have been slapping foul balls onto his lawn. For at least 50 years, he has been grabbing those balls and keeping them for his own.

Legend has it among the children of Auburn that Roche has barrels filled with foul balls, although Roche dismisses that with a wave of his hand. "I keep'm, and then I give'm to friends or my own grandchildren," he said.

There is no way, no how, he will ever throw them back.

Roche lives on North Division Street, immediately next to Auburn's shiny new ballpark. He has lived there all of his 74 years. He remembers the first Falcon Park going up in the 1920s. His father, a factory worker, didn't like it then. The stadium gave the family scant buffer, which the Roches maintain they deserved by right and courtesy.

Yet when the original Falcon Park was built, Stan Roche's father was not a U.S. citizen. That made him afraid to really rock the boat.

Stan Roche, however, does not have that inhibition. He eventually inherited ownership of the house. And if baseball has become a tradition at Falcon Park, so has Roche's refusal to part with foul balls.

The *Post-Standard*, Monday, June 26, 1995

"I've been a prisoner in this yard," Roche said. His family, he said, once had gardens and fruit trees out on the lawn. He said they were destroyed by ball-chasing children. "I'd come home, and there'd be 12 or 13 kids in the yard."

So he decided to put a stop to it. For decades, he and his wife, Ella, have pulled out lawn chairs for any Auburn home game. They put them in the shade of that majestic weeping willow. If a foul ball hits their property, Stan races to get to it before any of the kids.

Ella, for her part, admitted she actually likes watching baseball. "But it is hard on our yard," she quickly added, when Stan gave her a shocked-husband look.

Despite his—ahem—hardball stance, Stan is a pretty amiable guy. He readily admits that his own son, Andrew, and the neighbor's kid, Ben Konyk, spent much of their boyhood haunting the ballpark. Indeed, the now grown-up Konyk pulled up a chair with the Roches to watch the opener.

Stan laughs when he remembers how a foul ball once bonked him right on the head. "It had to happen," said Konyk. And Stan takes particular delight in a story from the late 1940s, when a man named Joe owned the Auburn minor-league team.

"He came over and told me, 'Look. Let's resolve this. I'll buy back any foul balls hit over here,'" Roche recalls. "'OK,' I told him. 'I want $200 for the whole summer.' He didn't like that, and he got mad and went back and built this wall of chicken wire to keep the foul balls in the park."

Roche paused for drama, and offered a big smile. "It didn't work. I got my foul balls."

There is, Roche maintains, an easy solution to his problem. He said the city was wrong in allowing the ballpark to push up to his yard. The right thing for the city to do, he said, would be to give him a good price for his house. Then he and Ella could get out, the city could knock his place down, and the kids could have all the foul balls they want.

While Roche said the city made a dinky bid to buy his house during stadium construction, Vijay Mital said he isn't aware of any offer. Mital, Auburn's economic development director, said there were some informal talks about buying the Roche property, in the event the city needed more stadium parking.

Those parking needs are satisfied, and Mital doesn't see any deal in the works. In response, Roche offered a grim, determined shrug. He is retired. He has a lawn chair. He has good shade and plenty of time. For as long as he remains a neighbor to Falcon Park, any foul ball is in his yard is still going, going, gone.

In 2001, Stanley Roche sold his house to his daughter and moved into a senior citizens tower in Auburn. Roche's son, Stanley Jr., says his sister and her husband erected a tall fence to keep most foul balls out of the yard, all but ending Stanley Sr.'s long vigil and his feud with city officials.

The tradition, however, is not completely forgotten. Every now and then, a foul ball still clears the fence. When it does, Stanley Jr. says, his sister keeps the ball.

◆ ◆ ◆

67　Cianfrocco Dreams Up a Fall Classic

For the past few nights, Archi Cianfrocco has struggled to sleep. He sprawls in bed in whatever hotel where he is staying. His thoughts drift back to when he was 9 or 10 years old, when he played Wiffle Ball on a vacant lot near Embargo Street

He grew up in Rome, N.Y. He'd play two-on-two Wiffle Ball with three of his best friends. They always made believe they were in the World Series. Those were beautiful autumn days, sweatshirt weather beneath the changing leaves, and the boys would fantasize about Reggie Jackson or Graig Nettles.

Nineteen years later, Archi (pronounced ARK-ee) is well past fantasy. He is a backup first baseman with the San Diego Padres. This year, he knocked in 32 runs while hitting .281, his best batting average for four years in the majors. On Tuesday, as the West Division champion Padres opened the National League playoffs with a 3-1 loss in St. Louis, Archi played in the eighth and ninth innings.

"It's a weird feeling," he said after the game. "It's almost like another person's life."

Archi has been invited back to Syracuse for an Oct. 13 alumni game at Onondaga Community College. He figures they'll understand why he can't make it. That game is exactly one week after Archi's 30th birthday.

The *Post-Standard*, Wednesday, October 2, 1996

He will spend his milestone living out a dream. Archi has not lost the glow of playing in the majors.

When the Padres are on the road and Archi gets up to bat, he knows his 6-year-old son, Angelo, is watching on TV. Archi always sends a little signal. "A lot of times," Archi said, "I'll reach up and rub my nose."

Before this year, when their son's schooling gave them reason to remain in San Diego, Archi and his wife, Maria, would return to Rome for the winter. Until five years ago, Archi would spend those winters working for the Rome Water Department, wearing rubber boots as he waded into icy overflows.

During last year's baseball strike, when the owners threatened to use replacement players, Archi was offered the opportunity to play as a scab. He was a minor leaguer who refused to cross the picket line. He feared that decision would alienate his bosses and destroy his career. Later, when he was called up to the majors, critics charged the Padres only chose him to placate the players union. Archi silenced the sniping by doing his job. He feels he's earned the right to enjoy these playoffs.

"I'm just trying to absorb as much as I can," Archi said. "Some guys never even get this chance."

He described last weekend's regular-season climax as his greatest thrill in baseball. He has spent the last couple of nights mentally replaying that dramatic series with the Dodgers. The Padres were underdogs in Los Angeles. They won three in a row to capture the division.

"That's what jumps to my mind, running out onto the field in L.A., throwing champagne in the clubhouse," Archi said. "Everyone had counted us out."

He was traded to San Diego from Montreal in 1993, in the middle of the notorious Padre "fire sale." He is one of the few Padres remaining from that bleak era, which was also endured by the great Tony Gwynn. Archi still makes a point of getting to the ballpark early to watch Gwynn take batting practice.

"I really think he's going to hit .400 someday," Archi said. "You watch him from the stands and it looks easy. What he's really taught me is (how) you have to focus and concentrate on every at-bat. A lot of young guys, they'll concentrate (for) two or three at-bats a game. The other two times, they don't really know what they're looking for up there.

"He videotapes every game. He's a big believer in videotape. He has a whole library. He videotapes himself, what he's done against every pitcher he's faced. He has film of every guy he's ever batted against. He's a professional hitter. That's why he's the best."

That kind of attitude, Archi said, explains why there is no despair among the Padres. The team has been through too much to get shook by one defeat. "We all know, if we split here, we'll still be all right," he said.

He was speaking on the phone from St. Louis, at 8 p.m. He planned on trying to get to sleep early, but he knew it would not happen. He knew he would close his eyes and immediately rewind to childhood, to throwing a ball again and again off his parents' roof, always pretending he was playing in the big leagues in October.

Even then, as a boy, he had one baseball dream. It is here. He is living it. He can't believe this is his life.

Archi Cianfrocco is retired now and living with his family in San Diego. He last played for the Padres in 1998, and he says he has lost none of his awe about his time in the Major Leagues. "I go to games," he says, "and I still can't believe I played. The last time we went, I turned to my wife and I said, 'Did I really used to do this?'"

He is also willing, in retirement, to make a confession: Rubbing his nose wasn't the only family message he'd send when he batted for the Padres. Cianfrocco has an aunt in Utica, N.Y., with a bawdy sense of humor, and he made contact with her in his own way, whenever he knew he was batting on national TV: "I'd adjust my cup as my signal to Aunt Donna," Cianfrocco says.

◆ ◆ ◆

68 Big Man of the Little League

WILLIAMSPORT, PA.— The folks from Easley, S.C., were taking no prisoners. Their mission was landing a "Big League" world series in their hometown, "Big League" being what Little League Inc. calls its teen-age baseball program.

The Easley crew was lobbying at the downtown Genetti Lycoming

---

Hotel. Little League big wheels stay there during the Little League World Series, whose championship game today could draw more than 40,000 fans. And the Easley guys struck gold when Luke LaPorta walked into a late-night reception.

"Doc! Doc! Doc!" hollered the fellas from Easley. They surrounded LaPorta, chairman of Little League's board of directors, and handed him pins and T-shirts. How about that Syracuse football team, Doc? And how about our proposal? Get a chance to read our proposal yet, Doc?

"No," LaPorta told them, "but I will." He took time to shake every hand and slap every arm, making sure to look every man in the eye, because that is the core of his philosophy.

"These are the people," as he puts it, "who go out and bust their cookies."

Then he turned to drift away in the ballroom, where he was immediately snared by some old Little League buddies from Puerto Rico.

"Doc! Doc!" they cried, while Tom Boyle smiled and watched his buddy work the room. Boyle is another Little League veteran, a guy whose business sense in the 1970s helped youth baseball explode in California.

"If you think of Little League," Boyle said, "there are certain names you always have to think of. You think of Carl Stotz, the founder. You think of Creighton Hale. You think of Peter McGovern. And you've got to think about Luke LaPorta."

He is back in Williamsport, shaking hands and slapping shoulders, despite 14 of the roughest months of his life.

LaPorta's mother died in May. She was 89. "It was hard," LaPorta said. "Very hard." She died 11 months after LaPorta survived another scare, which he lightly refers to now as "the quadruple."

He had open heart surgery, a quadruple bypass. That was a year ago in June. Stephen Keener, the Little League president who on Friday was named chief executive officer as of November, said LaPorta's illness sent a shock wave through Little League Baseball. It also became a personal challenge to LaPorta, whose daughter, Lisa Marie, was getting married in July. He had promised to walk her down the aisle.

"You've got to have goals," LaPorta said. "If you don't, why do you want to get up in the morning?"

Three weeks after surgery, he was waiting in the church. A year ago this month, his friend Joe Janowski of Liverpool flew LaPorta to Williamsport for the World Series. LaPorta wanted to be there. He is only the second chairman Little League Baseball has ever had, and his main duty is calming the emotions that sometimes roil on the board.

At the reception Wednesday night, at every table, Little League administrators from towns and counties across the U.S. sipped beer or soda from plastic cups. They agreed that LaPorta is easy to approach, his manner less intimidating than some of Little League's more corporate-styled leaders.

"He's one of us," said Harold Weissman, a district administrator from New York City. "He doesn't forget the guy holding the shovel."

Yet LaPorta's time as chairman is nearing an end. He plans to step down in 1997, although he'll stay on as a member of the board. "What I told Stephen Keener is that I'd like to go one more year as chairman, and then take a break," said LaPorta, who wants more time to travel with his wife.

Still, that leaves LaPorta plenty of time to enjoy a job he loves. On Thursday, at a big Little League breakfast, LaPorta sat at the head table, next to ESPN sportscaster Jim Rooker. He presented a "Parents of the Year" award to Malcolm and Eleanor Mussina, whose son Mike — the Oriole pitcher — is a Little League alumnus.

Around town, LaPorta was hailed constantly as "Doc," derived from his doctorate in education. He never went far without being stopped. He comforted the widow of Little League's long-time South American administrator. He waded into a group of Japanese officials, who laughed in recognition upon seeing LaPorta. He promised some Puerto Rican coaches he would soon visit their league.

He learned of Little League in 1948. He read an article in the Saturday Evening Post that profiled Carl Stotz, the Williamsport man who founded the first Little League. The idea fascinated LaPorta, who was in graduate school at Syracuse University.

LaPorta had a whole philosophy of education. He maintained sports could reinforce responsibility and character in children. Those same principles were central to Stotz's Little League approach. LaPorta saw a chance to put his thesis into practice.

He made a pilgrimage to Williamsport. He hit it off with Stotz. In Liverpool, LaPorta started an infant league. Within a few years, that fledgling program blossomed into new leagues across Central New York.

"Like throwing seeds in the wind," LaPorta often says.

He remained close to Stotz and other national leaders. In the early 1950s, LaPorta endured the painful split between Stotz and Peter McGovern, who carried Little League into the 1980s. Stotz was reluctant to change any of his rules and dimensions. Other Little League officials quietly insisted change had to happen, such as lengthening the distance between home plate and the mound.

Stotz objected, unhappy with the whole direction of the program. Until his death 40 years later, even as Little League swept across the globe, Stotz remained exiled from his own creation. On Thursday, LaPorta stopped by the small field where Stotz's league played for the first time in 1939. It has the feel of a shrine.

"He was a great guy," LaPorta said of Stotz. "He was the one who started it. You always have to give that to Carl."

In 1984, after McGovern's death, LaPorta was elevated to chairman of the board. "It isn't an easy job," said Bud Vanderburg of Michigan, another board member. "People don't always agree. Luke's taken some shots. But he's always managed to hold things together."

Which in Williamsport makes him an accessible legend.

LaPorta is seen as a pioneer, a throwback. He knew Stotz. He knew McGovern in the early days. He remembers when volunteers built fields from overgrown lots, when Little League was not a multi-million dollar business. He has pushed Little League into new countries. He still maintains the most important contributors are all the moms or dads who break their backs to make it go.

"Just to be a part of it, to have seen it grow, that's the most satisfying thing," said LaPorta.

Then he walked onto the street, where men and women of every language and nationality called his name, seeking just a few minutes of his time. Luke was always on his way, but he always stopped to talk.

Luke LaPorta, now 78, retired as Little League chairman in 1998. He still sits on the national board of directors, one of the few left in Little League who actually knew Stotz. LaPorta said the recent scandals in the game — including the celebrated case of Danny Almonte, a 14-year-old pitcher from New York whose Little League coaches maintained that he was 12 — have not jaded him about the importance of youth baseball.

"People fudge in the pros, and they fudge in college," LaPorta said. "People fudge. You don't like it, but these things happen. The important things are still there — the friendships and learning the rules of the game. Ninety-nine percent of the time, it's still a true and positive thing."

◆ ◆ ◆

69 Mother's Voice Guides Player

Robert Perez will definitely call his mom tomorrow, for Mother's Day. He is thousands of miles away from her, playing in a city foreign to everything he knew as a child. A few good words make it seem a lot less lonely, so he hasn't been shy about placing that call.

Perez is the best hitter on the Syracuse Chiefs, maybe the hottest hitter in the International League. His average is hovering around .370. For three years now, he has been the kind of steady, talented player that Triple-A fans dream about. In his last two seasons at Syracuse, his cumulative average is .299, with 309 hits and 130 runs batted in.

Armed with numbers like those, he figured he was finally done with the minors. Perez started the year with the Major League Toronto Blue Jays. Last month, just before the regular season began, the Jays returned him to MacArthur Stadium. Perez was stunned. He thought he had proven everything he could in Syracuse.

"It is all very ... confusing," said Perez, hunting for the right word.

Those phone calls to his mother, Luisa, help him get by. She has never seen him play a professional game, and she didn't want him to play baseball in the first place. She lives in his home city of Bolivar, in Venezuela. During his brief stay with the Jays, she would edge up to the television screen, trying to glimpse her Robert in the dugout.

"She's always been there for me," Perez said. His mother was waiting every day when he got home from school. She didn't want him to box, a sport beloved by other men in his family. She pushed him to do well in his studies. And he recalled how she made all the difference on the night he almost died

He was 15 years old. A grown man stuck a knife in Robert's belly. He was afraid he would never walk out of the hospital.

Perez had simply been walking home that night when he passed some men drinking hard at a party. Three of them started taunting the kid, challenging him to fight. Perez tried to wave them off. But they were drunk, and he was a hotshot young athlete, and they attacked. Perez put up a struggle. One of the men pulled out the knife and stabbed Perez in the stomach.

Perez knew he'd been cut pretty bad. They rushed him to the hospital, and he can still smell the gas that knocked him out for surgery. Perez, as he faded, wondered if he'd live through it.

"When I woke up," Perez said, "the first thing I saw was my mother's face."

It helps explain why he never quits. Next month, he will turn 26. He is no kid, and he worries his time is running out. These years are his window to make the Major Leagues, to earn the kind of money he could lavish on his family. "I'll give them everything," he said. "A big house, everything."

Robert is the third of four boys. His father, Jesus, loves boxing, and that was the sport favored by Robert's older brothers. But his dad, worried about his sons, told Robert to try baseball. Even though the kid thrived at the game, his mother didn't want him to be a ballplayer.

Robert was a good student. She wanted him to be in class.

She cried when Toronto signed him, when he quit school and went away. "She still cries every time I leave," Perez said. Eventually, as he climbed through the minors and his paychecks improved, she came to accept his choice. If he was going to play baseball, she told him, take it all the way.

Being a Latino ballplayer in Syracuse can be a lonely thing. Few ballplayers ever feel a part of this town, and Perez is a continent away from his home. He is still working on his English. When he isn't at the ballpark, he either stays in his apartment or hangs around with other Chiefs.

Whenever Perez goes home to Venezuela, his mom tries to make it all up to him. She does his laundry, irons his clothes, fixes his favorite dish of black beans. It is hard to find a good Venezuelan meal in Syracuse, and he said no one here does beans like Luisa.

He has spent a good part of his career in this city. This is where Perez first saw snow. He reacted like a kid. He had a teammate take pictures as he sprawled in the stuff, waving his arms and making an angel. The snapshots went straight to his family, who struggled to imagine their world covered with ice.

Still, seeing snow once was plenty for Perez. This spring, he felt sure he'd make the jump to the majors.

It didn't happen. Perez remains unsure of why Toronto sent him down. It was a hard thing, going from glamour in the SkyDome to the rust of Big Mac. As soon as Perez got the tough news, he picked up the phone and called his mother. She felt so bad that again she burst out in tears, but then she recovered to do a mother's job.

"Go there and play hard," she said. "Show them how they made a mistake."

He is a good son, and he is doing as she asked.

Robert Perez would go on to lead the 1996 Blue Jays in batting with a
.327 average in 202 at bats, although he soon began a five-team Major league
odyssey that would — as of this writing — land him back in the International
League, with the Columbus Clippers.

◆ ◆ ◆

70 A Runner Who Can't Get Home

Nothing much has changed since the last time Lenny Haymon saw his bedroom.

His bed has gone unused for the past three months. It remains covered by a blanket with a pattern of ballplayers. At the top of the bed is a faded Power Rangers pillow, a pillow that Lenny — at 14 — was not quite ready to throw out.

Sneakers and baseball cleats are still in a jumble near his old Cub Scout books. His mother, Joan Haymon, refuses to wash away the elaborate pencil signatures on the white paint of the bedroom door, where Lenny practiced a dramatic autograph.

Beneath red and green academic ribbons, beneath a nearly year-old 14th birthday card from his grandma and grandpa, a shelf holds Lenny's many trophies. Among them is a scuffed baseball, covered with childish signatures, from Auburn's Sandlot League. Four years ago, Lenny pitched and won the championship game.

Next to it, white and shiny, is a New York-Penn League baseball signed by all the Auburn Doubledays, a gift from the team first sent to Lenny's room at University Hospital.

It is the one thing in his bedroom Lenny's never touched.

The Pitch

Lenny Haymon was not among the 1,045 fans who pushed through the turnstiles June 30 at Auburn's Falcon Park, where the Doubledays played the Vermont Expos on a warm Friday night. But Lenny was there, milling around with other boys outside the North Division Street entrance to the ballpark, all of them hoping for a chance at a foul ball.

Some kids, such as 13-year-old Matt Dagnesi, planned to trade in their foul balls for two free tickets at the gate, a Doubledays policy aimed at salvaging high-quality baseballs. Others simply wanted a ball as a souvenir. Few spectators gave those boys a second thought. Over 42 years of minor league baseball in Auburn, no one could remember serious injuries caused by kids chasing foul balls.

The young men playing the game were hardly thinking of those boys beyond the gate. The Expos were more worried about Auburn pitcher Jose Calvo. He struck out the first five hitters he faced. By the top of the fourth, when Vermont's Phil Downing stepped to the plate with one away, Calvo still had not given up a hit.

Auburn catcher Ryan McGrath, 23, saw this next hitter as a problem. Downing, a lefty, was batting .346. In Vermont, he had hurt the Doubledays by pulling the ball hard to right.

Ahead on the count, with a ball and two strikes, McGrath called for a fastball, just outside.

Calvo, 20, a fastball pitcher, liked the call. For him, the game had become a celebration. He grew up in Panama City, often knocking around an old tennis ball with his buddies at a city park. The kids scrounged for tattered hand-me-down baseball gloves. For bats, they'd use tree limbs they cut down with machetes.

One day, a stranger, a grown man, watched Calvo playing catcher in a pickup game. The man was a scout. He was impressed by Calvo's arm. He helped Calvo evolve into a pitcher. In 1999, the Houston Astros assigned Calvo to Auburn, a little city in the Class A New York-Penn League, the lowest level of minor league ball.

"All of my dreams," Calvo said, "are of playing baseball."

On June 30, with two strikes on Downing, Calvo threw the fastball McGrath asked him to throw, placing it just a little bit outside.

Downing called it "a pitch that I could drive."

The Fan

Hours earlier, Lenny Haymon had waited for his mother and his older sister, Amanda, to come home. He wanted to tell them he was going to the Doubledays game. Lenny and Amanda are barely a year apart. They bickered constantly, although they shared a bond that made their mom laugh out loud — such as the night when they stayed up in Amanda's room until 4 a.m., hip-hop teens singing along to country and western, bellowing out the words to Deana Carter's "Did I Shave My Legs For This?"

"From the time they've been little," Joan said, "it's been just me and the kids."

A working mother, she raised her children by herself. Their father moved out when they were toddlers. The older kids helped Joan paint and fix up their small house. Eight years ago, Joan gave birth to her third child, Nicky, who quickly decided he would be just like his brother — even adopting Lenny's passion for the Dallas Cowboys.

Lenny, this fall, would have been starting the ninth grade at Auburn High School. He loved sports, and he loved going to Falcon Park. After his Little League team won a championship, Lenny got to stand on the field during the national anthem. As the boy grew older, Joan allowed Lenny to join his buddies at the games.

On June 30, Amanda was lying on the couch when Lenny left the house, in a good mood. He had a little money in his pocket for the game, a few dollars he had earned that day mowing a neighbor's lawn.

"You going to lie there all night, you lazy bum?" Lenny asked.

"You're a lazy bum," Amanda needled back.

Lenny walked past a 9-foot basket on a pole, near his driveway. More than anything, the boy wanted to dunk the ball. He practiced so often he wore away the grass, often leaping from a crate beneath the rim. Finally, one day, he asked Joan to come outside. She watched as Lenny, triumphantly, ran, jumped and jammed.

Three months later, beneath the hoop, the grass has all grown back.

The Hit

Phil Downing, the batter, was living his own dream.

He was still a little stunned just to have a pro contract. In his hometown of Salt Lake City, he never started on his high school team. The son of a dentist, he considered going into medicine. Instead, Downing became a "walk-on" starter at the University of Southern Utah. In his senior year, he transferred to Arizona State and batted .355. Montreal, impressed, drafted him in the 15th round.

Within days of graduating, he was with the Vermont Expos.

"From what I know, from high school, I'm the only one from my team still playing," said Downing, 22. "It makes you feel great. There was a time when nobody thought I was worth anything."

Calvo had struck out Downing in the first inning. Three innings later, Calvo recalls, he again picked up two quick strikes on Downing. When

Calvo threw the outside fastball, Downing went after it. He fouled the ball away. It sailed out of sight, beyond the third base bleachers.

In the street, it was exactly what the boys were waiting for. Matt Dagnesi felt that jolt of jubilation when a foul ball touches down. A crowd of boys bolted into the street. One of them was Lenny Haymon, a kid Dagnesi knew casually from playing football in a buddy's back yard. Dagnesi prepared to follow. He looked up, saw a car, stopped himself just at the curb.

Terrified, he shouted for his buddies to watch out.

From the mound, Calvo heard the squeal of brakes. Downing was already focused on the next pitch. He dug in and ripped a single, breaking up Calvo's no-hitter.

"I had no idea what was going on until they pulled us off the field," Downing said. "It didn't even dawn on me that it could have been my foul ball."

The Driver

Just minutes before Downing fouled off Calvo's pitch, Donald Pettit got into a blue 1986 Chevrolet parked outside the Ukrainian National Club on Cottage Street, according to Auburn police reports. On his way home, Pettit later told police, he drove toward the nearby ballpark.

Pettit, 50, of Port Byron, already had one alcohol-related mark on his record from 1995, a conviction for driving while ability impaired. He would later tell police he drank five beers in the hours before he got into his car. Cathy Simmons, the Ukrainian Club manager, said Pettit drank only two beers while she was bartending. He had seemed ready to leave earlier in the evening, Simmons said.

But Pettit bumped into a man he'd once worked with, Simmons said. The two men hung around and talked at the club. Simmons said it's pointless to wonder if that encounter made the difference, if Lenny Haymon might be laughing with his friends today if Pettit had skipped that last conversation.

"I'm a firm believer," Simmons said, "that what's going to be is going to be."

The Witness

William Breck, 43, was driving to a corner store, along North Division Street. He was approaching Falcon Park when a baseball bounced across the street. "Four or five boys" bolted directly into traffic, Breck said. Lenny, who was trailing the pack, was wearing a Walkman. Breck watched as a blue Chevrolet, two cars in front of him, smashed into Lenny and threw him, hard, into the air.

"I can still see it," Breck said. "Another second, and he would have been clear."

Breck hit the brakes. He ran to the side of the boy curled in the road. Breck and Bill Canino, another witness, both used their cell phones to call for an ambulance. "Help's coming," Breck said, but Lenny did not respond. The driver of the blue car, Breck said, walked out to look at Lenny. Several witnesses said the driver, as if in shock, went back to his car and lit up a cigarette.

The ball had settled in some tall grass across the street, where Canino saw one kid continuing to hunt for it. For everyone else, the ball had lost all meaning. Paramedics from the ballpark rushed to help the injured boy. Breck watched as emergency crews got out a stretcher. Breck had gone through all this before, with his own son. He knew—all too well—how the boy's family would feel.

Joshua Breck was 4 in 1983, playing in a sandbox on a November day, when an animal escaped from a neighbor's pen. The animal—described in newspaper reports as being half-dog and half-wolf—attacked the child. It locked its jaws around his head. Josh survived, with neurological damage.

Something in the face of Lenny Haymon made Breck think of his son. "Such a good-looking kid," Breck said, "with so much going for him."

The Aftermath

Terry Winslow, an Auburn fire captain, arrived quickly at Falcon Park. His firefighters helped to wheel the motionless boy toward the field, through a birthday party in the Doubledays' party tent. Dan Mahoney, the team's general manager at that time, hurried to home plate and spoke with Kenneth Durham, 23, a first-year umpire.

Durham waved both teams off the field.

No one in the bleachers or the dugouts made a sound. A chopper landed, pounding the air above the field, but emergency crews decided Lenny was too fragile to fly to Syracuse. He was taken by ambulance to Auburn Memorial Hospital. Paramedics established an airway for the boy, allowing Lenny to be flown to University Hospital.

Investigators took Pettit into custody. According to police reports, his blood alcohol level was 0.11 percent, making him legally drunk. Pettit, whose case is pending, would plead innocent to driving while intoxicated and vehicular assault.

Calvo, his arm tight from the long break in the game, went to the showers. Auburn wound up winning, 4-3. No one really cared, after what they all had seen. Calvo thought instead of his childhood in Panama, how he'd chase foul balls with his friends near a local stadium. He thought of his little nephew, back home, who now does the same thing.

Durham, the young umpire, was also lost in memory. Years ago, when he was a boy in Texas, his father had rushed home with terrifying news. Durham's little brother had been running to get ice cream at a Dairy Queen. He darted into the street without looking. A car ran down the boy. The doctors weren't sure he would make it.

The child lived. Lenny Haymon brought all of it back.

"I was in shock," Durham said. He hurried to his hotel and called his younger brother, the one who many years ago had survived the same thing.

"He told me to get (Lenny) a card, to try and see him, that it would mean something (to the family)," Durham said.

Phil Downing, who hit the ball, struggled most of all. He tried to call his parents. They were away, camping. Tim Leiper, Vermont's manager, took Downing aside. He told his young outfielder that it was not his fault. He told him that no human being can control the arc of a foul ball.

Downing was not so easy to console.

"It shouldn't have had to happen," Downing said, weeks later. "For a while, I couldn't stop thinking about it. Even now, it kind of keeps coming back to me. Any single thing could have made it different. If I get a curveball instead of a fastball. If the guy who hit the kid just took longer to get there.

"I wish," he said, "I could do something to make it different."

Lenny's Room

This is what you find on the walls of Lenny's bedroom:

A school project on Picasso, hanging above his bed.

A "phone tree" for his youth basketball team.

A Nerf backboard, rim missing from too many Lenny slams.

A rack holding every Little League and Babe Ruth League cap Lenny ever wore.

Behind those caps, half-hidden, a photograph of Lenny and Amanda, now 16, laughing together as babies.

A poster, handwritten in many different colors, listing what Lenny called, "RULES FOR MY ROOM."

    1.) Don't go through my stuff when I'm not there, or even when I'm there.

2.) No jumping on the bed.

3.) No calling names, especially sware words.

4.) If you want to fight, take it outside.

5.) Don't take my cards out of my card holders, especially my Todd Day. It's worth lots of money.

6.) No spitting.

Beneath those rules, Lenny drew a smiley face.

Behind his bed, inside a closet, you will find two brown shoe boxes.

Lenny used one of them to store all the baseball gloves he'd ever owned.

The other box is filled with grass-stained baseballs and softballs.

Some are foul balls Lenny brought home from Falcon Park, bearing the stamped signature of Robert Julian, New York-Penn League president.

They are treasures the boy put in a box, to keep them safe.

Joan's Wish

Lenny survived, despite profound head injuries. He has yet to come home from University Hospital. Visitors say he remains in a coma-like state. Three months after the accident, on her lawyer's orders, Joan Haymon cannot speak of Lenny's progress.

But Joan and her children make a daily drive to Syracuse, spending long hours with Lenny in his room.

The boy's condition remains on the mind of Durham, the umpire who put every ball in play that night. And McGrath, the catcher who called for the fastball, just outside. And Calvo, the pitcher who threw it so precisely. And Downing, who still suffers because he swung the bat.

As for Joan Haymon, Lenny's mom, she is the keeper of the wish, the wish that joins these strangers somehow linked by that foul ball:

They all wait, day by day, for Lenny to come home.

In the summer of 2002, two years after he was run down while chasing the foul ball, Lenny Haymon came home. He suffers from occasional seizures. Joan is still working. She needs nursing help at night, when she needs to sleep. Lenny has yet to talk, although Joan believes— at least once— Lenny tried to say, "Mom."

On the whole, his progress is beyond what his mother had expected. Lenny often smiles. He hums. He can clasp a visitor's hand. He blinks his eyes for yes and no. His mother describes his reactions, at times, as bordering on playful.

"He's in there," Joan says. "He's definitely in there."

As for Donald Pettit, he was convicted of a misdemeanor count of driving while intoxicated. He was sentenced to 60 days in jail and three years on probation.

◆ ◆ ◆

71 A Player, a Coach, a Lover of Game

The old Stars Park was off West Genesee Street, and the kids knew where all the baseballs would roll. Children would haunt the perimeter of the outfield fence, and sooner or later a home run would come their way. They'd grab it, rip off the cover, unwind the string to the core and tie it back into a clump.

Then they played in the street, using open palms to hit the ball, thus avoiding broken windows in the old West End of Syracuse.

That is how Adam Markowski learned the game. The Stars were the top farm club for the St. Louis Cardinals, and the boys collected the team's discarded broken bats, then nailed and taped them together. They ran suits to the cleaners for the Stars' equipment manager, who charged the players $1 for a 50-cent job but gave the young errand boys none of that cream.

The boys did it for free to be close to the team. The equipment man would name his favorites to be batboys. Young Adam became one. When Babe Ruth brought a barnstorming team through Syracuse, Markowski sat next to him on the bench. He has one crystal image of the big man laughing, patting him on the leg, telling the excited boy, "Take it easy, kid."

Seven decades later, with another spring thaw announcing the season, Markowski watches baseball in the dark wooden den of his Geddes home. It is a welcome change from what bothers him about basketball, ranting players and coaches in the mold of Bobby Knight. Markowski can't understand any man who acts bigger than the game.

Because the games go on. Always.

He was a coach himself and he is 79 years old, intimate with so much

of this city's sporting life. At one point, the mantle in his den was thick with trophies, but he has divided them among his three grown children. He is the kind of man who takes care of those things.

Markowski has cancer of the larynx. The doctors told him they could try to cut it away, but the surgery would come with no guarantees. He turned it down. He took the best of whatever time he might get.

His children wish he would come and stay with them. He prefers to watch the games in this den he built himself. He is a broad-shouldered man, quick in conversation, memory exact. He drives his car and gets around the house all right. Outside of his voice, which has been reduced to a whisper, he does not seem so ill. The whisper is his way of offering the truth.

"I'm on the list," he said. "Three, maybe four weeks." He shrugged, dark eyes focused on something outside. If what is coming frightens him, he offers no sign. "Scared of what?" Markowski asked. "When I was a young man, I would have been scared."

In those days, he had a wife and little ones to worry about. But his wife, Jean, has been gone for four years. His kids are adults. So he walks the house, and he works over the thing. He suspects when it ends, it really does end. "That's what I think," he said. "What about you?" The old coach listens carefully to the answer.

Markowski is what was once called a sportsman. He was a ballplayer, then a coach. He was born into trolleys and mitts without webbing. Now, the kids wear mirrored visors and swing metal bats. Still, some things are the same. Markowski watches the games. In conversation, he will pantomime a move to the hoop or casually step into a mock batting stance.

As a kid, when the thaw came, he picked up his glove. He was an outfielder, a small boy who hit for average. His father, a tailor who came to Syracuse from Austria, thought the game was a waste of time. Markowski kept playing.

These days, he worries about parents who push their children too hard, "Guys who couldn't play ball who see themselves in their kids." He spoke of a youth baseball coach who told Markowski's son to shift his back leg when he hit. "His back leg," Markowski exclaimed, dropping into a stance, shifting the wrong foot. "Imagine that."

At the old Central High he was a star athlete, and then he took a scholarship on the hill and played three sports. Markowski knew Bud Wilkinson when he was a young SU football assistant. He was a teammate

Opposite: **Adam Markowski (third from left, standing) on a semipro team from Auburn, N.Y., in the 1940s. (Judy Caputo)**

of Jim Konstanty, the major-league pitcher who played third base for the Orange.

He speaks of them, worried all the time about how his story will be told. "Don't overdo it, all right?" he asks.

Overdo it? In 1938, the New York Giants played an exhibition against some upstate all-stars in Truxton, the hometown of John McGraw. Markowski was in right field. The papers said he made a fine running catch. What he remembers more clearly is going 5-for-5 around that time in some factory league, in a game that ensured he'd get a few extra bucks.

He had an offer to play pro ball in the North Country. He turned it down to earn more in a blanket factory. He got out of SU with his master's in education, and he tried to get a teaching job, but he said nobody liked a name ending in "ski."

An SU counselor suggested he anglicize the spelling, and he became "Mark Adam." He got a job. Fifty years later, it gnaws at him that he had to make the change. When he returned from World War II, he again used his true name.

He taught for a while, then took a job at General Electric. He coached baseball and basketball at Sacred Heart in the late '50s, when the school was a Parochial League power. Crowds of 6,000 sometimes watched his team in the playoffs at the old War Memorial.

All of this is told in a whisper from his den. Baseball was his first love, always his favorite. For years, he had a friend tied to the New York Yankees who'd get him choice seats. That is how he and his son, Jody, came to be in Yankee Stadium for the fifth game of the 1956 World Series, when Don Larsen threw his perfect game at the Dodgers.

Markowski recalls the trajectory of the final pitch, the way Dale Mitchell watched it sail outside but was nailed with a called strike. The umpire's arm shot up, triggering an instant of communal disbelief. The unthinkable had happened, a feeling Markowski still struggles to describe.

"I had my boy with me," he said. "That was the best, to be with your son at a moment like that."

He and Jody joined with thousands flowing down upon the diamond. Markowski snapped a photo of the 10-year-old amid the infield crowd. No one broke down the walls, or ripped up the grass. They walked the field with respect, and they left when it was time.

Markowski died almost a month to the day after this column appeared in the Post-Standard.

◆ ◆ ◆

72 His Latest Case Hits Close to Home

Gerry Sabloski, in many ways, is the classic street cop. Baggy trench coat, hands in pockets, a dry and edgy humor. In 28 years of probing homicides, he learned to keep a philosopher's distance.

Until the Syracuse police sergeant was assigned to the killing of a friend he called "Pah-boots."

"I hope it hit him like an airplane," Sabloski said. "I hope he didn't feel it."

John Pobutkiewicz (pronounced pa-BOOT-kavich) died Sunday. He lived on Park Avenue, in the old Polish neighborhood where Sabloski grew up. Many people knew Pobutkiewicz by the nickname "Johnny Morgan." To childhood friends, however, he remained Pah-boots.

Pah-boots, 52, stood maybe 5-foot-2. He was attacked around 11 p.m. Friday. He had just left the Oakdale Grill on Apple Street, the bar Sabloski's steelworking father used to speak of as "the office."

Two teen-agers, police say, grabbed Pah-boots from behind. They kicked him, choked him, beat him with a wooden stick. They broke his pelvis, cracked his ribs, put him in a coma.

They took $10 from his pocket and left him lying there.

Sabloski learned early Saturday that he was on the case. He went to University Hospital to visit Pah-boots in the ICU. Officially, the doctors said, Pah-boots was alive. But it was clear, to Sabloski, that his friend's soul had moved on.

Later that day, police arrested Jamie Rolfe, 18, and Marcelle Smith, 17. Sabloski helped to question them. He is a realist. Sabloski isn't shocked anymore by assaults for a few dollars. But even Sabloski couldn't understand why Pah-boots had to die.

"He was the little guy you see at the end of the bar, the little guy you see in the grocery, the little guy who always comes around with the parlay," Sabloski said.

As a child, Pah-boots was the little guy at second base. "Like Luis Aparicio," Sabloski said, referring to a tiny legend of the major leagues.

More than anything, to Sabloski, Pah-boots is linked with baseball.

The *Post-Standard*, Monday, December 1, 1997

They played together in an era when mitts dangled from handlebars, when kids never gave up on a ball lost in tall grass, when the tramping of feet wore baselines in the weeds.

In the 1950s, many adults in their neighborhood still spoke Polish. The streets carried the sharp aroma of boiling sausage. The dads worked in factories and drank beer at the corner. And the kids lived for baseball, in the same way that so many city kids live for basketball today.

"We played sandlot ball at Frazer Park," Sabloski said. "We'd have five games going at once. We'd play until our mothers came and dragged us home. Pah-boots was a second baseman, 4-foot-5, 4-foot-6, who could really go after the ball.

"At the plate he was a slap hitter. No one moved back when he came up, but you'd pitch and he'd hit a Texas Leaguer to right field. Then he'd get on base and it'd be yip, yip, yip, yip, always talking."

When the kids finished, as dusk set in, they would all leap into the unfenced public pool they called "Polio Bay."

Mrs. Pobutkiewicz, Sabloski said, worked as a cook at the Sacred Heart cafeteria. The whole neighborhood knew her. The family had a big front porch. When it poured in the summer, the kids would gather at Pah-boots' to play cards and watch the rain.

All of this swept across Sabloski on a raw November weekend, as he tracked teen-age killers on the streets where he once played.

"Those were the days," Sabloski said, "of proprietary interest."

To Sabloski, those words describe the best way to fight crime. City neighbors, he said, once took care of their own. Mothers leaned out windows, scolding other people's kids. If a father was a bum and a mom was a big drinker, other families on the street gave safe haven to the kids.

Today? For a moment, the tough street cop didn't sound so tough. Sabloski reflected on absentee landlords and runaway fathers and 14-year-olds who settle petty beefs with handguns. "Proprietary interest," as he puts it, is often hard to find.

He last felt it in the ICU, above the waste of Pah-boots.

Gerry Sabloski, at 55, still works as a detective for the Syracuse Police Department. He thinks of "Pah-boots" all the time, he says.

"I'll still see a flower sometimes at the spot where it happened," Sabloski says. "I'll be traveling and I'll see the most remote thing, a ballfield or a red wagon, and it'll make me think of him. Anyplace, anywhere, anytime. Life goes on, but I think about it."

As for his police work, he plans to retire before long. "I seen enough,"

Sabloski says, speaking in the summer of 2002, when street violence in Syracuse is at a particularly crazed pitch. "Time to sit down, hang up the spikes, and let the other kids play."

◆ ◆ ◆

73 Johnny Does It All

Johnny O'Neill, the experts say, will never ride a bike. He wants that beyond anything, but it can't be done. How can a boy whose legs won't bend pump the pedals or turn corners? It is impossible, unthinkable.

In the meantime, there's karate.

"He loves speed," says Linda Pascarella-O'Neill, who has learned it does no good to warn her son to slow it down.

Johnny is a first-grader, and his life for six years has been filled with obstacles. The doctors told Linda there was no way Johnny would stand and walk, much less throw a baseball or climb stairs or shoot hoops or turn a cartwheel.

His right arm is half-formed. His left hand has three fingers. His legs cannot support him. Each one is pinned and braced. He was born with severe limb deformities. As an infant, he began a sequence of leg surgeries that will continue for the rest of his life. The alternative is amputation.

That all sounds very sad unless you talk to Johnny, who grabs your sleeve as he roars like his idol, the T-Rex.

Johnny walks. He climbs the stairs. He plays T-ball in Liverpool and throws a baseball like a rocket. He kicks a soccer ball endlessly off the garage wall. He is learning to play tennis. The karate lessons will start soon.

And his mother keeps looking for some way to get the kid onto a bike.

Johnny attends Blessed Sacrament Elementary School in Eastwood. Last year, in an "acrojazz" show for a school assembly, he took a running

start, dipped his shoulder and ripped off a full cartwheel. The place went nuts. Johnny glowed.

"Was I surprised?" asks his mother. "I'm always surprised."

Johnny lives in Liverpool. He is Linda's only child. He was born in California, after Linda left Syracuse and married Shane O'Neill.

The couple, from the outside, had an ideal life. Linda was administrative director of a cardiac surgery transplant center. She became pregnant. A child, to her, seemed the final, perfect piece.

Linda's old life ended in delivery. Johnny's limbs stopped developing in the first weeks of pregnancy. There was no warning. At first, Linda says, "I was in complete shock." She and Shane, quickly, had to make their choices.

A top California surgeon wanted to amputate Johnny's legs. The couple decided instead on a surgical process advanced by Dr. Dror Paley in Baltimore. It involved setting and resetting pins as Johnny's legs stretched out. Linda began a grueling schedule of flying coast to coast.

Linda quit her job, which she says had shaped her sense of self-esteem. She turned for support to her family in Liverpool. It made sense, with all the traveling, for Linda to move home. Shane stayed in California. The couple grew apart. They separated, without hard feelings. Shane remains a devoted, involved father.

As for Linda, she searched for meaning in the way everything changed. She sees Johnny's spirit, his courage, as a lesson from God. She does not pretend that she is always perfect or patient. But her mission is preparing her son for what he'll face.

"She's an amazing mother," says Andrea Polcaro, principal at Blessed Sacrament. "Sometimes we try to shelter our children so much they are unprepared for life. Johnny has not been raised to face life that way."

Johnny loves dinosaurs. He has a dinosaur village set up in his basement. Last summer, Linda called Steve Wilson—coach of a T-ball team in Liverpool—and asked if it was all right for her son to play. She explained his disabilities. Steve said it was fine, although he assumed Johnny wouldn't be much of a player.

He did not expect a kid who catches the ball left-handed, wedges his mitt beneath his right armpit, and then fires off a left-handed throw. "He might have had the best arm on our team," Wilson says.

Wilson was blown away by Johnny's sense of humor. When Johnny took the field for the first time, the other team stared. Johnny stared back.

Opposite: **Johnny O'Neill, Liverpool, N.Y., 1997. (Lisa Krantz, *Post-Standard.*)**

He dropped his mitt and bent forward and held his arms at a perfect angle. He was a dinosaur, a T-Rex, master of the Earth. He opened his mouth and let out a roar.

The kids bellowed with laughter. Then they all played ball.

Johnny, Linda says, is a normal little boy. He is good-natured and affectionate, but he is not a saint. When he wants something, he'll pester his mother. He'll whine and complain if he wants to delay bedtime. He stalls when his mom calls for him to come inside.

He is a 6-year-old first-grader, and Linda's glad he acts like one.

"He knows how to manipulate," Linda says. In a way, she admires that. She respects his courage. She respects his resilience. He is a handsome child. He is also bright. That intelligence, at times, will not make things easier.

Linda knows, pretty soon, he will start to wonder. Why he can't walk through a mall without all the stares. Why God made him so different from most of his friends. Why things most kids do easily are hard for him to master.

That time has not yet come. Today, Johnny is a kid who throws a baseball fast and true, who draws a smiling self-portrait that shows his arms just as they are. After school, in the parking lot, he tugs at his mom's coat, chattering about what he did in class that day, chattering until a kid zooms past on a bike.

Johnny stares at the bike, and his mother stares at Johnny. They say nothing. There is silence.

In the meantime, there's karate.

Johnny O'Neill is now 12 years old. He played two more years of Little League before he decided to give up baseball. His new passion is golf, another sport in which Johnny can still hit the ball hard.

In November 2002, in Syracuse, Johnny's legs were amputated. It was a decision that his parents allowed him to reach by himself. The first days after the surgery were difficult, as Johnny literally mourned for his missing legs.

Around Syracuse, the community rose up in support. Johnny received visits from such celebrities as Ronan Tynan, the famed Irish tenor and Paralympic champion who is also a double amputee. By June 2003, when Johnny graduated from elementary school, he was able to use his new prosthetic legs to walk to the altar in Blessed Sacrament Church, where he received his diploma.

And he was already hoping, in the coming months, to see if prosthetic legs just might make it possible for him to ride a bike.

◆ ◆ ◆

74 A Glove a Boy Will Love

It was Holy Saturday, and I was running late. I was supposed to buy a couple of baseball gloves for the boys, gloves that would be a surprise on Easter Sunday, and my wife expected me home within an hour. But the store had an entire wall of mitts and gloves, and my youngest son throws the ball left-handed, and none of this was something a dad does in a hurry.

Besides, I was jealous of the guy next to me.

He was my age, 40ish, and he was there with both his father and his own little boy. Buying a glove for the kid obviously meant as much to them as it meant to me, and my counterpart kept pulling gloves off the rack — patterned gloves, striped gloves, gloves smelling of rich leather — and the little boy would slide each one onto his hand.

The old man stood behind them, offering a final judgment: "Not that one," he would say. "His hand's going to grow."

I watched them, feeling lost. Hunting for a glove isn't what it used to be. I've coached Little League baseball for five or six years, and I'm amazed at the end of every season by the gloves some kids simply leave behind: Expensive gloves from big-name companies, gloves on which these kids never bothered to sign their names. I save them. Sooner or later, there's always a kid on my team who needs a glove.

Still, for some of us, a glove once had the importance of a wedding ring. I still have the glove I used in Little League, a tattered green Wilson from the early 1970s. I remember the moment in the store when I found it. I wore it with a pair of white spikes, a kind of steel town tribute to the Oakland A's, whose flamboyance first made that exotica all right.

A glove was precious. We all called them our "mitts," even if that wasn't technically correct, and we wrote our names on each one in big block letters. Once we'd get a glove, we'd keep it for years.

We'd break it in by slamming a ball into it, around the house. When we batted, we'd make sure we knew exactly where we put our glove. Leave your glove on the handlebars when you ran into the store, and it would often vanish before you got back.

We all knew kids growing up in chaos, kids who got beatings but never got a brand-new glove. Sometimes they'd show up after school with a "used" glove they'd say came from a brother or a friend, often with a big square of ink where someone else's name had been.

My second glove said everything about the way my mom and dad saw baseball. It was a gift for my confirmation, the ceremonial moment when a Catholic junior high kid officially accepts the Holy Spirit. Instead of a medal or a cross, my folks bought me this fine new Rawlings to use in our Babe Ruth League.

We were usually broke. We rented our house. Somehow, my folks found the cash to buy this glove. It is still my backup glove for softball, and it is the glove I hand to any visitor who wants to play some catch, and I keep it in the Little League equipment bag when I'm coaching — just because I kind of like to have it there.

But now, on this Holy Saturday, I needed gloves for my own little boys. I stood there, thinking of running home from school to join a flood of kids at a vacant lot called Jacob's Field, where over the years we wore the base paths into the grass. I thought of playing catch with my father in the street — a street that was all ours until the steel-plant whistle caused a flood of afternoon traffic- and how my father threw the ball while smoking a cigarette.

Then I thought of the last week of my father's life. My brothers weren't that alarmed as they sat with him in the hospital, watching the World Series between the Dodgers and the A's. I called and I got my father on the phone, and he said — in a voice from faraway, another world — "Where are you? I just saw you at the game."

I was four hours away, in Oswego. My father fell asleep and died.

In the store, the time to buy two new gloves was growing short. I knew my wife was already wondering where I was. I tried to stuff my adult hand into a little kid's left-handed glove, and I turned to my counterpart, standing next to me. "Can I borrow your son?" I asked, and he laughed and said sure, and his little boy tried on the left-handed glove for me. It fit, and that left me with one final task — to buy the first quality glove my 10-year-old boy would ever own.

It came down to a hard choice between buying a larger, more expensive Louisville Slugger glove or a smaller, cheaper glove that would fit him better now. I went back and forth, thinking about our budget and what the kid would really want, all the time knowing that my wife needed me home.

The decision was simply too much to make alone. I stuck the glove under my arm and hurried out into the store, where the grandfather was waiting for my counterpart to check out with their stuff. I tapped the old man on the back, and I said to him, "My 10-year-old needs a glove. I like this one, but I think maybe it's too big and it's too much."

The old man looked at me, and understood. He took the glove and ran his hand in and out many times, squeezed it, pounded it, all the time nodding his head.

"This," he said, "is the kind of glove a boy will love."

I bought it. He gave me that second confirmation.

◆ ◆ ◆

75 Ball Field Heroes Pay Respects to the Real Thing

The chance to meet a New York Yankee.

Tom Giordano had looked forward to that moment since his childhood in Brooklyn, since the days when he'd go out in the street with his buddies and swing a broomstick at a rubber ball they'd cut in half, so the kid who was pitching could make the "ball" dive and hook.

That was 30 years ago. Giordano's uncle loved the Yankees, and the boy absorbed the passion. He didn't care that the team was going nowhere. He didn't care that Tom Seaver's New York Mets owned the spotlight and the glamour, out in Queens.

"Horace Clarke, Jake Gibbs, I made it through all those years," Giordano said, recalling not-so-famous Yankee mainstays of the time. He stuck with the Yanks when they were down, and he watched them slowly build to this newest dynasty, to this team of resilient grace now battling Seattle.

Two weeks ago, three of those Yankees—including Derek Jeter—came unannounced to Giordano's place of work. He couldn't be there. He is fire captain for the "Red Hook Raiders" in Brooklyn, home to Ladder Company 101. When the Yankees walked in, shocking all the regulars, Giordano was at the home of Linda Maffeo.

The *Post-Standard*, Friday, October 19, 2001

"I was at the right place," Giordano said. "That's where I was supposed to be."

On Sept. 11, as the twin towers burned, Linda's husband, Joe, and six other Red Hook firefighters rushed to the World Trade Center. Giordano, off duty, was walking his dog. He learned of the attacks when he snapped on the radio.

Giordano sped to work, got his equipment and raced into Manhattan. The towers had collapsed. The city was lost in smoke.

"I find one of my guys, just a kid, sitting on the curb, covered with dust, just sitting there," Giordano said. "He's saying, over and over, "Cap. They're all gone.'"

Seven guys lost. Giordano went through their lockers at the firehouse. With the permission of the families, he made a little shrine. He started off with a Sal Calabro cigar, because Sal loved a good smoke, and he found small tools or photographs in the other lockers, and he kept going until he kept a piece of each of them.

Then, with his men, he started "visiting the wives," a routine that has continued every night for the last month. Giordano would eventually guide those women, as a group, through the rubble of "ground zero," the only place where they could fully comprehend why their husbands have not been found.

"Pretty tough," Giordano said. "I find myself coming to work and being angry. All these guys, and they aren't going to come back."

Two weeks ago, he was at the Maffeo house—comforting Joe's wife and playing with their 1-year-old son—when Derek Jeter, Tino Martinez and Gerald Williams walked in the firehouse door.

The startled Red Hook firefighters quickly called their captain.

"My guy calls and says, "Cap, I got someone who wants to talk to you,' and he puts on Jeter," Giordano said. "He gets on and he's calling me sir. He says, "This is Derek Jeter, sir,' and I tell him (expletive) and he says, "No, sir, this is Derek Jeter.' Calling me sir! What a gentleman! What a guy! You know he's got parents who brought him up right.

"I got tongue-tied. I didn't know what to say. I just told him to take a lot of pictures with the guys, and he said, "Yes, sir,' and that was it."

That conversation means more than Giordano can explain. With these Yankees, October baseball has become almost routine. Last year brought the most electric New York series of them all, with the firehouse split between the Mets and the Yanks. Feelings were so intense that fans of the two teams watched the games in separate rooms.

At Red Hook, Giordano said, the sport is like religion. The ladder company softball team, the Red Hook Raiders, plays in a league based near

Coney Island. Last summer, the Raiders went deep into the playoffs. Calabro, Tommy Kennedy and Patrick Byrne — three of the seven men lost at the twin towers— played important roles in that success.

At first, Giordano didn't want the team to play again. "Now I think next year, maybe (we play) and dedicate it to them," he said.

The three guys from the softball team were also Yankee fans. They would have loved to know how Jeter stopped by and called them "heroes." The captain takes comfort in that thought, when he can. Each new shift brings raw grief from 23 firefighters "who are more like my own kids," and then Giordano goes out to "visit with the wives," before he goes home and tries to smile for his family.

Amid all that, it's nice to know the Yanks are still alive.

Epilogue

It ends amid gray tombstones on a hot Saturday afternoon in August, a few drops of rain falling from a pewter sky. Not far away, the Tapanzee Bridge carries New York State Thruway traffic across the Hudson River. Cars and trucks are backed up in an hour-long nightmare.

But it is almost closing time at Kensico Cemetery in Valhalla, the final resting place of Lou and Eleanor Gehrig, a place you have wanted to visit since childhood. You stop and look at the visitors' book, where just that day a man from Michigan signed his name, stating that he had made the long journey "to pay respects to Lou Gehrig."

To reach the grave you pass the tomb of famed "Big Band" leader Tommy Dorsey, whose monument includes a stone trombone. Lou and Eleanor's grave is simpler, without flourish. That does not stop the pilgrims from leaving behind such tokens as faded Yankee caps, plastic bats, a couple of yellowed balls. On one of them, someone wrote, "LOU. YOUR THE GREATEST."

You cannot see the penny in the lock that changed George Pollack's mind. It no longer matters. Whatever happened, this is where Lou and Eleanor belong.

In death, as in life, Babe Ruth is more flamboyant.

He is buried alongside his wife, Claire, in the Gate of Heaven Cemetery, maybe a five-minute drive from Gehrig's grave. Ruth's elaborate tomb features an heroic figure of Christ with his arm around a boy in a baseball uniform.

A visitor has left a lipstick kiss upon the boy's stone cheek.

Around the grave is a chaotic jumble, even bigger than the pile of talismans at Gehrig's tomb. John Clark, 78, a security guard at Gate of Heaven, stops and tells you how the cemetery regularly cleans up hot dogs and sauerkraut put there as homage to the Babe's big appetite.

Fifty-four years after Ruth's death, someone has left a bottle of a brew made in Cooperstown. There are crumbling cigars. There are ticket stubs *from minor league games and even a $37 ticket, never used, to a 2002 game at Yankee Stadium against the Arizona Diamondbacks.*

There is the faded cover of a book about Ruth, still carrying the stickers and warnings from a public library. There are many baseballs, some with scrawled messages that sound more like desperate prayers: "BABE, YOUR THE MAN. YOU ARE THE BIG BAMBINO. PLEASE HELP US."

And then there are the photographs, mostly of children: Children in Little League uniforms, and children holding bats, and a couple of smiling children in hospital gowns, maybe children whose struggles are tied to the written pleas for help upon the balls.

One photo, an old Polaroid, is blurred by sun and water. At first it seems to be a photograph of Ruth or an imposter in a Yankees uniform, until you pick up the photo and turn it in your hand. The Polaroid is fragile, brittle. It definitely carries the image of someone in a baseball uniform, the features distorted and faded from the rain, making it impossible to even guess the age.

You realize, as you leave, that it could be one of us.

Index